School Refusal

Related Titles of Interest

Teaching Social Skills to Children and Youth: Innovative Approaches, Third Edition
Gwendolyn Cartledge and JoAnne Fellows Milburn (Editors)
ISBN: 0-205-16507-9   Paper   0-205-16073-5   Cloth

School Consultation: Practice and Training, Second Edition
Jane Close Conoley and Collie W. Conoley
ISBN: 0-205-14561-2

The Handbook of Family-School Intervention: A Systems Perspective
Marvin J. Fine and Cindy Carlson (Editors)
ISBN: 0-205-13024-0

Counseling for Diversity: A Guide for School Counselors and Related Professionals
Courtland C. Lee (Editor)
ISBN: 0-205-15321-6

Behavioral Family Intervention
Matthew R. Sanders and Mark R. Dadds
ISBN: 0-205-14600-7

Behavior Management in the Schools: Principles and Procedures, Second Edition
Richard M. Wielkiewicz
ISBN: 0-205-16459-5   Paper   0-205-16458-7   Cloth

► School Refusal

Assessment
and Treatment

Neville J. King, Ph.D.
Monash University
Australia

Thomas H. Ollendick, Ph.D.
Virginia Polytechnic Institute and State University

Bruce J. Tonge, M.D.
Monash University and Monash Medical Centre
Australia

Allyn and Bacon
Boston • London • Toronto • Sydney • Tokyo • Singapore

We wish to dedicate this effort to our children and families.

Copyright © 1995 by Allyn & Bacon
A Simon & Schuster Company
Needham Heights, Massachusetts 02194

Library of Congress Cataloging-in-Publication Data

King, Neville J.
    School refusal : assessment and treatment / Neville J. King,
Thomas H. Ollendick, Bruce J. Tonge.
        p.   cm.
    Includes bibliographical references and index.
    ISBN 0-205-16071-9
    1. School phobia.   I. Ollendick, Thomas H.   II. Tonge, Bruce J.
(Bruce John)   III. Title.
RJ506.S33K54   1995
618.92´89—dc20   94-34941
                                                                         CIP

Printed in the United States of America
10 9 8 7 6 5 4 3 2 1   99 98 97 96 95

► Contents

Preface   *vii*

Acknowledgments   *ix*

List of Tables   *x*

List of Figures   *xi*

About the Authors   *xiii*

1   Overview of School Refusal   1
Introduction   *1*
Developmental, Gender, and Socioeconomic Considerations   *3*
Clinical Presentation   *7*
Diagnostic Considerations   *10*
Etiology   *15*
Epidemiology   *19*
Relationship to Adult Psychopathology   *22*
Summary   *24*

2   Behavioral Assessment   27
Introduction   *27*
Assessment Procedures   *29*
    Behavioral Interviews   *31*
    Diagnostic Interviews   *34*
    Self-Report Instruments   *39*
    Self-Monitoring   *51*
    Behavioral Ratings   *54*
    Behavioral Observations   *57*
    Family Assessment Measures   *60*
Summary   *63*

3   Behavioral Treatment Strategies   65
Introduction   65
Behavioral Treatment Strategies   68
      Relaxation Training   68
      Systematic Desensitization   76
      Emotive Imagery   81
      Shaping and Contingency Management   84
      Modeling   88
      Cognitive Restructuring   91
Case Illustrations   94
      Case A   95
      Case B   101
Research Support   105
Summary   112

4   Pharmacotherapy   113
Introduction   113
      Indications for Drug Use   114
      Action of Drugs   115
      Drug Safety and Side Effects   116
      Administration of Medication   117
Pharmacotherapy of School Refusal   120
      Antidepressants   120
      Anxiolytics   126
      Neuroleptics   128
      Stimulants   128
      Cautions   129
Case Illustration   130
Summary   132

5   Epilogue   135
Concluding Remarks   135
The School-Refusing Child in Treatment   136
      Case Illustration   139
The Family Context   140
      Case Illustration   142
School Consultancy   144
      Case Illustration   147
Maintaining Treatment Gains   149
      Case Illustration   151
Summary   152

References   155

Author Index   173

Subject Index   177

▶ Preface

School attendance difficulties associated with emotional distress have been chronicled for many years, by both school authorities and mental health workers. This book is written from a clinical behavioral perspective and draws on our experience at the Monash Medical Centre School Refusal Clinic and the Virginia Polytechnic Institute and State University Childhood Anxiety Disorders Clinic. The primary objective of our book is to assist professionals, particularly mental health therapists and school practitioners, who are responsible for the management of school-refusing children. To help achieve this goal, we provide literature reviews on important aspects of school refusal, as well as practical guidelines for assessment and treatment. Another objective is to facilitate systematic and controlled research on the efficacy of behavioral treatment for school-refusing children ("scientist-practitioner").

Chapter 1 furnishes an internationally accepted definition of school refusal, according to which the major characteristics of the problem are prolonged school absenteeism and heightened emotional distress ("negative affectivity"). We elaborate on the clinical presentation of school refusal and examine findings on the diagnostic profile of these distressed children, thus confirming the heterogeneity of the problem. The etiology of school refusal is approached from a cognitive-behavioral perspective, it being argued that school avoidance is usually occasioned by a complex interaction of many factors ranging from biological vulnerability to schoolwide system influences. Epidemiology and relationship to adult psychopathology are also discussed in the opening chapter. Chapter 2 provides an account of our assessment approach, in which there is an emphasis on individual functional analysis. Suggestions are given for the use of assessment instruments and diagnostic procedures. Many instruments and protocols are reproduced for the benefit of the clinician-researcher, with comments on their reliability and validity.

Chapter 3 outlines behavioral and cognitive treatment strategies that may be used in the management of school-refusing children: relaxation training, systematic desensitization, emotive imagery, shaping and contingency management, modeling, and cognitive restructuring. Practical suggestions and clinical tips are provided for each of these treatment procedures. To further illustrate the clinical application of the treatment procedures, two detailed case studies are provided in which intervention successfully effected school return and anxiety reduction. Research findings in support of this treatment approach are critically reviewed. Given that school-refusing children are often medicated, the next chapter (Chapter 4) is devoted to pharmacotherapy. We believe that practitioners need to be aware of the commonly prescribed drugs (e.g., tricyclic antidepressants) and their side effects. The final chapter addresses significant clinical issues that arise in the assessment and treatment of school-refusing children. For example, the cooperation of all three parties—child, parents, and school—is crucial for successful intervention. However, for a variety of reasons, cooperation is not always forthcoming. We discuss some of the barriers to treatment that we have experienced and show how they were resolved in our clinics. Another important clinical and scientific issue is the durability of treatment gains. Chapter 5 examines strategies for facilitating the maintenance of treatment gains for school-refusing children.

Acknowledgments

We wish to thank the following reviewers for their comments on an earlier draft of this manuscript: Richard E. Maurer, Principal at the Anne M. Dorner Middle School, Ossining, NY; Richard M. Wielkiewicz, College of Saint Benedict, St. Joseph, MN; and Michael Cauley, Harvard Medical School and Massachusetts General Hospital. Their comments were invaluable in helping the authors bring this manuscript to fruition. We also wish to thank Susan Hutchinson, Editorial Assistant, and Mylan Jaixen, Editor, Allyn and Bacon. Their guidance, patience, and friendship throughout the project were greatly appreciated. We are grateful to the funding bodies that have supported our research on school refusal, including the National Health and Medical Research Council and the Ian Potter Foundation. Finally, we thank the many children and adolescents who, perhaps unwittingly, provided us the stimulus to undertake this project and the reinforcement in doing so.

▶ List of Tables

Table 2-1   ADIS—C School Refusal Behavior

Table 2-2   ADIS—P School Refusal Behavior

Table 2-3   The Fear Survey Schedule for Children—Revised

Table 2-4   The Failure and Criticism Factor of the FSSC—R

Table 2-5   School Refusal Assessment Scale

Table 2-6   Sample Items from the Preschool Observation Scale of Anxiety

Table 3-1   Pretest to determine readiness for relaxation training

Table 3-2   Examples of anxiety hierarchies

Table 3-3   Steps in the treatment of a school-refusing boy

Table 3-4   Procedural and behavioral progression during the treatment of school refusal

Table 3-5   Factors that enhance modeling

Table 3-6   Analysis of cognitions and coping statements of parents and children

Table 4-1   Possible psychotropic drug side effects

Table 4-2   Imipramine dose schedule and side effects for school-refusing child

▶ List of Figures

Figure 1-1   Age trends in school-related fears

Figure 1-2   Age of onset for school refusal

Figure 2-1   Sample diary page illustratiang directions and proper recording procedures

Figure 2-2   Sample Fear Thermometer

Figure 3-1   Increase in lesson attendance and self-confidence

Figure 3-2   Rates of appropriate and inappropriate behaviors across experimental conditions in the treatment of a child with social phobia

Figure 3-3   Acceptability ratings provided by students, parents, and professionals regarding treatment options for school refusal

▶ About the Authors

Neville J. King, Ph.D., is Associate Professor in the Faculty of Education, School of Graduate Studies, Monash University. His current research and clinical interests focus on school refusal. Dr. King's work on children's fears and anxiety disorders has been published in leading international journals such as the *Journal of Child Psychology and Psychiatry, Behaviour Research and Therapy,* and *Clinical Psychology Review.* Dr. King co-authored *Children's Phobias: A Behavioural Perspective* (Wiley, 1988) with David Hamilton and Thomas Ollendick. In addition, he has co-edited *Health Care: A Behavioural Approach* (Grune and Stratton, 1986) and *Psychology for the Health Sciences* (Thomas Nelson, 1989), both with Andrew Remenyi. He was also the founding editor of *Behaviour Change,* a journal of the Australian Behaviour Modification Association. Currently he is an Associate Editor for the *Australian Psychologist.*

Thomas H. Ollendick, Ph.D., is Professor of Psychology and Director of Clinical Training at Virginia Polytechnic Institute and State University. He formerly held positions at the Devereux Foundation, Indiana State University, and the Western Psychiatric Institute and Clinic. He has co-authored *Clinical Behavior Therapy with Children* (Plenum, 1981) with Jerome Cerny, *Enhancing Children's Social Skills* (Pergamon, 1988) with Johnny Matson, and *Children's Phobias: A Behavioural Perspective* with Neville King and David Hamilton. In addition, he has co-edited *Child Behavioral Assessment: Principles and Procedures* (Pergamon, 1984), the *Handbook of Child Psychopathology* (Plenum, 1989), and the *Handbook of Child and Adolescent Assessment* (Allyn and Bacon, 1993), all with Michel Hersen. The author of numerous research articles and chapters, he serves on the editorial board of 10 journals, including *Behaviour Change, Journal of Clinical Child Psychology,* and *Journal of Consulting and Clinical Psychology.* He is the Past

President of the American Psychological Association's Section on Clinical Child Psychology and the current President of the Association for the Advancement of Behavior Therapy. His work is concentrated on the understanding, assessment, and treatment of diverse child disorders, with special reference to childhood anxiety and phobic disorders.

Bruce J. Tonge, M.B.B.S., M.D., D.P.M., M.R.C.Psych., FRANZCP, is Professor of Child and Adolescent Psychiatry, Head of the Monash University Centre for Developmental Psychiatry and Department of Psychological Medicine, and Chairperson of the Monash Medical Centre, Division of Psychiatry. Previously he was the Foundation Professor of Child and Adolescent Psychiatry, University of Sydney, and also served as the Director of Child and Adolescent Psychiatry, Austin Hospital, Heidelberg, Victoria, Australia. He is the author of numerous research papers and is the principal editor of the *Handbook of Child Psychiatry* (Elsevier, 1991) with G. Burrows and J. Werry. Dr. Tonge is a Fellow of the Royal Australian and New Zealand College of Psychiatrists and has served as the Chairperson of the Committee for Training in Child Psychiatry, and is currently the Chairperson of the Faculty of Child Psychiatry (Victorian Branch) RANZCP. His research and clinical interests lie in the fields of the psychiatry of intellectual disability, pervasive developmental disorders, postnatal mood states and mother-infant interaction, and childhood anxiety disorders, centered on a school refusal clinic. He was a co-recipient of the 1992 Australian Society for the Study of Intellectual Disability research prize.

► 1
Overview of School Refusal

INTRODUCTION

School attendance difficulties have long been recognized to be a problem for children and adolescents. In fact, even before mandatory education became prominent, Shakespeare wrote of "the whining schoolboy with his satchel and shining morning face creeping like a snail unwillingly to school" (*As You Like It*, Act II). Several authors, including Blagg (1987) and Ollendick and Mayer (1984), have outlined the major historical developments necessary to an understanding of school refusal. In brief, early thinking about school attendance difficulties focused on truancy, and pioneering studies by Healy (1915) and Burt (1925) linked truancy with delinquency.

In 1932, however, Broadwin described a variant of truancy that highlighted the role of anxiety in school attendance difficulties:

> The child is absent from school for periods varying from several months to a year. The absence is consistent. At all times the parents know where the child is. It is near the mother or near the home. The reason for the truancy is incomprehensible to the parents and the school. The child may say that it is afraid to go to school, afraid of the teacher or say that it does not know why it will not go to school. (p. 254)

A few years later, Partridge (1939) labeled this particular kind of reluctance to go to school "psychoneurotic truancy" and described it as a form of "mother-following syndrome." The term *school phobia* was first used in the professional literature by Johnson and her coworkers in 1941. These American psychodynamic-oriented clinicians emphasized that school phobia was due to "deep seated neurosis of the obsessional type" and that fear of school represented a form of "displacement" of anxiety from its real source (separation from mother) to a source more palatable to the child (the school). Further, from this perspective, the mother of the school-phobic child was thought to be "unconsciously" supporting the child's fear by strongly sympathizing with complaints about school. The mother herself was thought to view school as an impersonal and unpleasant place, indirectly communicating the message that she wished the child to remain at home with her. In fact, at a later stage, Estes, Haylett, and Johnson (1956) concluded that school phobia was a variant of separation anxiety. Since then, the term *school phobia* has been used widely in the literature, along with frequent and unquestioning acceptance of the separation anxiety hypothesis of school avoidance.

However, like some other clinicians and researchers, we prefer the term *school refusal* as a label for the school attendance difficulties in question (Atkinson, Quarrington, & Cyr, 1985; Burke & Silverman, 1987; Hersov, 1977). This term has appeal because of its descriptive merits and recognition of the heterogeneity of the problem. Calling these youngsters school refusers or school avoiders is also consistent with the British empirical tradition (Hersov, 1977). The British have taken a more empirical stance and have posited a wide array of etiologic agents including events at school as well as separation problems at home. In this tradition, school-avoidant behavior might result from the child being afraid of specific aspects of the school situation, such as taking a test, speaking in front of class, being bullied by a peer, or dressing and undressing for physical education activities. It is now quite clear that school refusal can result from various causes, only one of which is separation problems at home (Ollendick & King, 1990). Clearly, how we label these children and adolescents is not a minor point and affects our understanding of school attendance difficulties.

An issue for clinicians and researchers has been the lack of objective guidelines for the identification of school-refusing children. In response to this lack, we have endorsed criteria for school refusal originally put forth by Berg, Nichols, and Pritchard (1969):

1. Severe difficulty attending school, often resulting in prolonged absence
2. Severe emotional upset, including excessive fearfulness, temper outbursts, or complaints of feeling ill when faced with the prospect of going to school
3. Staying at home with the parent's knowledge when the youngster should be at school

4. Absence of antisocial characteristics such as stealing, lying, and destructiveness

These criteria are important because they maintain the distinction between school truancy, which is often associated with conduct disorders, and school refusal, which is frequently associated with anxiety disorders. Further, the criteria call for evidence of prolonged absence, excessive fearfulness, somatic complaints, and adamant refusal to attend school—all characteristics that are commonly observed in children experiencing school attendance difficulties. What is equally important is that the criteria do not prejudge etiology; rather, they allow for a multiplicity of causal patterns. In our own work we have elaborated upon these criteria by operationalizing prolonged absence as absenteeism that is characterized by two or more absences, on average, per week and that persists over a four-week period. Thus, the child must be absent from school 40 percent of the time or more over a four-week period to meet our criteria. Of course, other children may be highly fearful and refuse to go to school on a less frequent basis (e.g., one day a week or one day every two weeks) or actually go to school every day but report excessive fears or worries in doing so. Obviously, the fears, worries, and anxieties of these children are of concern and these children may well benefit from the treatment strategies described later in this book. However, it is important to establish from the outset what we mean by "severe" school refusal. These other patterns of absenteeism may represent mild or moderate variants of school refusal and are in need of careful assessment and treatment in their own right.

Finally, consistent with the criteria put forth by Berg, Nichols, and Pritchard (1969), we require that our children and adolescents who refuse to go to school also report heightened levels of negative affect and emotional distress (e.g., anxiety, fear, depression) about going to school in order to be officially identified as school refusers. Levels of distress are determined through clinical interviews, self-report measures, parent rating scales, and behavioral observations conducted in the school and home settings, as described in Chapter 2. Thus, we look for persistent school absenteeism that is associated with considerable emotional distress in defining the problem of "school refusal."

DEVELOPMENTAL, GENDER, AND SOCIOECONOMIC CONSIDERATIONS

The social and educational merits of school attendance are widely agreed upon in society, as reflected in legal statutes governing school attendance. While school attendance can be a rewarding and satisfying experience for many children, it produces fear and apprehension for others. Ollendick and

Mayer (1984) point out that it is quite common for children to evidence a large number of fears, including an initial fear of attending school and separating from one's parents. In fact, the distress experienced by a child when separated from the person who cares for him or her (typically the mother) is a normal developmental phenomenon (Bauer, 1980; Gittelman-Klein & Klein, 1980). For most children this fear of separation occurs after the age of 6 to 8 months and persists, in varying degrees, until the child is 2 or 3 years of age. Generally this fear subsides as the child develops the cognitive properties to "grasp" the meaning of mother's absence and as the child is gradually exposed to increasingly longer periods of separation (i.e., from a few minutes to a few hours). Similarly, it is a normal developmental phenomenon for the child to be fearful of imaginary creatures, being alone, and strange places (Ollendick, 1979). For many children, school is a strange place, inhabited by imaginary creatures and characterized by unknown dimensions. As with fear of separation, this fear generally diminishes as the child becomes cognitively able to assimilate what was unknown and strange and as he or she becomes gradually desensitized to feared aspects of the school situation. However, fears such as taking a test and getting poor grades become more prominent in older children and adolescents. This is not surprising in view of the emphasis that is placed on academic performance by teachers and parents as the youngster progresses through school.

Researchers have examined the school-related fears of children using various self-report procedures (e.g., Angelino, Dollins, & Mech, 1956; Granell de Aldaz et al., 1987; Jersild, Goldman, & Loftus, 1941; King, Ollendick, & Gullone, 1990). For example, Granell de Aldaz and colleagues studied a large representative sample of Venezuelan children between 3 and 14 years of age. Nearly one-fifth of the children expressed intense fear of school on a self-report instrument (Fear Survey Schedule for Children), and some interesting developmental differences were observed in relation to specific school-related fears (see Figure 1-1). Older children were particularly fearful of the school evaluation system and the possibility of failure. On the other hand, the younger children expressed greater apprehension about more concrete situations such as being scolded at school or performing before a group. However, as noted by the researchers, parents completed the fear survey schedule for the younger children, whereas the older ones completed the schedule themselves. This difference in procedure may have resulted in some distortion of the findings. Nonetheless, these findings illustrate the range of school-related fears experienced by children and their relationship to age.

Venezuelan data on self-reported fears are comparable to those obtained in studies in which we administered the Revised Fear Survey Schedule for

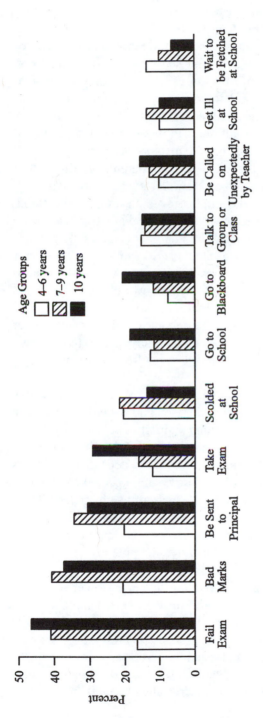

FIGURE 1-1   Age Trends in School-Related Fears

Source: E. Granell de Aldaz, L. Feldman, E. Vivas, D. M. Gelfand, "Characteristics of Venezuelan School Refusers: Toward the Development of a High-Risk Profile, *Journal of Nervous and Mental Disease,* 175, 402–407 (1987). © Williams & Wilkins, 1987.

Children (FSSC—R) to British, American, and Australian children and adolescents (King et al., 1989; Ollendick, King, & Frary, 1989; Ollendick, Yule, & Ollier, 1990). This instrument requires the child to rate his or her level of fear to each of 80 stimulus items on a 3-point scale: none, some, or a lot. Five factors have emerged in children's responses to the stimulus items: fear of failure and criticism, fear of the unknown, fear of injury and small animals, fear of death and danger, and medical fears (Ollendick, 1983; Ollendick et al., 1989). When analyses included all items on the instrument, we found an age-related decline in self-reported fears. This was particularly true for stimulus events or situations such as separation from parents, getting lost in a strange place, or being sent to the principal. However, examination of school-related items concerned with tests and grades revealed an opposite trend. Similar to the findings of the Venezuelan study, school evaluation fears were observed to be more common in older children and adolescents. These particular fears can be found on the fear of failure and criticism factor. The factor structure was shown to be robust and generalized across American, Australian, and British youngsters, as were the patterns of self-reported fears (Ollendick et al., 1989; Ollendick et al., 1990).

In addition to age, children's school-related fears are influenced by other factors, particularly sex and socioeconomic status. Many studies have shown girls to be more fearful than boys in relation to school-related stimuli (e.g., Granell de Aldaz et al., 1987; King et al., 1989; Ollendick & King, 1989). However, these findings have been challenged on the grounds that they may reflect differences in sex role stereotyping. Sarason and his colleagues have argued that in Western cultures we expect and support admissions of fear in girls in ways different from boys (Sarason et al., 1960). It is in keeping with "feminine character" for girls to be anxious or fearful and dependent on others for help and reassurance. On the other hand, boys are expected to be brave and fearless, consistent with our stereotype of "masculine character." Thus, differences in self-reported fear scores may reflect a difference in attitude between boys and girls toward admitting fear rather than real differences in actual fear. An often cited study which illustrates the potency of socioeconomic status is that of Angelino, Dollins, and Mech (1956). In this investigation a large sample of children were grouped into upper or lower socioeconomic status levels on predetermined criteria. In relation to school settings, lower socioeconomic status children were afraid of teachers and susceptible to stage fright, whereas the upper socioeconomic status children were more worried about schoolwork and grades. Several issues have also been raised about the interpretation of such findings, including the lack of standardization as to how socioeconomic status is defined (see Morris & Kratochwill, 1983).

Parents and teachers report that children experience various school-related fears, although not necessarily to the degree reported by children themselves (Granell de Aldaz et al., 1984; Lapouse & Monk, 1959). Typically, parents and teachers underreport such fears. Sex differences and socioeconomic status differences are also evident in teacher and parent reports (e.g., Lapouse & Monk, 1959; Staley & O'Donnell, 1984), with more fears ascribed to girls and to children from lower socioeconomic status levels. Parents and teachers, however, tend to notice the more overt behavioral expressions of fear that cause disruption in school or at home. Thus, in a longitudinal study of children attending primary school in London, Moore (1966) found that most parents perceived their child as being reluctant to attend school at least in the early years of school attendance. This difficulty was attributed chiefly to overdependence on parents (or fear of separation). However, reluctance to attend school along with other difficulties concerning teachers and schoolwork was reported less frequently by the parents as the children progressed through school, even though subjective worries and concerns persisted. Interestingly, parents reported being firm with their children about school attendance despite anxiety or dislike of school on the part of the child (Mitchell & Shepherd, 1967). Obviously, this is a vital factor in the maintenance of school attendance, and it deserves further exploration. More recently, research has focused on the importance of an adaptive and cohesive family pattern for positive school adjustment (Elizur, 1986). This is consonant with the call for more expansive research on the developmental and normative aspects of childhood phobias and school refusal (reviews by Graziano, De Giovanni, & Garcia, 1979; King, Hamilton, & Ollendick, 1988; Ollendick & Mayer, 1984).

CLINICAL PRESENTATION

School refusers are usually referred to our clinics by school authorities, family physicians, or parents following unsuccessful attempts at school return. Typically parents report that when pressure is placed on the child to attend school, he or she shows signs of anxiety or even panic. Our own behavioral observations as well as parent and teacher reports indicate that children show marked physiological changes—for example, muscular tension, breathing irregularities, and pallor—consistent with sympathetic arousal. Frequently there are complaints of physical illness such as headache and stomach pain for which there is no organic cause (e.g., Granell de Aldaz et al., 1987; Lang, 1982) and, when the children are forced to go to school, visits to the school nurse are common. Verbal protests, whining, and temper tantrums are common resistive behaviors. Although many children refuse to leave home for school, some set out for school but rush home in a state of anxiety before getting to school or refuse to enter the school building once there (Hersov, 1977). Others telephone home and request to be retrieved. Another feature of school refusal has been that the child typically stays at home through the day under the care of the mother or other family members. In more recent years, increasingly more school-refusing children stay at home alone. As noted, school refusers do not usually exhibit antisocial behaviors such as stealing and destructiveness, and they typically remain in the secure environment of the home while out of school. An acute onset of school refusal (e.g., school refusal following an illness, move to a new home) is usually seen in younger children, whereas chronic presentations of school refusal are more typical of older children and adolescents (Coolidge, Hahn, & Peck, 1957; Kennedy, 1965). Perhaps this distinction in age between acute and chronic presentation should not be unexpected. For the most part, "chronic" refusers were "acute" at one time, and the chronicity reflects the accumulation of emotional distress and school refusal over time. As we shall see later, chronic refusers who are persistent in their refusal pattern are more difficult to treat.

In the clinical presentation of school refusal we see children with various maladaptive fears and excessive anxiety similar to reports in the literature (Chazan, 1962; Granell de Aldaz et al., 1987; Kearney & Silverman, 1990; Smith, 1970). Some children are afraid of separation from their parents (usually the mother) and fear some kind of harm befalling their parents. Many children have exaggerated fears of specific events or situations in the school setting such as being bullied by peers or punished by teachers. Yet other children have extreme fears of taking tests and performing other evaluation tasks in the classroom. Fear of entering a new school, fear of vomiting, fear of interpersonal interaction, and fear of undressing for sports are also frequently evidenced in school refusal cases. Further, school refusers often display multiple and diffuse fears in relation to home and/or school settings (King, Ollendick, & Gullone, 1990). The clinical presentation of school refusal also appears to be influenced by developmental factors (Granell de Aldaz et al., 1987; Last et al., 1987). Fear of separation from parents is more typical of the clinical presentation of young children. On the other hand, fear of teachers or other children is seen more frequently in older school refusers. Social-evaluative fears are also seen more frequently in older school refusers.

Consistent with these fears, especially fear of separation from parents, school refusers often show excessive dependency on their mother or other family members. Equally often, mothers or other caregivers are sometimes overprotective and can present as being anxious or worried about various aspects of their child's well-being. For example, the mother of a 9-year-old boy referred to the Monash Medical Centre School Refusal Clinic repeatedly expressed fear of her child having an "undetected illness" and worried about his ability to cope at school. On those days the child managed to attend school, the mother would visit or telephone the school for reassurance about her child. Similarly, the mother of a 7-year-old boy referred to the Child Anxiety Disorder Clinic at Virginia Polytechnic Institute and State University worried excessively about harm befalling her child and that he would be bullied by larger boys. In fact, her worries were unfounded. Yet they were transmitted to her son, who, in turn, became overly dependent on her and developed separation concerns and subsequent school refusal. In 1974, Berg developed a self-administered dependency questionnaire for caregivers that assesses dependency in four primary areas: affection, communication, assistance, and travel from home. In a series of controlled investigations of separation-anxious school refusers, Berg and his colleagues confirmed that school refusal was frequently confounded by dependency and maternal overprotection (Berg, 1980; Berg & McGuire, 1971, 1974). Also, it appeared that chronic school refusers who were separation-anxious were more dependent than were acute school refusers (Berg, Nichols, & Pritchard, 1969).

School refusers may also present with depressive features including dysphoria, irritability, tearfulness, feelings of worthlessness, guilt, and sleep disturbance (e.g., Agras, 1959; Bernstein, 1991). Any reports of suicidal thoughts or suicide attempts are of concern, particularly as a few school refusers have actually committed suicide (Shaffer, 1974). The incidence and severity of depression among school refusers vary enormously, although we concur with other clinicians and researchers who have observed depressive symptomatology to be more characteristic of adolescent school refusers (Bernstein & Garfinkel, 1986). Social maladjustment is evident in certain cases of school refusal. For example, a 12-year-old girl presenting with school refusal had problems in interactions with peers and teachers (Esveldt-Dawson et al., 1982). She displayed various inappropriate behaviors including stiffness in the trunk and limbs, nervous giggling, inadequate eye contact, and inappropriate affect. We have observed similar deficits in many of our school refusers. To our knowledge, there have been no controlled investigations of social functioning in school refusers, although children with internalizing disorders frequently have low peer status and often lack social skills (Strauss, 1988). Given their emotional distress and school attendance difficulties, it is not surprising that school refusers often experience low self-esteem and poor image problems. In one of the few studies on this issue, Nichols and Berg (1970) found that chronic (but not acute) school refusers experienced lowered self-esteem compared to other clinic-referred children. Interestingly, their findings are contrary to the predictions of those researchers who believe that school refusers overvalue themselves and their achievements and hence possess heightened, if not unrealistic, levels of self-esteem (Leventhal & Sills, 1964). In conclusion, the clinical presentation of school refusal is heterogeneous and does not represent a fixed set of symptoms, let alone a unitary syndrome.

DIAGNOSTIC CONSIDERATIONS

As is evident, there is considerable heterogeneity in the clinical picture of children and adolescents who present with school refusal. Some children and adolescents who refuse school present with long and complicated histories of separation anxiety, depression, and, at times, oppositional and conduct problems. Others present with relatively circumscribed fears or phobias about aspects of the school itself (e.g., taking tests, speaking in front of class, riding the bus to school, being teased by other children). Still others present with combinations of specific fears and phobias and depression or separation anxiety. Such heterogeneity in clinical presentation demands thoughtful and sensitive considerations regarding the formulation of the clinical problem, the assessment to be pursued, and the treatment to be undertaken. Here, we shall comment briefly about diagnostic considerations; issues of assessment and treatment will be pursued more fully in subsequent chapters.

For the most part, children and adolescents who present with school refusal meet criteria for one or more of the anxiety or affective disorders described in the *International Classification of Diseases (ICD-9, ICD-10)* developed by the World Health Organization or the *Diagnostic and Statistical Manual (DSM-III-R, DSM-IV)* put forth by the American Psychiatric Association. Although differences exist between these systems, they are similar in the coverage afforded major anxiety and affective disorders. In our own clinics in Australia and the United States we use the *DSM* system.

A wide variety of anxiety disorders are presented in the *DSM-III-R* (American Psychiatric Association, 1987) and its recent revision, *DSM-IV* (APA, 1994): separation anxiety disorder, overanxious disorder, avoidant disorder, panic disorder, agoraphobia, social phobia, simple phobia, obsessive-compulsive disorder, post-traumatic stress disorder, generalized anxiety disorder, and anxiety disorder not otherwise specified. Although the first three disorders are commonly referred to as "anxiety disorders of childhood or adolescence," these disorders can exist in adults if onset occurs prior to age 18. In addition, the other anxiety disorders described in *DSM* and typically referred to as adult disorders (e.g., simple phobia, generalized anxiety disorder, panic disorder) can and do exist in children and adolescents even though they are not mentioned in the section on anxiety disorders of childhood or adolescence. Thus, any of the anxiety disorders listed above can be observed in children and adolescents, and their presence should be routinely explored in school-refusing children and adolescents. However, it should be noted that several of these disorders have much in common (e.g., avoidant disorder and social phobia, overanxious disorder and generalized anxiety disorder), and, as a result, the disorders frequently co-occur in the same children or adolescents. This co-occurrence is referred to as comorbidity in the literature.

Fortunately the number of affective disorders in the *DSM-III-R* are more limited and are not differentiated for children and adults. For our purposes here, two primary affective disorders are most relevant: major depressive disorder and dysthymia. The primary distinction between them is the gradual onset and chronic course of depression in dysthymia. Major depressive disorder is more short-lived and typically of acute or sudden onset.

As will be documented shortly, the most frequently observed diagnoses in children and adolescents who present with school refusal are separation anxiety disorder, simple or social phobia, and major depressive disorder. Frequently these diagnoses co-occur in the same children or adolescents, and diagnostic heterogeneity prevails. In an early study of 37 school refusers, Ollendick and Mayer (1984) identified two primary types of children and adolescents who refused school and who met our expanded criteria for "serious" school refusal: separation-anxious school refusers ($n = 13$) and phobic school refusers ($n = 15$). In the former group, children and adolescents were concerned with harm befalling themselves or their parents. Such concerns are the hallmark of separation anxiety disorder. In the latter group the children and adolescents were more concerned about and fearful of specific aspects of the school itself (e.g., entering a new school, taking tests, participating in physical education classes, sarcastic teachers, being teased by peers). They displayed the characteristics of simple or social phobia. A third, smaller group ($n = 9$) showed the characteristics of both separation anxiety disorder and simple or social phobia. That is, they were worried about harm befalling their major attachment figure (or themselves) and dreaded some specific aspect of the school itself. Unfortunately the presence of depressive disorders was not determined in this sample of school refusers. However, it is likely that this latter group would have been characterized by depressive disorders as well. They were also more chronic and less acute than their separation-anxious and phobic counterparts.

In a more recent study, Last and her colleagues (1987) undertook a systematic study of 48 children and adolescents presenting with separation anxiety disorder and 19 children and adolescents presenting with a phobic disorder of school. Chronicity of refusal was not reported. Although age and gender differences between the two groups were noted (the separation-anxious group was younger and included more girls than the phobic disorder group), the children and adolescents in both groups were equally likely to present with an additional anxiety disorder (50 percent of the children and adolescents with separation anxiety disorder and 53 percent of the children with a phobic disorder of school) and a concurrent affective disorder (33 percent of the children and adolescents with separation anxiety disorder and 32 percent of the children and adolescents with a phobic disorder of school). Overanxious disorder and major depressive disorder were the most frequent co-occurring disorders for both groups. Because some children and adolescents in both groups evinced multiple co-occurring disorders, it was possible to determine the absolute per cent of children and adolescents in each group who evinced at least one co-occurring disorder. In such an analysis, Last and her colleagues demonstrated that the separation anxiety group was more likely overall to have a concurrent psychiatric disorder (92 percent) than was the phobic group (63 percent). In addition, these investigators explored the lifetime history of psychiatric disorders, as well as the presence of current psychiatric disorders, in the mothers of these child and adolescent patients. Although the lifetime and current rates of disorder in the mothers were high in both groups, they were significantly higher in the mothers of the separation anxiety disorder patients. Based on the comorbid rates in the children and adolescents and the presence of lifetime and current rates of psychiatric disorders in the mothers, Last and her colleagues concluded that the children and adolescents in the separation anxiety disorder group, and their mothers, were more severely disturbed than those in the phobic disorder group.

In this same study, Last et al. (1987) explored the presence of school refusal in the separation anxiety disorder and school phobic groups. As noted earlier by Ollendick and Mayer (1984), not all separation-anxious children and adolescents exhibit school refusal, nor, for that matter, do all children and adolescents phobic of school show separation concerns. Consistent with this notion, 100 percent of the phobic youngsters showed school refusal whereas 73 percent of the separation anxious youth did so. Thus, over 25 percent of the separation youngsters did not evidence school refusal, indicating the need to maintain clinical distinctions between the two disorders. Of course, based on our comments, it would also be important to determine the history and chronicity of the school refusal, as well as the presence of major depressive disorders in these subgroups of school refusers.

In a more recent report, Last and Strauss (1990) expanded on their earlier study by examining the specific anxiety disorders associated with 63 cases of school refusers. That is, children and adolescents presenting with school refusal were identified and then the prevalence of anxiety disorders was determined. In addition, they reported comorbidity estimates for their school refusal sample and examined the childhood histories of mothers of the school refusers. Regarding specific anxiety disorders, Last and Strauss reported that separation anxiety disorder was the most common diagnosis (38 percent, 24 of the 63 youth), with social phobia (30 percent, 19 of 63) a close second, and followed in order by simple phobia (22 percent, 14 of 63), panic disorder (6 percent, 4 of 63), and post-traumatic stress disorder (2 percent, 2 of 63). As is evident, over 60 percent of school refusers presented with a primary anxiety diagnosis other than separation anxiety disorder. If we combine those children and adolescents with social and simple phobia into a phobic school refusal group, it can be seen that 52 percent meet such criteria. Clearly, the distinctions offered by Ollendick and Mayer (1984) and Last et al. (1987) are affirmed in this study.

In reference to comorbidity, Last and Strauss (1990) reported that overanxious disorder was most common (25 percent), followed by major depressive disorder (13 percent), non-school related social phobia (13 percent), non-school related simple phobia (also 13 percent), and avoidant disorder (11 percent). In examining maternal histories of the school-refusing children and adolescents, they found that 33 percent of their mothers had a history of such refusal. Additional analyses revealed that most of the offspring of mothers with a school refusal history fell in the separation anxiety group. To wit, systematic comparison of the separation-anxious school refusers and the combined social and simple phobic school refusers indicated that mothers of separation-anxious youth (75 percent) were more likely than mothers of the combined phobic group (18 percent) to have a history of school refusal. These findings, combined with others in the study, led Last and Strauss to conclude, as in their earlier study, that the separation-anxious group was more severely disturbed than the phobic group.

These findings have been largely supported in a series of studies undertaken by Bernstein and her colleagues (Bernstein, 1991; Bernstein & Garfinkel, 1986; Bernstein, Svingen, & Garfinkel, 1990). In her most recent study, Bernstein (1991) evaluated 96 children and adolescents with (for the most part) chronic school refusal. On the basis of her earlier work (Bernstein & Garfinkel, 1986), she formed four groups of school refusers: an anxiety disorder only group (separation anxiety disorder and/or overanxious disorder, $n = 27$), a depressive disorder only group (major depressive disorder or dysthymia, $n = 27$), an anxiety and depressive disorder group (comorbid for anxiety and depression, $n = 24$), and a no anxiety or depressive disorder group (an absence of anxiety/depressive disorders, $n = 18$). The majority of the children and adolescents in the latter group met criteria for one of the disruptive behavior disorders (e.g., conduct disorder, oppositional defiant disorder). Although some sociodemographic differences among the groups on age and family status were noted, the groups were equivalent in gender, urban versus rural residence, socioeconomic status, duration of school refusal symptoms, referral source, and whether or not a truancy petition had been filed by the child or adolescent's school.

Of special interest, Bernstein reported very few phobic school refusers in her anxiety disorder only and combined anxiety/depressive disorder groups. Rather, separation anxiety disorder was the most frequent anxiety disorder in both the anxiety plus depressive disorders group (50 percent) and in the anxiety disorder only group (63 percent). Overanxious disorder was the second most common disorder in both groups (29 percent and 15 percent, respectively). Although Bernstein notes that other anxiety disorders such as simple phobia and panic disorder could not be tracked because of insufficient chart information, it is probable that her sample of school refusers differed from those studied by Ollendick and Mayer (1984) and Last and her colleagues (Last et al., 1987; Last & Strauss, 1990). Inspection of sample characteristics reveals that her sample was somewhat older, possessed a longer duration of school refusal symptoms (i.e., were more chronic), and was more pathological (i.e., also depressed). These differences should be recalled when interpreting the results.

Basically, Bernstein (1991) showed that the group comorbid for anxiety and depression scored the highest on a series of rating scales for anxiety and depression, with the no anxiety or depression group scoring the lowest. For the most part, the anxiety only and depression only groups scored similarly, with scores that were intermediate between the other two groups. In effect, the findings suggest a difference in symptom severity among the four diagnostic groups of school refusers. The comorbidity of anxiety and depressive disorders is associated with more severe symptomatology. This pattern was also found in her earlier studies (Bernstein & Garfinkel, 1986). Moreover, in another study (Bernstein, 1990), she has shown that the comorbid group is characterized by greater family dysfunction, particularly in the areas of role performance and values and norms. She argues that the boundaries between parental and child roles are obscured in such families and that the parents are not effective in their roles to facilitate return to school. She further notes that the parents of such children and adolescents may give "contradictory messages regarding school attendance, independence, separation from one another, and response to somatization" (p. 28).

What appears to be clear from these various diagnostic studies is that the formulation of school refusal is complex, variable, and highly individualized. Yet, there appears to be support for three primary and distinguishable clinical groups of severe school refusers: phobic school refusers, separation-anxious school refusers, and anxious/depressed school refusers. Of course, it should be evident that these various clinical groups might also differ on the acuteness or chronicity of their disorder. In general, however, it might be supposed that the separation-anxious and phobic disorder groups will be more acute in their presentation, while the anxious/depressed group will be more chronic. Other, minor groups of school refusers exist as well, including those who might be characterized best by post-traumatic stress disorder, panic disorder, and, in some rare instances, medical disorders that result in school refusal (see Blackman and Wheler, 1987, for discussion of a case of school refusal in a 12-year-old boy with a fourth ventricular tumor). It is also possible, albeit unlikely, that some school refusers will be devoid of diagnostic status. In such rare instances the "problem" of school refusal might reside in the psychopathology of the parent or in some systemic problem in the school itself (see Chapter 5). Regardless, as is evident in the assessment chapter, the diagnostic formulation is greatly enriched by the use of developmentally sensitive and psychometrically sound assessment strategies. Moreover, the assessment process itself is informed by the diagnostic formulation. In short, a dynamic interplay exists between the diagnostic formulation and the assessment process. In turn, both of these activities affect selection of efficacious treatment strategies, as we shall illustrate in Chapter 3.

ETIOLOGY

The etiology of school refusal is complexly determined, with many factors contributing to the development and maintenance of the problem. Certain children probably have a constitutional or inborn vulnerability that places them at risk for the development of emotional disturbance. Recent years have witnessed much research on temperament as a determinant of child psychopathology. It is evident that children at an early age exhibit quite different behavioral styles or emotional reactivity in their interactions with the environment. Various temperament characteristics—for example, activity level, mood, and adaptability—have been identified by Thomas and Chess (1977). A follow-up study of previously identified "temperamentally difficult" children found that the children displayed various symptomatology in home and school settings (Maziade et al., 1985). Whereas there was a preponderance of oppositional behavior and other outwardly directed symptoms at home, these children showed a preponderance of inwardly directed symptoms at school. Teachers described them as worried, unhappy, tearful, solitary, and fearful (a picture very similar to that of the school refuser). The findings also revealed that temperament is not a fixed or unmodifiable entity throughout the course of development, as parenting skills seemed to offset the risk of severe psychopathology. The relationship of school refusal to temperament deserves closer empirical investigation. Certainly, we have found in our own clinics that behaviorally inhibited children appear to be at risk for the development of school refusal. As show by the work of Kagan and his colleagues, children with this temperamental quality are unusually shy and fearful (Kagan, Reznick, & Snidman, 1987; Reznick et al., 1986). Consistent with our own observations, these researchers have also found that behaviorally inhibited children experience school attendance difficulties, with many of them having an actual anxiety disorder (Hirshfeld et al., 1992).

Stressful life events at home and/or school invariably precede the onset of school refusal. In a study of 50 cases of school refusal seen in the Children's Department at the Maudsley Hospital, for example, Hersov (1960b) reported that the most common precipitating factor was a change to a new school, followed by an illness, accident, or operation that led to the child spending a period of time in hospital or at home, and then by the death, departure, or illness of a parent (usually the mother). Moreover, Blagg (1987) and others have observed that school refusal is often the manifestation of an *accumulation* of stressful events at home or school. Illustratively, Lazarus, Davison, and Polefka (1965) have detailed the history of a school refuser that included a life-threatening incident, a serious appendectomy, the sudden death of a family friend, witnessing a drowning, and a stressful home atmosphere. Poznanski (1973) has reported some interesting impressions on the emergence of excessive fears (including "school phobia") in a group of children from an outpatient psychiatric clinic. The charts for these children were carefully examined for "subjective impressions" of the circumstances surrounding the onset of their maladaptive fears. In contrast to a control group drawn from the same population, the phobic group showed a definite history of stressful life events and subsequent development of excessive fears. Among the stressful events that preceded the onset of the phobias were, for example, witnessing the slaughtering of a pet cow, watching the Kennedy funeral on television, and having a brother sent to the Vietnam War. It was also noted that most of the children who were excessively fearful seemed to have more than the usual amount of anxiety prior to the onset of excessive fears. In other words, situational stress appeared to precipitate a more open display of fears and anxiety. Although methodological limitations are apparent in the study, the findings support the view that stressful life events play a significant role in the etiology of school refusal.

From a learning theory perspective, the principles of classical, operant, and vicarious conditioning can be usefully employed in descriptions of the etiology and maintenance of school refusal (e.g., Miller, Barrett, & Hampe, 1974; Ollendick & King, 1990; Yates, 1970). Such principles have been used to account for problems in separation as well as specific fears about the school situation itself. For example, Yates (1970) acknowledged the potential importance of mother-child relationships and separation anxiety from an operant perspective. Since parents act as strong reinforcers for children during the preschool years, the children see them as a refuge to which they may turn when frightened, uncertain, or placed in novel situations. Feelings of anxiety about separation may be both prompted and reinforced by mothers (or fathers) who are overly concerned about the safety of their child. Consequently, many children will feel some anxiety in separation from the mother when first attending school. Whether or not this anxiety develops into a fear of school will depend on the availability of reinforcers in the school, which effectively compete with anxiety reactions, and on the response of the mother to the fears of the child. Hence, the genesis of school refusal may be complexly determined, if not overdetermined (Ollendick, 1979), by the following factors: "separation anxiety leading to over-dependence on the home as a safe refuge; insufficient rewards or actual anxiety-arousing experiences at school; and possibly, of course, actual traumatic events at school" (Yates, 1970, p. 152). This account of school refusal signifies that behavioral formulations can often accommodate separation anxiety. Moreover, even when separation anxiety is not a contributing factor, conditioning principles may be useful in understanding the development and maintenance of school refusal from other causes.

In an influential theoretical paper, Rachman (1977) suggested that fears can be acquired through three major pathways: direct conditioning (e.g., child developing a fear of school after being assaulted by peers at school), vicarious conditioning (e.g., child imitating the school-related fears of a sibling), and transmission of fear messages (e.g., child showing a fear of school as a result of hearing negative accounts of school from parents). Rachman believes that direct conditioning is probably the most crucial to the onset of severe phobias. Recently we have documented the importance of such pathways in the acquisition of children's fears (Ollendick & King, 1991) and have shown that they are frequently overdetermined (i.e., the result of several interacting forces). Eysenck (1968, 1979) has noted that for some individuals there is no immediate display of conditioned fear after the original traumatic event. Instead, the fear seems to grow over time even in the absence of further trauma (this process has been labeled "incubation"). Among the major parameters that facilitate incubation, Eysenck points to very short exposures to the conditioned stimulus and certain genetically determined personality characteristics (cf. temperament) that make the person susceptible to fear arousal. As just noted, a learning theory approach to school refusal also emphasizes the role of reinforcement. Parental attention, television viewing, and a host of other activities make staying at home a rewarding experience for many children.

Although neglected early on by traditional learning theory, it is now evident that the study of cognitive processes provides us with valuable insights into questions of etiology and maintenance. The findings of several controlled investigations (Prins, 1985, 1986; Zatz & Chassin, 1983, 1985) show that anxious children engage in negative self-talk when faced with fear-producing situations. For example, Zatz and Chassin (1983, 1985) examined the cognitions of low, moderate, and high test-anxious children under analog and naturalistic test-taking conditions. They found that high test-anxious children showed more task-debilitating cognitions during testing, including negative self-evaluations (e.g., "I'm doing poorly") and off-task thoughts (e.g., "I wish I were home") and fewer positive self-evaluations (e.g., "I'm doing the best that I can do"). Evidence for dysfunctional thinking in school refusers, however, is limited to case reports such as that of Mansdorf and Lukens (1987). Cognitive analysis of two children presenting with school refusal revealed quite different mediating beliefs, a finding that is not surprising in view of the heterogeneity of school refusal. Clearly, dysfunctional thinking should be examined in controlled studies with school-refusing children.

School refusal frequently occurs in a family context in which there is marked pathology and distress (Bernstein & Garfinkel, 1988; Bernstein, Svingen, & Garfinkel, 1990; Lang, 1982). As noted, particular interest has been expressed in child-mother relations, which are often characterized by dependency and maternal overprotectiveness. Also, it is not uncommon for parents to have a history of school refusal or for siblings to have current or previous school attendance difficulties (Gittelman-Klein, 1975b; Granell de Aldaz et al., 1987). Further, marital conflict and psychopathology (e.g., anxiety, depression, and alcohol abuse) are frequently present in parents (Berg, Butler, & Pritchard, 1974; Lang, 1982; Last et al., 1987). Thus, in these adverse family circumstances, parents are often unwilling or ill-equipped to manage school attendance difficulties. Typically, parents do not work as a mutually supportive team and appear incapable of problem solving and developing constructive solutions for school return. Lang (1982) has observed that families often display attitudes that are antithetical to educational values and school attendance. Although we should be cautious of making generalizations about the family situation, it is undoubtedly a consideration in the etiology and maintenance of school refusal (see Chapter 5).

EPIDEMIOLOGY

School refusal has a low prevalence among school-age children. In the United States, Kennedy (1965) estimated the prevalence to be 1.7 percent of school-age children. However, it is unclear how this estimate was derived. Ollendick and Mayer (1984) examined the prevalence of school refusal in a sample of school-age children in southwest Virginia. They found the prevalence of severe school refusal to be 0.4 percent using the criteria specified by Berg, Nichols, and Pritchard (1969) and elaborated upon here. Studies in other countries have also confirmed that school refusal has a low prevalence in the general population of children and adolescents (e.g., Granell de Aldaz et al., 1984; Mitchell & Shepherd, 1967; Rutter, Tizard, & Whitemore, 1970). The study reported by Granell de Aldaz et al. (1984) on Venezuelan children and adolescents is of particular interest because of the use of multiple informants (children, parents, and teachers). When using a strict definition of school refusal, the researchers found that 0.4 percent of the sample could be classified as school refusers. This definition required that *all* informants (i.e., parents, teachers, and child) agree that the child's absences were attributable to extreme fear. However, when the researchers combined school-avoidant children with children with high absenteeism who were judged to be fearful by *any* one of the informants, the prevalence rate increased to 5.4 percent. Thus, it is evident that how we operationalize our definition of school refusal has a profound influence on prevalence estimates. Although school refusal has a low prevalence, it is still consistently represented in referrals to clinical services (Baker & Wills, 1978; Chazan, 1962; Smith, 1970).

School refusal can occur throughout the entire range of school years, but major peaks are evident at certain ages. To illustrate, Smith (1970) has presented a histogram on age at intake and age of onset for 63 school refusers assessed at the Maudsley Hospital (see Figure 1-2). Although the children presented with school refusal across the school years, it is evident that the peak age at presentation was 11 to 12 years. However, a different picture emerged for age at onset, where two peaks were evident: 5 to 6 years and 11

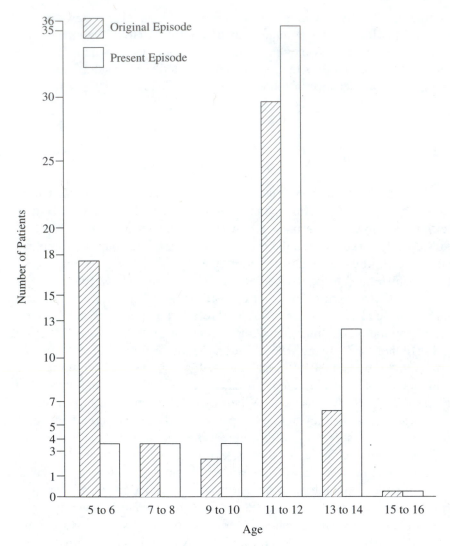

FIGURE 1-2   **Age of Onset for School Refusal**

Source: S. L. Smith, "School Refusal with Anxiety: A Review of Sixty-Three Cases," *Canadian Psychiatry Association Journal, 15,* 257–264 (1970). Used with permission.

to 12 years. It will be recognized that these two peaks coincide with school entry and major school transitions. We have also pointed out earlier that age has a bearing on the clinical presentation of school refusal, particularly in relation to separation anxiety symptomatology, which is frequently associated with young school refusers, and phobic behavior, which appears to be more typical of older school refusers (Last et al., 1987; Smith, 1970).

While males outnumber females for most types of child behavior disorders (Ollendick & Hersen, 1983; Quay & Werry, 1979), school refusal tends to be mixed (e.g., Berg & Fielding, 1978; Granell de Aldaz et al., 1984; Kennedy, 1965), with some studies showing a predominance of males (e.g., Atkinson et al., 1989; Baker & Wills, 1978; Rodriguez, Rodriguez, & Eisenberg, 1959) and others indicating a predominance of females (e.g., Adams, McDonald, & Huey, 1966; Berg, Nichols, & Pritchard, 1969; Warnecke, 1964). Quite validly, some have pointed out that these discrepant findings might be due to differences in the diagnostic composition of the samples. Indeed, research findings indicate that separation-anxious children are predominantly female, while the majority of school phobic children are male (Last & Francis, 1988; Last et al., 1987).

Last and Francis (1988) have observed that until recently there have been few empirical assessments of the socioeconomic status of school refusers. However, there have been some studies that have done so. Socioeconomic status was one of the variables used to classify a large sample of British school-refusing children in a study reported by Baker and Wills (1978), for example. The researchers reported that 18 percent of their sample were from social classes I and II (highest classes), 24 percent from class III, 33 percent from class IV, and 20 percent from class V (remainder were unidentified). Presumably this classification was based on occupation of parents. More recently, American researchers have drawn on the work of Hollingshead and Redlich (1958), who introduced an "Index of Social Position" based on three indicators: residential address, occupational position, and educational standard. A more pragmatic variant is the two-factor index that requires only knowledge of occupation and education. Thus, Last and Strauss (1990) found that approximately one-half of their sample of school refusers came from lower socioeconomic status families (Hollingshead ratings IV and V). Consistent with these findings, an Australian study found that school refusers came more from families of lower socioeconomic status (determined by father's occupation) compared to a control group of children without school attendance difficulties (Lang, 1982).

The early literature suggested that school refusers were of above average intelligence (e.g., Adams, McDonald, & Huey, 1966; Leton, 1962; Rodriguez, Rodriguez, & Eisenberg, 1959). In his review, however, Trueman (1984) noted several methodological issues about these early studies, including sample bias and a reliance on clinical impressions in the assessment of intelligence. To date, the most systematic investigation of school refusers on this issue is that of Hampe, Miller, and colleagues (1973). Using a sample of 57 school refusers across a wide age range, the researchers found a WISC Full Scale IQ of 98.9, with a Verbal IQ of 96.7 and a Performance IQ of 101.6. These findings, together with those of several other studies (e.g., Hersov, 1960a; Warnecke, 1964), indicate that school refusers show a normal distribution of intelligence. Also no significant differences in IQ have been found between acute and chronic school refusers (Baker & Wills, 1978; Berg, Nichols, & Pritchard, 1969; Nichols & Berg, 1970). Unfortunately, intelligence levels of separation-anxious, phobic, and anxious/depressed subgroups have not been reported. Overall, our own samples of school refusers have come from all intellectual levels and from varying socioeconomic status levels. Slightly more boys than girls have presented.

RELATIONSHIP TO ADULT PSYCHOPATHOLOGY

The long-term adjustment of school refusers is a major concern for educational authorities and mental health workers, particularly in relation to employment prospects and social-emotional difficulties. In this vein, it has been proposed that school refusal may be a precursor to disturbance in adult life. Before we review the studies on the relationship of school refusal to adult psychopathology, we should emphasize that the prognosis for school refusal is undoubtedly affected by many variables. As recently restated by Atkinson, Quarrington, and Cyr (1985), and Last and Francis (1988), the major prognostic indicators include severity of the disorder, age of onset, intellectual functioning, and time until treatment is obtained. Young and intelligent children presenting with school refusal are most responsive to treatment, while adolescents with chronic presentations of school refusal and accompanying depression are less likely to evidence symptom improvement and/or return to school (cf. Berg & Jackson, 1985; Jacobsen, 1948; Miller et al., 1972; Smith, 1970).

Several follow-up studies have been reported on previously hospitalized adolescent school refusers (Berg, Butler, & Hall, 1976; Berg & Jackson, 1985; Warren, 1965). Of 125 school refusers treated in a psychiatric unit for young adolescents, Berg, Butler, and Hall (1976) have reported data on 100 cases that were re-examined at three-year follow-up. About a third of the cases were found to have experienced little or no improvement. These youngsters continued to exhibit symptoms of emotional disturbance and were significantly impaired in their social functioning (some had received further psychiatric treatment). Also, these youngsters experienced marked school attendance difficulties over the follow-up period. Another third of the cases were found to have improved moderately but were affected by persistent "neurotic" symptoms such as anxiety, depression, and obsessions. The other third were found to have improved substantially or completely as evidenced by few difficulties in school attendance and social functioning. The researchers noted that the best indicator of follow-up status was improved clinical condition on discharge (however, half of these cases did not change during the follow-up period). Berg and Jackson (1985) have also reported follow-up data on a large sample of adolescent school refusers, approximately 10 years after inpatient treatment. Almost half were well or much improved throughout the follow-up period. However, about one-third required psychiatric treatment during the follow-up period. Nonetheless, the findings of the latter study convey a more optimistic long-term picture of school refusers. Given the sample bias apparent in these studies, we should be cautious about extrapolation to the general population of school refusers.

More recently, Flakierska, Lindström, and Gillberg (1988) reported a 15- to 20-year follow-up study of Swedish children who had received treatment for school refusal. The children were 7 to 12 years of age at the time of treatment (14 inpatient and 21 outpatient). In their follow-up of these children the researchers relied on public health records and national registers. Also, a matched control group of children was selected from school health records. There were no differences between the two groups on many indices, including school completion, marital status, criminal offenses, and contact with social authorities. In relation to psychiatric care, however, a greater proportion of school refusers received outpatient treatment than the control group (31 percent v. 11 percent). In the absence of a detailed clinical assessment, the nature and severity of the difficulties experienced over the follow-up period are unknown. In all studies we reviewed, it can be noted that although the youngsters had received various forms of treatment, the findings point to continued psychopathology in adult life for a significant number of school refusers.

For many years, clinicians and researchers have proposed a relationship between school refusal and adult agoraphobia. Several studies have examined the retrospective reports of adult agoraphobic patients for a possible history of school refusal (e.g., Berg et al., 1974; Tyrer & Tyrer, 1974). In the Berg et al. study, for example, the incidence of past school refusal was surveyed by questionnaire in a large sample of women who were members of an agoraphobic correspondence club. School refusal was assumed to have been present when subjects answered "yes" to the question "Did you ever stay away from school for at least two weeks with a great reluctance or fear about going back?" Twenty-two percent of respondents indicated a history of school refusal. These individuals recalled experiencing a fear of leaving their parents as well as fears of teachers, schoolwork, other children, and physical education. However, a similar proportion of nonagoraphobic "neurotic" controls also reported a history of school refusal. Tyrer and Tyrer interviewed 240 adult psychiatric patients about problems of school attendance during childhood. The psychiatric patient sample comprised individuals with agoraphobia, chronic anxiety states, or depression. Patient reports of school refusal were validated by relatives, hospital records, and general practitioners. A control group of orthopedic and dental patients, matched for age and sex with the psychiatric sample, was also interviewed. Although the psychiatric patients reported a greater incidence of school refusal than did the control group, school refusal was not associated with agoraphobia in particular. Rather, school refusal was predictive of adult neurotic disturbance in general. Clinical and research issues on the relationship of school refusal to adult psychopathology have been discussed in greater detail by Klein and Last (1989).

SUMMARY

In keeping with society's expectations concerning education and school attendance, most children attend school on a regular and voluntary basis. However, for some children, school attendance is so distressing emotionally that they have difficulty attending school, often resulting in prolonged absence from school. We emphasized that school refusal is a heterogeneous problem and does not involve a fixed set of symptoms or constitute a unitary syndrome. In clinical presentation, for example, some children are separation-anxious while others might be fearful of specific events in the school setting such as tests or bullying. Yet other children exhibit depressive features along with their school attendance difficulties. Indeed, school-refusing children often meet *DSM-III-R/DSM-IV* criteria for separation anxiety disorder, social or simple phobia, or major depressive disorder. Also, many children have concurrent disorders such as separation anxiety disorder and major depressive disorder (labeled comorbidity). For some the school refusal is acute and short-lived; for others, however, it is chronic and persistent over years. The etiology of school refusal involves a complex interaction of many factors, including, for example, temperament characteristics, stressful life events, learning history, parental psychopathology, family dysfunction, and schoolwide system variables.

School refusal has a low prevalence among school-age children, although prevalence estimates depend very much on how we operationally define school refusal. While school refusal can occur throughout the entire school years, some research findings suggest peak onset periods at 5 to 6 years and 11 to 12 years. Contrary to early thinking, school-refusing children show a normal distribution of intelligence. Depending on a range of factors, school refusal may be a precursor to disturbance in adult life. In fact, it has been hypothesized that school refusal may be a forerunner to agoraphobia. Although a specific relationship between school refusal and agoraphobia has not been supported empirically, it is still worrying that a number of children with school attendance problems are at risk of continued psychopathology in adult life.

▶ 2

Behavioral
Assessment

INTRODUCTION

Before describing specific assessment procedures that we have found useful in working with school-refusing children, we shall comment briefly on the nature of behavioral assessment with children and adolescents in general. As frequently noted, the evaluation of effective behavioral interventions for child behavioral problems relies on the use of developmentally sensitive and psychometrically sound assessment tools. Yet, while treatment strategies derived from behavioral principles have a long and rich tradition in psychology (e.g., Holmes, 1936; Jones, 1924a; Watson & Rayner, 1920), assessment procedures based on these same principles have lagged behind. Moreover, most behavioral assessment procedures for children have been adopted, sometimes indiscriminately, from those used with adults. This "adultmorphic" practice is of dubious merit and has retarded advances in the theory and practice of child behavioral assessment. The need to develop and evaluate behavioral assessment procedures *for children* has been acknowledged recently by several authors (e.g., Mash & Terdal, 1981, 1988; Ollendick & Hersen, 1984, 1993).

As first described by Mash and Terdal (1981) and expanded on by Ollendick and Hersen (1984), child behavioral assessment can be described as *an exploratory, hypothesis-testing process in which a range of specific procedures is used in order to understand a given child, group, or social ecology, and to formulate and evaluate specific treatment strategies.* As such, child behavioral assessment entails more than the identification of discrete target behaviors and their controlling variables. While the importance of direct observation of target behaviors should not be underestimated, recent advances in child behavioral assessment have incorporated a wide range of assessment procedures, including behavioral and diagnostic interviews, self-reports, ratings by significant others, self-monitoring, and behavioral observations. This *multimethod approach* results in a composite "picture" of the child that is useful in both the understanding and treatment of specific child behavior problems (Ollendick & Cerny, 1981).

Two primary features characterize good child behavioral assessment procedures. First, they should be sensitive to rapid developmental changes, and, second, they should be validated empirically. Probably the most important and distinguishing characteristic of children is change. Whether such change is based on hypothesized stages of growth (e.g., Piagetian theory) or assumed principles of learning (e.g., operant theory, social learning theory), it has direct implications for the selection of assessment procedures and for their use in the evaluation of treatment outcome. Behavioral and diagnostic interviews, self-reports, other-reports, self-monitoring, and behavioral observation are all affected by rapidly changing developmental processes. Further, some of these assessment procedures are more useful at one age than at another. For example, diagnostic interviews may be more difficult to conduct and self-reports may be less reliable with younger children (Achenbach, McConaughy, & Howell, 1987), whereas self-monitoring and behavioral observations may be more reactive with adolescents (Ollendick & Hersen, 1984). Age-related constraints are numerous and must be taken into considerations when selecting methods of assessment.

Child behavioral assessment procedures must be psychometrically sound and empirically validated. All too frequently, professionals working with children have used assessment methods out of convenience without due regard for their psychometric properties, including their reliability, validity, and clinical utility. Although child behavior assessors have fared somewhat better in this regard than their psychodynamically oriented counterparts, they too have tended to develop and use assessment tools designed for very specific purposes, often without regard for their psychometric characteristics. As we have noted elsewhere (Ollendick & Hersen, 1984, 1993), comparison across studies is difficult, and the advancement of an assessment technology, let alone an understanding of child behavior disorders, is less possible with such an approach.

While a multimethod approach based on developmentally sensitive and empirically validated procedures is espoused, it should be clear that a "test battery" approach is not being recommended. The specific procedures to be used depend on a variety of factors including the age of the child; the reason for the referral; and the personnel, time, and resources available (Ollendick & Cerny, 1981). Nonetheless, given the inherent limitations of the various procedures as well as the desirability of obtaining as complete a picture of the child as possible, we recommend multimethod assessment whenever feasible. Any one procedure is not sufficient to provide a composite view of the child. The multimethod approach is not only helpful in assessing specific target behaviors and in determining response to behavior change, but also in understanding child behavior disorders and advancing our data base in this area of study.

Based on these considerations, we offer the following assumptions about child behavioral assessment:

1. Children are a special population. The automatic extension of adult behavioral assessment methods to children is not warranted and may in many instances be inappropriate. Age-related variables affect the choice of methods as well as the procedures employed.

2. Given rapid developmental change in children, normative comparisons are required to ensure that appropriate target behaviors are selected and that change in behavior is related to treatment, not to normal developmental change. Such comparisons require identification of suitable reference groups and information about the "natural course" of child behavior problems.

3. Thorough child behavioral assessment involves multiple targets of change including overt behavior, affective states, and cognitive processes. Further, such assessment entails determining the context (e.g., developmental, familial, social, cultural) in which the child's behavior occurs and the function that the targeted behaviors serve.

4. Given the wide range of targets for change, multimethod assessment is desirable. Multimethod assessment should not be viewed simply as a test battery approach; rather, methods should be selected on the basis of their appropriateness to the referral question. Regardless of the measures used, they should be developmentally sensitive and empirically validated (Weist, Ollendick, & Finney, 1991).

ASSESSMENT PROCEDURES

As emphasized in Chapter 1, school refusal in children is complex and does not represent a unitary syndrome. Some children who refuse school present with specific fears or phobias about aspects of the school itself (e.g., speaking in front of class, being teased by a bully), whereas others present with long and complicated histories of separation anxiety, depression, and, at times, oppositional or defiant problems. Further, it is clear that the problems related to school refusal can result from a variety of causes and that they may be "explained" by different theoretical approaches. As a result, the factors that are deemed important in a thorough assessment vary according to one's theoretical perspective. From a behavioral point of view, school refusal can be viewed as a complex set of learned responses that have specific affective, behavioral, and cognitive referents (King, Hamilton, & Ollendick, 1988).

Accordingly, comprehensive assessment of school refusal includes measures of affective, behavioral, and cognitive responding as well as determination of the context in which the refusal occurs. Our strategy is to begin with a broad assessment of the child and his or her environment (e.g., family, peers, school) and move toward obtaining more specific information about stimulus features, response modes, antecedents and consequences, severity, duration, and pervasiveness of the school refusal. Thus, the assessment procedure begins with a thorough behavioral interview conducted with the child and his or her parents and utilizes a multimethod, problem-solving approach (Mash & Terdal, 1981; Ollendick & Hersen, 1984).

As noted earlier, multimethod behavioral assessment of children entails the use of a range of procedures. As behavioral approaches with children evolved from sole reliance on operant procedures to those involving cognitive and self-control procedures, the methods of assessment changed accordingly. The identification of discrete target behaviors has been expanded to include assessment of cognitions and affects as well as large-scale social systems that affect the child (e.g., families, schools, communities).

Information about these additional areas can be obtained most efficiently through interviews, self-reports, and other-reports. Cone (1978) has described these assessment methods as *indirect*; that is, while they may be used to measure behaviors of clinical relevance, they are obtained at a time and place different from that when the actual behaviors occurred. In both behavioral interviews and self-report questionnaires a verbal representation of the behaviors of interest is obtained. Other-reports or ratings by others are also included in the indirect category because they involve retrospective descriptions of behavior. Generally a significant person in the child's environment (e.g., parent, teacher) is asked to rate the child based on previous observations (recollections).

As noted by Cone (1978), ratings such as these should not be confused with direct observation methods that assess the behaviors of interest at the time and place of their occurrence. Of course, information regarding cognition and affects, as well as the situations or settings in which they occur, can be obtained through direct behavioral observations, either by self-monitoring or through trained observers. In the sections that follow, both indirect and direct methods are examined, and guidelines for their use are presented.

Behavioral Interviews

Of the many procedures employed by behavioral clinicians, the problem-focused behavioral interview is the most widely used (Swann & MacDonald, 1978) and is generally considered an indispensable part of case formulation (Gross, 1984; Linehan, 1977). Behavioral interviews are structured to obtain detailed information about the target behaviors and their controlling variables, to begin the formulation of specific treatment plans, and to develop a relationship with the child and his or her family (Ollendick & Cerny, 1981). While the primary purpose of the behavioral interview is to obtain information, we have found that traditional "helping" skills including reflections, clarifications, and summary statements help put the child and parents at ease and greatly facilitate the collection of this information.

The popularity of the behavioral interview derives from a number of practical considerations as well as specific advantages it offers over other procedures (Gross, 1984). While direct observations of target behaviors are the hallmark of behavioral assessment, such observations are not always practical or feasible. At times, especially in outpatient therapy, the clinician must rely on the child's self-report as well as that of his or her parents to initiate assessment and treatment. Further, the interview allows the clinician to obtain a broad band of information regarding overall functioning as well as detailed information about specific areas of concern. The flexibility inherent in the interview also allows the clinician to build a relationship with the child and family and to obtain information that might otherwise not be revealed. As noted by Linehan (1977), some family members may be more likely to divulge information verbally in the context of a professional relationship than to write it down on a form to be entered into a permanent file.

In addition, the interview allows the clinician the opportunity to observe the family as a whole and obtain information about the context in which the problem behaviors of the identified client (i.e., the school-refusing child) occur. Several interrelated issues may arise when child behavioral assessment is expanded to include the family unit (Evans & Nelson, 1977; Ollendick & Cerny, 1981). First, children rarely refer themselves for treatment; invariably, they are referred by adults, whose perceptions of problems may not coincide with those of the referred children. A second issue, related to the first, is the determination of when child behaviors are problematic and when they are not. Normative developmental comparisons are useful in this regard. It is not uncommon for parents to refer 5-year-olds who reverse letters, 3-year-olds who wet the bed, and 13-year-olds who are concerned about their physical appearance. Over the years we have also had several parents contact us because their child misses school occasionally and apparently feigns illness in order to stay home or avoid unpleasant circumstances at school. It is, of course, quite common for children to miss school occasionally and even to pretend that they are sick to determine their parents' response (Berganza & Anders, 1978). Frequently these referrals are based on parental uneasiness or unrealistic expectations rather than genuine problems (see Campbell, 1989, for further discussion of these issues). Finally, problematic family interactions (especially parent-child interactions) are frequently observed in families in which a particular child has been identified for treatment (cf. Patterson, 1976, 1982). These interactions may not be a part of the parents' original perception of the problematic behavior. However, assessment of such interactions allows the clinician the opportunity to observe the verbal and nonverbal behaviors of the family unit in response to a variety of topics and of family members in response to each other.

Evaluations of parental perceptions and parent-child interactions may enable the clinician to conceptualize the problematic behavior and formulate possible treatment alternatives from a more comprehensive, integrated perspective. However, the preceding discussion is not meant to imply that the behavioral interview should be limited to the family; in many instances, including that of school refusal, the issues and practices described here need to be extended to adults outside the family unit, such as teachers, principals, and physicians, and to environments beyond the home, including schools or daycare centers. With school refusal it is particularly important to assess the perceptions of teachers as well as specific teacher-child interactions. Thus, the clinician should approach the behavioral interview with caution and avoid blind acceptance of the premise that "school refusal" exists solely in the child. Information obtained in a comprehensive assessment may reveal that the school refusal is only a component of a more complex clinical picture involving siblings, parents, peers, other adults, and school systems. Of course, in undertaking such an extended and global assessment, issues of confidentiality must be considered and the rights of the child and family protected. Obviously, permission to secure information from these additional sources should be obtained.

In conducting a problem-focused behavioral interview with children who refuse school and with their parents, it is important to recognize that such children frequently present as timid, shy, fearful, and anxious and that they may be relatively unresponsive in the interview situation. As a result, it is usually necessary to phrase questions in specific, direct terms that the child will understand. It is also necessary to provide support and encouragement for responding. Open-ended questions such as "How do you feel about school?" or "How are things going in school?" generally result in unelaborated responses such as "I don't know" or "OK." More specific questions such as "What exactly makes you afraid in school?," "What do you think first caused you to be afraid in school?," "What happened?," and "What do your parents usually do when you tell them you are sick and do not want to go to school?" are more easily and readily responded to by the child. In addition, it is helpful to use the child's own words when phrasing these questions. Some children distinguish "nervous" feelings (scared, upset) from "anxious" (eager, anticipatory) ones. Of course, it is always important to keep developmental considerations in mind and to ensure that the child understands the questions.

In order to help the child describe aspects related to the school refusal, we have found it useful to have the child imagine himself or herself in the school situation and to describe what actually happens. For example, the child might be asked to describe all aspects of the dreaded classroom including the position of the teacher's desk, how the seats are arranged, the furnishings in the classroom, and the location of the classroom in the school. Then the child might be asked to describe in detail what leads up to his or her fear and what consequences ensue. In doing so, we observe the child for overt signs of fear such as crying, tremors, or flushing. At times this procedure is useful in delineating the specific cues that occasion the refusal behavior.

In sum, an attempt is made during the initial behavioral interview to obtain as complete a picture as possible of the child, his or her family, and other important individuals and environments. While the interview is focused around specific target behaviors, adult-child interactions and adult perceptions of the problem are also assessed. These perceptions should be considered tentative, however, and used primarily to formulate hypotheses about target behaviors and their controlling variables and to select additional assessment methods to explore target behaviors in greater depth (e.g., diagnostic interviews, rating scales, self-reports, self-monitoring, and behavioral observations). The behavioral interview, conducted in our outpatient clinics with both the school-refusing child and his or her parents in attendance, is the first step in the assessment process. Of course, this interview can be conducted in the school itself, as suggested by Blagg (1987).

Diagnostic Interviews

When possible, we recommend that the behavioral interview be followed by one of the more structured or semistructured diagnostic interviews. In general, these interview schedules allow for the standardized administration of questions and observations of prescribed behaviors. They also facilitate greater reliability of diagnosis (Edelbrock & Costello, 1984; Silverman, 1991) and acknowledge that children can provide valuable information about their thoughts, feelings, and behaviors that are useful in diagnostic decision making (Ollendick & Greene, 1990; Silverman, 1991). Effective diagnostic interviews must be reliable, valid, and clinically and educationally useful.

A variety of diagnostic interviews exist: the Interview Schedule for Children (Kovacs, 1978), the Children's Assessment Schedule (Hodges, 1978), the Diagnostic Interview Schedule for Children (Costello et al., 1984), the Diagnostic Interview for Children and Adolescents (Herjanic & Reich, 1982), and the Anxiety Disorders Interview Schedule for Children (Silverman, 1991a,b; Silverman & Nelles, 1988). Each possesses particular strengths and weaknesses (see recent review by Silverman, 1991c). In our work with anxious and phobic children we have found the Anxiety Disorders Interview Schedule for Children (ADIS) and its recent revision to be the most useful. It is the only diagnostic interview designed specifically for anxiety disorders and, as a result, it is more extensive in its coverage. There are two versions of the ADIS, a child version (ADIS—C) and a parent version (ADIS—P). Both are downward extensions of a similar schedule used with adults (DiNardo et al., 1983). The interviews, which are organized by diagnosis, permit differential diagnosis among the major *DSM* anxiety disorders (both childhood and adulthood disorders) from the perspective of both the child and the parent. Although Silverman and Nelles (1988) recommend interviewing the child first, followed by the parent, we have not found this practice to be essential. Whenever possible, we have one clinician interview the child while another interviews the parent. Interview questions from the School Refusal Behavior section of the ADIS—C and ADIS—P are reproduced for illustrative purposes in Table 2-1 and Table 2-2, respectively.

In examining the School Refusal Behavior sections of the ADIS, note that the same questions are addressed to both the child and his or her parents. Also note that visual prompts (i.e., Fear Thermometer, Interference Thermometer) are used to help the child report his or her symptomatology. Furthermore, the parent interview asks specific questions that potentially lead to a functional analysis of the school refusal behavior. Similar detail is addressed for the major anxiety disorders and the major depressive disorders. Finally,

TABLE 2-1 • ADIS—C School Refusal Behavior

1. Do you get very nervous or scared about having to go to school?
    _____ Yes   _____ No   _____ Other

2. Do you stay home from school because you are nervous or scared?
    _____ Yes   _____ No   _____ Other
    If "Yes," ask: How many times has that happened this year? _____
    If "Yes," ask 2A; otherwise skip to question 3.

    A. Can you give me an example of a "typical" day when you wake up and don't go
        to school? [What happens? What do you do? What do your parents do?]
        _____
        _____

3. Do you get very nervous or scared when you are in school?
    _____ Yes   _____ No   _____ Other

    A. If child responds "Yes," ask: Have you ever left school because of this?
        _____ Yes   _____ No   _____ Other

    If "Yes," ask: How many times has that happened this year? _____

    Ask child to elaborate on "Yes" response to 3 or 3A.

    Record as "No" responses that reflect "typical" child school-related anxiety and do
    not appear to be excessively interfering (e.g., "a little nervous before tests," "a little
    nervous when I forget my homework").

    If "Yes" to any of Questions 1–3, go to Question 4.

    If "No" to Questions 1–3, skip to SEPARATION ANXIETY.

4. Do you miss school or leave school because you like it better at home?
    _____ Yes   _____ No   _____ Other

5. Has anyone ever given you any medicine to help you go to school?
    _____ Yes   _____ No   _____ Other

    If "Yes," Could you tell me about that? _____
    _____
    _____

6. What exactly is it that makes school scary for you? If younger child, ask: If I had a
    magic wand, is there anything I could do to make school less scary? _____
    _____
    _____

7. I am going to give you a list of a few things and I'd like you to tell me if any of
    them may be what makes you nervous about school. OK?

    For each "Yes" response below, use Fear Thermometer to obtain severity rating
    (0–4-point scale).

    For those items with a severity rating of 2 or greater, a rating of interference should
    also be obtained. Interviewer should use the following instructions to explain
    "interference," pointing to "Interference Thermometer" during explanation. Other-
    wise, skip to Question 8.

(Continued)

TABLE 2-1 • *(Continued)*

A. OK, I want to know how much the fears you have told me about upset you or bother you; that is, how much they have messed things up for you, how much it stops you from doing things in school you would like to do, and so on. OK? I want you to tell me how much (0–4-point scale) by using this "Mess Things Up Thermometer," OK? If necessary, interviewer should review the scale with child. Show child "Interference Thermometer."

		Severity Rating	*Interference Rating*
The teacher(s) or principal	__ Yes __ No __ Other	_____	_____
The other kids	__ Yes __ No __ Other	_____	_____
Speaking to other people	__ Yes __ No __ Other	_____	_____
Having to talk in class or in front of the class	__ Yes __ No __ Other	_____	_____
Taking tests	__ Yes __ No __ Other	_____	_____
Writing on the blackboard	__ Yes __ No __ Other	_____	_____
Being away from your parents because you are in school	__ Yes __ No __ Other	_____	_____
The bell ringing	__ Yes __ No __ Other	_____	_____
Gym class	__ Yes __ No __ Other	_____	_____
Riding on the school bus	__ Yes __ No __ Other	_____	_____
Anything else?			
_____	__ Yes __ No __ Other	_____	_____

Objects/situations specified by child in Question 6 if not mentioned above

_____		_____	_____
_____		_____	_____

8. Is there anything else about school that bothers you a lot and may help us understand why you have trouble being in school?
   _____ Yes   _____ No   _____ Other

If the child reports "Yes" or almost Yes via "Other" to *any* of questions 6–8, continue inquiry.

If the child reports "No" to all questions 7–8, ask him/her why he/she reported problems in questions 1–4. Repeat questions 7–8 if necessary to obtain clarification. Otherwise, skip to SEPARATION ANXIETY DISORDER.

   A. How long have you had problems going to (or staying in) school? _____

   To be viewed as having clinically significant school refusal behavior, one of the following conditions must hold: (a) Interference of 2 or greater for any item in Question 7A, (b) child misses, leaves, or has trouble going to school enough times to constitute an interference rating of 2 or greater.

TABLE 2-2 • ADIS—P School Refusal Behavior

1. Does your child get very nervous or scared about having to go to school?
   _____ Yes   _____ No   _____ Other

2. Does your child stay home from school because he/she is nervous or scared?
   _____ Yes   _____ No   _____ Other

   If "Yes," ask: How many times has that happened this year? _____

3. Does your child tell you that he/she gets very nervous or scared when he/she is in school?
   _____ Yes   _____ No   _____ Other

   A. If parents respond "Yes," ask: Has your child ever left school because of this?
      _____ Yes   _____ No   _____ Other

      If "Yes," ask: How many times has that happened this year? _____

   Ask parent to elaborate on "Yes" response to 3 or 3A.

   Record as "No" responses that reflect "typical" child school-related anxiety and do not appear to be excessively interfering (e.g., "a little nervous before tests," "a little nervous when he/she forgets his/her homework").

   If "Yes" to any of Questions 1–3, go to Question 4. If "No" to Questions 1–3, skip to SEPARATION ANXIETY.

4. Do you think your child misses school or tries to stay out of school because she/he likes it better at home?
   _____ Yes   _____ No   _____ Other

   If "Yes," ask: How many times has that happened this year? _____

   If "Yes" or "Other," explain: _____
   _____

5. What does your child do when she/he is not in school? Can you give me an example of a "typical" day when your child wakes up and doesn't go to school? (What happens? What do you or other family members do when your child does not want to go to school?) _____
   _____

6. Has your child ever been on medication for this problem of being nervous about school?
   _____ Yes   _____ No   _____ Other

   If "Yes," Could you tell me about that? _____
   _____

7. What do you think it is that makes school scary for your child? _____
   _____

8. I am going to give you a list of a few things, and I'd like you to tell me if you think any of them may be what makes your child nervous about school, OK? Ask parent to elaborate on each "Yes" response. Also, use 0–4 rating scale to obtain severity rating.

(Continued)

TABLE 2-2 • *(Continued)*

For those items with a severity rating of 2 or greater, a rating of interference should also be obtained. The following instructions should be used to obtain interference rating.

A. OK, (parent's name), for those things that you told me "2" or more to, I want you to tell me, again on a 0–4 scale, how much do you think this fear of your child interferes in his/her life, meaning that it interferes with his/her doing things at school, and how much it bothers him/her.

		Severity Rating	*Interference Rating*
The teacher(s) or principal	__ Yes __ No __ Other	_____	_____
The other kids	__ Yes __ No __ Other	_____	_____
Speaking to other people	__ Yes __ No __ Other	_____	_____
Having to talk in class or in front of the class	__ Yes __ No __ Other	_____	_____
Taking tests	__ Yes __ No __ Other	_____	_____
Writing on the blackboard	__ Yes __ No __ Other	_____	_____
Being away from your parents because you are in school	__ Yes __ No __ Other	_____	_____
The bell ringing	__ Yes __ No __ Other	_____	_____
Gym class	__ Yes __ No __ Other	_____	_____
Riding on the school bus	__ Yes __ No __ Other	_____	_____
Anything else? _____	__ Yes __ No __ Other	_____	_____
Objects/situations specified by parent in Question 7 if not mentioned above			
_____		_____	_____
_____		_____	_____

9. Is there anything else about school that you think may bother your child and may help us understand why he/she has trouble being in school?
   _____ Yes   _____ No   _____ Other

   If "Yes" or "Other," explain: _____
   _____

   If the parent reports "Yes" or almost Yes via "Other" to *any* of Questions 7–9, continue inquiry.

   If the parent reports "No" to all items of Question 8A and Question 9, ask him/her why he/she reported problems in Questions 1–4. Repeat Questions 8A–9 if necessary to obtain clarification. Otherwise, skip to SEPARATION ANXIETY DISORDER.

10. How long has your child had problems going to (or staying in) school?

    To be viewed as having clinically significant school refusal behavior, one of the following conditions must hold: (a) Interference of 2 or greater for any item in Question 8A; (b) child misses, leaves, or has trouble going to school enough times to constitute an interference rating of 2 or greater.

Source: W. K. Silverman (1991b), *Anxiety Disorders Interview Schedule for Children (Parent Version).* Albany, New York: Graywind Publications. Reprinted with permission. All rights reserved.

the parent version includes additional questions and diagnostic criteria for disruptive behavior disorders. Guidelines for combining the parent and child data to arrive at composite diagnoses are provided.

For the ADIS—C alone, ADIS—P alone, and Composite Diagnosis, Silverman and Nelles (1988) report moderate to high reliability estimates (Kappa coefficients between .78 and .84). Reliability estimates for specific disorders are somewhat lower but remain in the good to high ranges (Kappa coefficients range from .54 to 1.00 for the specific disorders). In a recent study, Silverman and Eisen (1992) reported the test-retest (10-day to 2-week retest interval) reliabilities to be similarly good (overall Kappas ranged from .67 to .76, while specific disorder Kappas ranged from .64 to .84). The utility of the schedule has been illustrated in several clinical case studies (Beidel, 1991; Ollendick, Hagopian, & Huntzinger, 1991). Attention to developmental issues (i.e., the wording of the questions, the use of visual prompts) may be particularly important for the enhanced reliability and validity of this schedule. As we have noted elsewhere, many of the other structured diagnostic interviews possess questionable reliability and validity, especially for the anxiety and phobic disorders (Ollendick & Francis, 1988).

In sum, structured diagnostic interviews are useful in providing a more complete diagnostic picture of the school-refusing child. In particular, the interviews are useful in drawing our attention to related disorders and characteristics. In many instances we might fail to ask relevant questions that would lead to these associated diagnoses; the diagnostic interviews, of course, provide specific cues to elicit such information. Although many schedules exist, we have found the ADIS designed by Silverman and her colleagues to be the most useful. Typically, these interviews are administered separately to the child and to his or her parents, providing important information from each point of view. As with the behavioral interview, the diagnostic interview is only one step in the process of obtaining a complete picture of the school-refusing child.

Self-Report Instruments

Following the behavioral and diagnostic interviews, we focus our attention on the children's self-reports of the situations that provoke the school refusal and the subjective experiences (both affective and cognitive) associated with the school refusal behavior (concurrently, assessment of family functioning and parent rating scales is undertaken; see following sections). A variety of self-report instruments for children and adolescents are available. Among the instruments that we have found most useful are measures of fear, anxiety, and depression; specifically, the Fear Survey Schedule for Children, the Children's Manifest Anxiety Scale, and the Children's Depression Inventory. More recently, we have also incorporated the School Refusal Assessment Scale (SRAS). The SRAS helps us explore the motivational factors involved in school refusal behavior and assists in arriving at a functional analysis of the behavior.

Fear Survey Schedule for Children.   Scherer and Nakamura (1968) developed the Fear Survey Schedule for Children (FSSC), modeled after the Wolpe-Lang Fear Survey Schedule for Adults (Wolpe & Lang, 1964). On this scale, children are instructed to rate their fear of each of 80 items on a 5-point scale. Factor-analytic studies of the FSSC show that this scale taps major fears: fear of death, fear of the dark, and home and school fears (Scherer & Nakamura, 1968). It was originally developed for children between 9 and 12 years of age.

Modified versions of the FSSC have been developed by Ryall and Dietiker (1979) and Ollendick (1983). The Children's Fear Survey Schedule developed by Ryall and Dietiker (1979) is a short form of the FSSC that contains 48 specific fear items and two blanks for children to indicate additional fears not already listed. Each item is rated on a 3-point scale ranging from not scared or nervous or afraid to a little scared to very scared. It was modified for use with younger children and is reported to be useful with children between 5 and 12 years of age. Although no information is available as to the validity of this revised Children's Fear Survey Schedule, it possesses good test-retest reliability and internal consistency.

The revision of the Fear Survey Schedule for Children undertaken by Ollendick (FSSR—R; Ollendick, 1983) is another useful tool for determining specific fear stimuli related to children's phobic behavior (Table 2-3). School-age children are instructed to rate their fear of the 80 items on a 3-point scale ranging from being frightened by the item none, some, or a lot. Normative data for children between 7 and 18 years of age are available. Further, the instrument has been used in cross-cultural studies in Australia, the United Kingdom, and the United States (King et al., 1989; Ollendick, King, & Frary, 1989; Ollendick, Matson, & Helsel, 1985; Ollendick, Yule, & Ollier, 1990). An examination of the scale suggests that it is a reliable and valid revision of the FSSC. For example, high scores on the survey are positively related to measures of anxiety and negatively related to internal locus of control and positive self-concept. Further, Ollendick and Mayer (1984) reported that it discriminated between "school phobic" children whose fears were related to separation anxiety and children whose fears appeared to be related to specific aspects of the school situation itself.

TABLE 2-3 • **The Fear Survey Schedule for Children—Revised**

SELF-RATING QUESTIONNAIRE (FSSC—R)

Name: _____   Age: _____   Date: _____

DIRECTIONS: A number of statements that boys and girls use to describe the fears they have are given below. Read each fear carefully and put an X in the box in front of the words that best describe your fear. There are no right or wrong answers. Remember, find the words that best describe how much fear you have.

		None		Some		A lot
1.	Giving an oral report	☐		☐		☐
2.	Riding in the car or bus	☐		☐		☐
3.	Getting punished by my mother	☐		☐		☐
4.	Lizards	☐		☐		☐
5.	Looking foolish	☐		☐		☐
6.	Ghosts or spooky things	☐		☐		☐
7.	Sharp objects	☐		☐		☐
8.	Having to go to the hospital	☐		☐		☐
9.	Death or dead people	☐		☐		☐
10.	Getting lost in a strange place	☐		☐		☐
11.	Snakes	☐		☐		☐
12.	Talking on the telephone	☐		☐		☐
13.	Roller coaster or carnival rides	☐		☐		☐
14.	Getting sick at school	☐		☐		☐
15.	Being sent to the principal	☐		☐		☐
16.	Riding on the train	☐		☐		☐
17.	Being left at home with a sitter	☐		☐		☐
18.	Bears or wolves	☐		☐		☐
19.	Meeting someone for the first time	☐		☐		☐
20.	Bombing attacks—being invaded	☐		☐		☐
21.	Getting a shot from the nurse or doctor	☐		☐		☐
22.	Going to the dentist	☐		☐		☐
23.	High places like mountains	☐		☐		☐
24.	Being teased	☐		☐		☐
25.	Spiders	☐		☐		☐
26.	A burglar breaking into our house	☐		☐		☐
27.	Flying in a plane	☐		☐		☐
28.	Being called on by the teacher	☐		☐		☐
29.	Getting poor grades	☐		☐		☐
30.	Bats or birds	☐		☐		☐
31.	My parents criticizing me	☐		☐		☐
32.	Guns	☐		☐		☐
33.	Being in a fight	☐		☐		☐
34.	Fire—getting burned	☐		☐		☐
35.	Getting a cut or injury	☐		☐		☐
36.	Being in a big crowd	☐		☐		☐
37.	Thunderstorms	☐		☐		☐
38.	Having to eat some food I don't like	☐		☐		☐
39.	Cats	☐		☐		☐
40.	Failing a test	☐		☐		☐

(Continued)

TABLE 2-3 • *(Continued)*

41.	Being hit by a car or truck	☐	None	☐	Some	☐	A lot
42.	Having to go to school	☐	None	☐	Some	☐	A lot
43.	Playing rough games during recess	☐	None	☐	Some	☐	A lot
44.	Having my parents argue	☐	None	☐	Some	☐	A lot
45.	Dark rooms or closets	☐	None	☐	Some	☐	A lot
46.	Having to put on a recital	☐	None	☐	Some	☐	A lot
47.	Ants or beetles	☐	None	☐	Some	☐	A lot
48.	Being criticized by others	☐	None	☐	Some	☐	A lot
49.	Strange-looking people	☐	None	☐	Some	☐	A lot
50.	The sight of blood	☐	None	☐	Some	☐	A lot
51.	Going to the doctor	☐	None	☐	Some	☐	A lot
52.	Strange or mean-looking dogs	☐	None	☐	Some	☐	A lot
53.	Cemeteries	☐	None	☐	Some	☐	A lot
54.	Getting a report card	☐	None	☐	Some	☐	A lot
55.	Getting a haircut	☐	None	☐	Some	☐	A lot
56.	Deep water or the ocean	☐	None	☐	Some	☐	A lot
57.	Nightmares	☐	None	☐	Some	☐	A lot
58.	Falling from high places	☐	None	☐	Some	☐	A lot
59.	Getting a shock from electricity	☐	None	☐	Some	☐	A lot
60.	Going to bed in the dark	☐	None	☐	Some	☐	A lot
61.	Getting car sick	☐	None	☐	Some	☐	A lot
62.	Being alone	☐	None	☐	Some	☐	A lot
63.	Having to wear clothes different from others	☐	None	☐	Some	☐	A lot
64.	Getting punished by my father	☐	None	☐	Some	☐	A lot
65.	Having to stay after school	☐	None	☐	Some	☐	A lot
66.	Making mistakes	☐	None	☐	Some	☐	A lot
67.	Mystery movies	☐	None	☐	Some	☐	A lot
68.	Loud sirens	☐	None	☐	Some	☐	A lot
69.	Doing something new	☐	None	☐	Some	☐	A lot
70.	Germs or getting a serious illness	☐	None	☐	Some	☐	A lot
71.	Closed spaces	☐	None	☐	Some	☐	A lot
72.	Earthquakes	☐	None	☐	Some	☐	A lot
73.	Russia	☐	None	☐	Some	☐	A lot
74.	Elevators	☐	None	☐	Some	☐	A lot
75.	Dark places	☐	None	☐	Some	☐	A lot
76.	Not being able to breathe	☐	None	☐	Some	☐	A lot
77.	Getting a bee sting	☐	None	☐	Some	☐	A lot
78.	Worms or snails	☐	None	☐	Some	☐	A lot
79.	Rats or mice	☐	None	☐	Some	☐	A lot
80.	Taking a test	☐	None	☐	Some	☐	A lot

Source: T. H. Ollendick, "Reliability and Validity of the Revised Fear Survey Schedule for Children (FSSC—R)," *Behaviour Research and Therapy, 21,* 685–692 (1983). Copyright 1983, with kind permission from Elsevier Science Ltd., The Boulevard, Langford Lane, Kidlington 0X51GB, UK.

Children whose school refusal was related to separation anxiety checked as fear-inspiring items such as "Getting lost in a strange place," "Being left at home with a sitter," "My parents criticizing me," and "Having to stay after school." Children whose school refusal was related to specific aspects of the school itself more frequently checked items such as "Giving an oral report," "Being sent to the principal," "Being called on by the teacher," and "Taking a test." In some cases this latter group of children also checked items related to "Being in a fight" and "Playing rough games during recess." Both groups of children claimed fear of "Having to go to school" and "Getting sick at school." Last, Francis, and Strauss (1989) recently reported similar findings and have shown that fear of similar items is related to differential diagnosis of school refusal, separation anxiety disorder, and overanxious disorder. In addition to these indications of the schedule's validity, Ollendick (1983) has shown that the measure possesses acceptable test-retest reliability and that it is internally consistent.

Finally, the instrument has been found to possess factorial invariance across wide age ranges in English-speaking cultures (Ollendick, Matson, & Helsel, 1985; Ollendick, King, & Frary, 1989; Ollendick, Yule, & Ollier, 1990). A five-factor solution has been obtained: Fear of Failure and Criticism, Fear of the Unknown, Fear of Injury and Small Animals, Fear of Danger and Death, and Medical Fears. Items contained on the Fear of Failure and Criticism factor are presented in Table 2-4. As can be seen, many of these fear items are directly related to those reported by children who refuse school because of specific factors at the school itself. Children who refuse school because of separation concerns frequently report these fears as well as those on the Fear of the Unknown factor.

Children's Manifest Anxiety Scale.   In contrast to the fear survey schedules, measures of anxiety have been used to determine the subjectively experienced effects of being in unknown or fearful situations. The Children's Manifest Anxiety Scale (CMAS; Casteneda, McCandless, & Palmero, 1956), a scaled-down version of the Manifest Anxiety Scale for Adults (Taylor, 1951), consists of 42 anxiety items and 11 lie items that assess a child's report of pervasive anxiety. In recent years, Reynolds and Richmond (1978) developed a revised version of the CMAS titled "What I Think and Feel" (RCMAS). The purpose of this 37-item revision (28 anxiety items, 9 lie items) was to clarify the wording of items, decrease administration time, and lower the reading level of the items. Representative anxiety items include, "I have trouble making up my mind," "It is hard for me to keep my mind on my school work," and "Often I feel sick in my stomach." Children respond to each of the items in a yes/no format. The RCMAS is suitable for children and

TABLE 2-4 • **The Failure and Criticism Factor of the FSSC—R**

1. Giving an oral report
3. Getting punished by my mother
5. Looking foolish
14. Getting sick at school
15. Being sent to the principal
19. Meeting someone for the first time
24. Being teased
28. Being called on by the teacher
29. Getting poor grades
31. My parents criticizing me
38. Having to eat some food I don't like
40. Failing a test
42. Having to go to school
44. Having my parents argue
46. Having to put on a recital
48. Being criticized by others
54. Getting a report card
63. Having to wear clothes different from others
64. Getting punished by my father
65. Having to stay after school
66. Making mistakes
69. Doing something new
80. Taking a test

Source: T. H. Ollendick, N. J. King, and R. B. Frary, "Fears in Children and Adolescents," *Behaviour Research and Therapy, 27,* 19–26 (1989). Copyright 1983, with kind permission from Elsevier Science Ltd., The Boulevard, Langford Lane, Kidlington 0X5 1GB, UK.

adolescents between 6 and 18 years of age; normative information for a variety of child groups from diverse cultures is available (Reynolds & Paget, 1983; Richmond & Millar, 1984; Richmond et al., 1984). Recently we have extended its use to Australian and British children (Ollendick, Yule, & Ollier, 1990). The scale yields three anxiety factors: physiological, worry/oversensitivity, and concentration (Reynolds & Richmond, 1978). We have found the factor scales to be particularly useful in determining targets of intervention. Some children who refuse school report high levels of physiological arousal, whereas others report few problems with physiological arousal but extreme difficulties with concentration or general overarousal and worry. Chapter 3 describes the use of this scale for intervention purposes in more detail.

Children's Depression Inventory.   As noted in Chapter 1, depression is frequently observed in children who refuse school. Several self-report measures of childhood and adolescent depression have emerged in recent years, including the Children's Depression Inventory (Kovacs & Beck, 1977), the Short Children's Depression Inventory (Carlson & Cantwell, 1979), the Beck Depression Inventory (Beck et al., 1961) and its modified adolescent form (Chiles, Miller, & Cox, 1980), the Children's Depression Scale (Lang & Tisher, 1978), and the Self-Rating Scale (Birleson, 1981). These measures and their psychometric characteristics have been reviewed thoroughly by Kazdin (1981) and Kazdin and Petti (1982). In his 1981 review, Kazdin concluded, "Because of the few studies that have examined basic psychometric properties of the assessment devices, the measurement of childhood depression is still at a very preliminary stage" (p. 366). Fortunately, much research has occurred since his seminal review, and we can now conclude that reliable, valid, and clinically useful assessment devices exist. Among the most frequently used and psychometrically sound instruments are the Children's Depression Inventory (CDI) and, for adolescents, the scale from which the CDI was derived, the Beck Depression Inventory (BDI). We will examine the CDI only, as the psychometric characteristics and clinical utility of the BDI are similar to those of the CDI. Although additional psychometric work remains to be conducted, the CDI is the most widely used clinical and research measure of childhood depression (Kazdin, 1988).

The CDI consists of 27 items designed to assess a variety of symptoms of depression such as sleep disturbance, appetite loss, suicidal thoughts, and general dysphoria. Each item consists of three brief statements that describe a range of endorsements, from normal responses to indications of moderate depressive symptoms or severe depressive symptoms. The child chooses the statement that best describes him or her (e.g., Item 15: "Doing schoolwork is not a big problem," "I have to push myself many times to do my schoolwork," "I have to push myself all the time to do my schoolwork" and Item 21: "I have fun at school many times," "I have fun at school only once in a while," "I never have fun at school"). The items are scored 0, 1, or 2, respectively, yielding a total score ranging from 0 to 54. Although normative studies have shown that boys report fewer depressive symptoms than girls and that younger children report fewer symptoms than older children (Finch, Saylor, & Edwards, 1985; Smucker et al., 1986), the size and clinical significance of these differences are small. In general, it is quite common for boys and girls of all ages to report mild to moderate symptoms of depression (average scores across age and gender hover around 9–10, with a standard deviation of 7). Using a cutoff score of 19 on the CDI, however, has been useful in identifying groups of children who are clinically different from their normal peers. Doerfler and colleagues (1988) found that such children report more anxiety, a lower self-concept, and a greater external locus of control than do children in the mid-range of the CDI. Strauss et al. (1984) indicated that children in their sample with high CDI scores also reported more anxiety and a lower self-concept. Furthermore, they were viewed by their teachers as doing less well academically and by their peers as less popular and less preferred as playmates. Finally, Ollendick and Yule (1990) found that both British and American children who scored high on the CDI evinced clinically significant levels of anxiety and fear. In explaining their findings, they invoked the construct of negative affectivity (Watson & Clark, 1984; Wolfe et al., 1987). In brief, these collective findings suggest that self-report measures of depression, anxiety, and fear are part of a broader construct, labeled *negative affectivity,* that measures negative emotional states in general (cf. King, Ollendick, & Gullone, 1991; Malcarne & Ingram, in press). Yet it is clear that all children who are depressed are not necessarily clinically anxious or fearful. Some are; some are not. As a result, we recommend the continued measurement of depression, anxiety, and fear as meaningfully distinct constructs.

In our experience, it is common for school-refusing children to report a high level of depression on the CDI. This is especially true of children whose school refusal is related to separation concerns. Although children whose school refusal is related to aspects of the school itself (e.g., taking tests, being bullied) usually report lower levels of depression, we occasionally observe these children to develop symptoms of depression over time. Perhaps as a result of their feelings of inefficaciousness in the school setting they develop depressogenic attributions as suggested by Seligman et al. (1984).

In brief, fear survey schedules and measures of anxiety and depression appear useful as instruments to identify specific fear sensitivities and anxiety or depressive experiences in children, as normative instruments for selecting children for treatment, and as outcome measures of treatment. Of course, they all possess limitations attendant on self-report instruments (Finch & Rogers, 1984).

School Refusal Assessment Scale.   Recently, Silverman and her colleagues (Burke & Silverman, 1987; Kearney & Silverman, 1988, 1990, 1993) have developed the School Refusal Assessment Scale (SRAS), an instrument designed to identify maintaining variables associated with school refusal. As such, the instrument attempts to provide a functional analysis of the school refusal behavior. As reviewed in Chapter 1, school refusal is not a unitary syndrome; rather, its causes and maintaining variables are complex and heterogeneous. Early on, Broadwin (1932) noted that school refusal "may represent an act of defiance, an attempt to obtain love, or escapes from real situations to which it is difficult to adjust" (p. 254). In describing school refusal in this way, Broadwin clearly set the stage for viewing acts of absenteeism as heterogeneous in origin.

The SRAS was designed to capture this heterogeneity. The measure assesses four primary hypothesized maintaining variables for school refusal behavior: (1) avoidance of stimuli that provoke specific fearfulness or general anxiousness, (2) escape from aversive social or evaluative situations, (3) attention-getting behaviors that reflect separation concerns, and (4) behaviors that procure positive reinforcement. Children of the first functional category include those who are fearful of some specific stimulus in the school setting (e.g., riding the school bus, being bullied by a peer, dressing for physical education class), whereas those in the second functional category include those who are socially anxious and who are apprehensive about evaluative settings in school (e.g., taking a test, performing in a recital, speaking in front of class). Both of these functional categories describe children who refuse to attend school for negative reinforcement (Kearney & Silverman, 1993). Children of the third and fourth functional categories, on the other hand, refuse to attend school for positive reinforcement, typically from the home setting (Kearney & Silverman, 1993). For example, children in the third category include those who engage in behavior designed to stay home with a particular caregiver (e.g., tantruming, getting sick), whereas those in the fourth functional category include those who remain home for other, more specific reasons such as watching television or playing with friends. This latter category appears to be analogous to the category of truancy, in which children refuse to attend school for reasons other than fearfulness or anxiety.

The SRAS is made up of 16 questions, 4 questions for each of the hypothesized maintaining conditions. Each question is rated on a Likert-type scale from 0 to 6, from *never* to *always*. The child version of the scale is reproduced in Table 2-5. Items 1, 5, 9, and 13 make up the first functional category (avoidance of fear-producing stimuli in the school setting), items 2, 6, 10, and 14 the second functional category (escape from aversive social or evaluative situations), items 3, 7, 11, and 15 the third functional category (attention-getting behaviors to be with caregiver), and items 4, 8, 12, and 16 the fourth functional category (positive tangible reinforcement that is not related to fear or anxiety). Item means for the four functional conditions are computed (range from 0 to 6) and compared to each other. The highest scoring condition is considered to be the primary maintaining variable of school refusal for a particular child. The differences in scale responses reflect the heterogeneity of school refusal behavior; one child's refusal behavior may be motivated primarily by avoidance of fear-producing events in the school

TABLE 2-5 • **The School Refusal Assessment Scale**

SCHOOL REFUSAL ASSESSMENT SCALE (C)

Your name: _____

Date: _____

Please circle the answer that best fits the following questions:

1. How often do you have trouble going to school because you are afraid of something in the school building (for example, a fire alarm, room, etc.)?

Never		Seldom		Half the Time		Usually		Always
0	1		2	3	4		5	6

2. Do you have trouble speaking with the other kids at school?

Never		Seldom		Half the Time		Usually		Always
0	1		2	3	4		5	6

3. Do you often do things that upset or annoy your family?

Never		Seldom		Half the Time		Usually		Always
0	1		2	3	4		5	6

4. How often do you go out of the house when not in school during the week (Monday to Friday)?

Never		Seldom		Half the Time		Usually		Always
0	1		2	3	4		5	6

5. Are you afraid of the teachers or others at school?

Never		Seldom		Half the Time		Usually		Always
0	1		2	3	4		5	6

6. Do you often feel embarrassed or scared in front of other people at school?

Never		Seldom		Half the Time		Usually		Always
0	1		2	3	4		5	6

7. How often do you feel that you would rather be with your parents than attend school?

Never		Seldom		Half the Time		Usually		Always
0	1		2	3	4		5	6

(Continued)

TABLE 2-5 • *(Continued)*

8. Do you ever talk to or see other people when not in school during the week (Monday to Friday)?

Never		Seldom		Half the Time		Usually		Always
0	1		2	3	4		5	6

9. Do you feel more nervous with your friends at school than with your friends somewhere else (e.g., at a party or at home)?

Never		Seldom		Half the Time		Usually		Always
0	1		2	3	4		5	6

10. Do you have trouble making friends?

Never		Seldom		Half the Time		Usually		Always
0	1		2	3	4		5	6

11. Do you ever think about your parents or family when in school or when they are away from you?

Never		Seldom		Half the Time		Usually		Always
0	1		2	3	4		5	6

12. Do you enjoy doing different things when not in school during the week (Monday to Friday)?

Never		Seldom		Half the Time		Usually		Always
0	1		2	3	4		5	6

13. Do you feel scared about school when you think about it on Saturday and Sunday?

Never		Seldom		Half the Time		Usually		Always
0	1		2	3	4		5	6

14. Do you often stay away from places where you would have to talk to someone?

Never		Seldom		Half the Time		Usually		Always
0	1		2	3	4		5	6

15. Do you ever refuse to go to school in order to be with your parents?

Never		Seldom		Half the Time		Usually		Always
0	1		2	3	4		5	6

(Continued)

TABLE 2-5 • *(Continued)*

16. Do you ever skip school because it's more fun to be out of school?

Never		Seldom		Half the Time		Usually		Always
0	1		2	3	4		5	6

Do not write below this line

ANA	ESE	AGB	PTR
1. _____	2. _____	3. _____	4. _____
5. _____	6. _____	7. _____	8. _____
9. _____	10. _____	11. _____	12. _____
13. _____	14. _____	15. _____	16. _____
Total Score = _____	_____	_____	_____
Mean Score = _____	_____	_____	_____
Relative Ranking = _____	_____	_____	_____

Source: C. A. Kearney and W. K. Silverman, "Measuring the Function of School Refusal Behavior," paper presented at annual meeting of the Association for the Advancement of Behavior Therapy, 1988. Reprinted with permission of Christopher A. Kearney, W. K. Silverman, and Lawrence Erlbaum Association, Inc.

setting, whereas another child's refusal behavior may be motivated primarily by positive reinforcement associated with attention from caregivers.

Kearney and Silverman have shown the scale to possess good test-retest and interrater reliability (Kearney & Silverman, 1988, 1993) and to have solid concurrent validity with the Anxiety Disorders Interview Schedule for Children, the Fear Survey Schedule for Children, and the Revised Children's Manifest Anxiety Scale (Kearney & Silverman, 1993). Moreover, it has been shown to possess good treatment validity (see Hayes, Nelson, & Jarrett, 1987) and to maximize treatment outcome through highly specific, individualized, and prescriptive treatment modalities (Kearney & Silverman, 1990). Finally, the scale has child, parent, and teacher versions.

The development of the SRAS represents one of the most exciting developments in the assessment of school refusal behavior in recent years. By focusing on specific maintaining variables, it provides an elegant entry into a functional analysis of the school refusal. In turn, the functional analysis can be related to the specific subgroups of school refusal described earlier (e.g., separation-anxious, phobic, and anxious/depressed) and reviewed in terms of whether the refusal is acute or chronic. Moreover, it can lead to specific treatment interventions, as will be seen in Chapter 3. When combined with other sources of information described in this chapter, it leads to a well-rounded as well as functional view of the child and his or her school refusal.

Self-Monitoring

Self-monitoring differs from self-report in that it constitutes an observation of the *clinically relevant target behavior* at the time of its occurrence (Cone, 1978). Self-monitoring requires the child to observe his or her own behavior and then to record its occurrence systematically. Typically the child is asked to keep a diary, place marks on a card, or push the plunger on a counter as the behavior occurs or immediately thereafter. Self-monitoring procedures have been used frequently with children and adolescents. At least three considerations must be attended to when such procedures are used with very young children (Shapiro, 1984): The behaviors should be clearly defined, prompts to use the procedures should be readily available, and rewards for their use should be provided. Younger children may have difficulty remembering exactly what behaviors to monitor and how those behaviors are defined. For these reasons it is generally considered desirable to give the child a brief description of the target behavior or, better yet, a visual depiction of it, and to have the child record only one or two behaviors at a time. In an exceptionally sensitive application of these guidelines, Kunzelman (1970) recommended the use of Countoons, simple stick figure drawings that depict the specific behaviors to be self-monitored. Children are instructed to place a tally mark next to the picture when the behavior occurs. For example, a girl monitoring stomachaches on school days may be given an index card with a drawing of a girl and instructed to mark each day that her stomach feels upset (as depicted in the picture). Such pictorial cues serve as visual prompts for self-monitoring. Finally, children should be reinforced following the successful use of self-monitoring.

In our work with school-refusing children we request children to monitor their feelings about going to school in the morning and then to report on their success in attending school at the day's end. They are given an index card entitled "Feelings about going to school" and are asked to circle a number from 1 to 5 regarding their feelings: 1—"I feel happy and good about going to school," 2—"I'm a little nervous and upset today, but I can still go to school," 3—"I'm nervous and upset and I'm not sure if I can go to school today," 4—"I'm very nervous and upset and I don't think I can go to school today," and 5—"I'm so nervous and upset that I know I cannot go to school today." In addition, they are asked to complete a second rating (on the back of the "Feelings" card) on how sick they feel: 1—"I don't feel sick today," 2—"I feel a little bit sick but not enough to bother me," 3—"I feel sick and it bothers me," 4—"I feel very sick and it bothers me a lot," and 5—"I feel like I'm going to throw up and that I won't be able to go to school today." At the end of the day they are asked to complete another index card that simply asks them to indicate whether (1) they went to school today, (2) they stayed in school all day, and (3) what the day in school was like. With such self-monitoring a diary of the child's feelings and school attendance is obtained. Frequently the diary is useful in identifying antecedent variables and consequent conditions that maintain the school refusal. For example, a 10-year-old school-refusing boy reported that he was very nervous and upset and that he didn't think he would be able to go to school on 9 of 10 days during a baseline period. On each of these 9 days he also indicated that he felt very sick and that he would likely throw up (parental report indicated that he got sick to his stomach and threw up on 4 of the 9 days). This information was helpful in two ways: First, the one day out of the 10 when he didn't report feeling upset or that he would throw up occurred on a day when a field trip was planned; and second, for three of the four days on which he actually threw up, tests were scheduled. For the remaining day no discernible pattern was evident. As reported in his end-of-the-day diary, he actually went to school on 6 of the 10 days (confirmed by parents and school authorities). However, he missed all of the days on which he actually threw up. This information allowed us to examine hypotheses related to taking tests and his subsequent school refusal.

A somewhat more elegant use of self-monitoring is evident in the work of Beidel and her colleagues. Recently, Beidel, Neal, and Lederer (1991) reported on the feasibility and validity of a daily diary for the assessment of anxiety in school children. Because anxiety associated with events in school is frequently related to the development of school refusal, this daily diary is of considerable interest and importance. As noted by Beidel, Neal, and Lederer (1991), the daily diary assesses parameters related to the occurrence of anxious events, including time of the day, location, specific anxiety-producing events, and behavioral responses to the event. A sample daily diary page is presented in Figure 2-1. The specific locations include school, school cafeteria, home, outside, or with friends. Specific events range from taking a test to reading out loud to performing in front of others. Responses to the events range from positive (i.e., told myself not to be nervous) to negative (i.e.,

This is your Daily Diary. Every time you feel scared, nervous, anxious or tense I want you to mark X in your diary. It's easy!

Here is an example:

On Tuesday morning, Sally's math teacher said she was going to have people come to the board and do math problems. Sally got real scared and nervous. Her stomach began to do flip-flops and she worried that the teacher would call on her. When the teacher called on her, Sally went to the board and did the math problem. After class Sally marked in her Daily Diary. This is how Sally marked her Daily Diary:

Daily Diary   Date **Jan 3, Tues** .

    Morning__ **X** __   Afternoon_____   Evening_____

Where were you? Class-Which one? **Math** __Home_____Cafeteria_____

    Outside_____ with friends_____ Other-Where?_____

What happened?
_____ I had a test.
_____ The teacher called on me to answer a question.
_____ I had to read out loud.
_____ I had to give a report.
X I had to write on the board.
_____ The teacher handed back a test.
_____ I had to perform in front of other people. (sing, dance, play an instrument, play a sport.)
_____ Other–What?_____

What did you do?
_____ Cried.
_____ Got a stomachache or headache.
_____ Refused to do what was asked.
_____ Hid my eyes so I was not called on.
_____ Got someone else to do it for me.
_____ Did not go to the place (baseball game, school, recital) so I would not have to do it.
X Did what I was suppose to do.
_____ Told myself not to be nervous it would be okay.
_____ Pretended I was sick so I did not have to go.
_____ Practiced extra hard ahead of time so I would not be afraid.
_____ Other-What?_____

Sally's math class was in the morning so she put an X by morning.

Sally was in math class so she put an X by class and wrote math.

Sally's teacher asked her to go to the board so Sally put an X by I had to write on the board.

Sally went to the board so she put an X by did what I was suppose to do.

Sally was nervous and her stomach was doing flip-flops. She put an X under the second picture.

Remember to mark in your Daily Diary any time you feel scared, nervous, anxious or tense. It's easy and fun!

FIGURE 2-1 Sample Daily Diary Page Illustrating Directions and Proper Recording Procedures

Reproduced from D. C. Beidel, A. M. Neal, and A. S. Lederer, "The Feasibility and Validity of a Daily Diary for the Assessment of Anxiety in Children," *Behavior Therapy, 22,* 505–517 (1991). Copyright 1991 by the Association of Behavior Therapy. Reprinted by permission of the publisher and the authors.

pretended I was sick so I wouldn't have to go) to neutral (i.e., did what was asked) behaviors. In addition, as can be seen in Figure 2-1, the children were asked to rate the degree of distress that they experienced by using a Self-Assessment Manikin (Lang & Cutherbert, 1984), similar to Kunzelman's (1970) Countoons, that depicted increasing degrees of anxious arousal ranging from 1 = relaxed to 5 = very scared or anxious. Again, such information can be invaluable in determining the situations and responses characteristic of a given child in an anxiety-producing situation.

In addition to these procedures, the Fear Thermometer has been used frequently in self-monitoring. In its original usage with adults the Fear Thermometer involved a sheet of paper that depicted a thermometer-like figure with a 1-to-10 rating scale (Lang & Lazovik, 1963; Walk, 1956). In controlled laboratory settings the subject is asked to provide a self-rating on the Fear Thermometer after presentation of a feared stimulus, as in a behavioral avoidance test (e.g., Lang & Lazovik, 1963). We used a variant of the Fear Thermometer in the assessment of an 8-year-old boy referred because of "school anxiety." After the child was interviewed, he was requested to provide daily ratings for one week on the level of fear experienced before leaving for school, since this was the most difficult part of the school day for him. A picture of a fear "thermometer" was used in order to facilitate the child's understanding and cooperation (see Figure 2-2). In a similar vein, Wolpe (1969) introduced a 1–100 self-rating scale to assess "subjective units of disturbance" (SUDs), a procedure that has been adopted successfully in the assessment of older school refusers (e.g., Kearney & Silverman, 1990; McNamara, 1988). Given its simplicity and cost-efficiency, the Fear Thermometer and its variants have much appeal in self-monitoring.

In sum, self-monitoring procedures, including fear thermometers, are direct ways to obtain information about target behaviors as well as their antecedents and consequences. While specific monitoring methods may vary, any procedure that allows the child to record the presence of the targeted behaviors can be used. When appropriate procedures are used, self-monitoring is a direct and elegant method of assessment.

Behavioral Ratings

While children are completing the self-report measures described here, we request the parents to complete specific rating forms describing their children's behavior (typically, similar forms are completed by the child's teacher as well). A variety of parent and teacher rating scales and checklists have been used in the assessment of fears and anxieties in children. Among the more

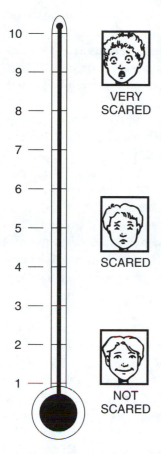

FIGURE 2-2   **Sample Fear Thermometer**

frequently used are the Child Behavior Checklist, the Behavior Problem Checklist, and the Fear Survey for Children. Each of these rating forms has been developed and standardized for use with children between 4 and 18 years of age.

The Child Behavior Checklist (CBCL; Achenbach, 1978; Achenbach & Edelbrock, 1979) has been used extensively in factor-analytic studies by Achenbach and his colleagues. Parents or teachers fill out this 138-item scale that taps both behavior problems and social competence. Social competency items assess the child's participation in social organizations, activities, and school. The behavior problem items are rated on a 3-point scale as to how well each describes the child. The inclusion of social competency and behavior problem items allows for a comprehensive assessment of the child's strengths and weaknesses. In addition, the scale allows for identification of children who display withdrawal, anxiety/depression, somatic complaints, social problems, thought problems, attention problems, aggressive behavior, and delinquent behavior. Specific anxiety items include "clings to adults," "school fears," and "shy, timid." This scale has been found to be reliable and valid and provides important normative data for boys and girls of varying ages (see Achenbach, 1985, for additional detail regarding the use of the CBCL with anxious and fearful children and Achenbach, 1991, for recent interpretive guidelines on these cross-informant scales).

The Revised Behavior Problem Checklist (Quay & Peterson, 1983) consists of 89 problem behaviors that are also rated on a 3-point scale ranging from "not a problem" through "mild problem" to "severe problem." Factor analyses of the scale yield the following dimensions: conduct problem, socialized aggression, attention problem—immaturity, anxiety/withdrawal, psychotic behavior, and motor excess. Like the CBCL, the Problem Behavior Checklist is a reliable and valid tool with which to assess reports of children's anxious behavior (anxiety/withdrawal factor) and its relationship to other deviant or pathological behavior.

Finally, the Louisville Fear Survey for Children (LFSC; Miller et al., 1971) is an 81-item scale covering a variety of specific fears. It also is appropriate for use with children between 4 and 16 years of age. In this survey the rater (parent, teacher) is instructed to indicate the child's level of fear on a 3-point scale ranging from "no fear" through "normal or reasonable fear" to "unrealistic or excessive fear." Limited evidence suggests that these ratings allow differentiation of school refusal into categories based on specific school fears and separation anxiety (Miller, Barrett, & Hampe, 1974). This finding is similar to the results of Ollendick and Mayer (1984) in which subtypes of school refusal were identified using the revised Fear Survey Schedule for Children.

It is beyond the scope of this chapter to address the many other instruments designed for parents or teachers. In view of the proliferation of such measures, McMahon (1984) recommends that clinicians and researchers be selective in the use of such instruments. We certainly agree. We usually prefer the Child Behavior Checklist or the Revised Behavioral Problem Checklist since they give us a more comprehensive picture of the child and his or her associated behavioral problems at home (parents) and school (teachers). Caution must be exercised, however, since the reliability and validity of even the better researched instruments are affected by a variety of factors. For example, parents and teachers may rate children as more deviant at the initial assessment to access treatment and, in turn, rate them as less deviant at the conclusion of treatment in order to please the clinician. Further, the extent to which these parent and teacher reports correspond to self-reports and behavioral interviews has not yet been investigated sufficiently to help us determine how to proceed when the various measures are discordant with one another. Still, such "other"-reports are necessary to obtain as complete a picture as possible of the child in these various settings.

Behavioral Observations

The hallmark of behavioral assessment is the direct observation of the child's behavior in the setting in which it occurs. In this tradition, assessment has ranged from unobtrusive observation in the child's home or school to direct observation in the laboratory (Lick & Katkin, 1976). Such observation provides a direct sample of the child's behavior and thus is the least inferential of data collection methods (Cone, 1978; Goldfried & Kent, 1972). In behavioral observation systems a behavior or set of behaviors that are indicative of school refusal are operationally defined, observed, and recorded systematically.

Illustratively, Neisworth, Madle, and Goeke (1975) conducted a behavioral assessment of a young girl's separation anxiety in a preschool setting. When left at school, she began to cry, sob, and scream until her mother returned to retrieve her. These behaviors (crying, screaming, and sobbing) were operationally defined and their intensity and duration measured in the preschool setting throughout baseline, treatment, and follow-up phases. For our purposes here, school refusal (labeled separation anxiety) was defined as a set of observable behaviors. These fearful behaviors occurred only in school, where the mother, as well as the preschool staff, found it difficult to endure the child's distress without attending to her. Neisworth and colleagues indicated that records and additional observations supported the notion that this attention played a role in the maintenance and development of "separation anxiety." Thus, in this case, specific behaviors were identified and observed; further, these observations suggested a specific treatment based on the antecedent (preschool setting only) and consequent (attention) conditions under which the behaviors occurred. Typically school-refusing children have stopped attending school by the time they are assessed. Nonetheless, behavioral observations of the child in the school setting are advised as soon as the child returns to school. At school it is likely the child will be highly anxious and require much support. Hence, behavioral observations can provide information on the child's specific fear behavior as well as the negative and positive influences on adjustment to school.

Behavioral observations in the home also provide valuable assessment information on the child's school refusal and controlling antecedent and consequent events. Such observations may be directed at the various stages of the "behavior chain" at which school refusal becomes evident. For example, Ayllon, Smith, and Rogers (1970) instigated systematic behavioral observations in the home of a school-refusing girl who had been absent from school for a prolonged period of time. In this case, the mother left for work approximately one hour after the girl (Valerie) and her siblings went to school. Although her siblings went to school on time, Valerie was observed to sleep late and then to "cling" to Mother until she left for work. "Valerie typically followed her mother around the house, from room to room, spending approximately 80 percent of her time within 10 feet of her mother. During these times, there was little or no conversation" (Ayllon, Smith, & Rogers, 1970, p. 128). Upon leaving for work, mother took Valerie to a neighbor's apartment to stay until she returned from work (the mother had long abandoned any hope of Valerie's going to school). When the mother left the neighbor's apartment, Valerie would follow. Observations indicated that this pattern continued with Valerie "following her mother at a 10-foot distance." Frequently the mother had to return Valerie to the neighbor's apartment. This daily pattern was usually concluded with the mother "literally running to get out of sight of Valerie" so that she would not follow her into traffic.

At the neighbor's apartment, observations revealed that Valerie was free to do whatever she pleased for the remainder of the day. As noted by the authors, "Her day was one which would be considered ideal by many grade-school children—she could be outdoors and play as she chose all day long. No demands of any type were made on Val" (Ayllon, Smith, & Rogers, p. 129). Since Valerie was not attending school, the authors arranged a simulated school setting to determine the extent of fear associated with academically related materials. Much to their surprise, Valerie exhibited little or no fear in the presence of these materials. Based on these observations, the authors hypothesized that Valerie's refusal to attend school was maintained by the attention from her mother and the pleasant and undemanding atmosphere of the neighbor's apartment.

Although not mentioned in the studies just described, behavioral observations can also help identify the extent to which poor household rules and routines contribute to school refusal (antecedent events). Further compounding the problem, parents may lack instruction-giving competencies with their child. In fact, Forehand and McMahon (1981) outline five types of commands that can lower compliance in children. These include long chains of commands, vague commands, question commands, "let's" commands, and commands followed by a rationale or other verbalization. Obviously, antecedent events as significant as these need to be identified in the assessment of school refusal.

Behavioral observation systems designed for other childhood fears and anxieties may also be useful with school-refusing children. Notable among them is the Preschool Observation Scale of Anxiety (POSA) developed by Glennon and Weisz (1978). The POSA includes 30 specific behavioral indices of anxiety to be observed using a standard time-sampling procedure. The behavioral indices include nail biting, avoidance of eye contact, silence to questions, and rigid posture (see Table 2-6). Although more information is needed regarding reliability and validity, this scale appears to be a promising clinical tool. We are currently using a variant of this system to code fearful and anxious behavior of children called to the principal's office. (Being sent to the principal is No. 1 of the 10 most common fears in children.) In addition to the actual route and time taken to arrive at the principal's office, a trembling voice, lip licking, and gratuitous hand movements are being reliably recorded and associated with high levels of reported fear about going to the principal's office. For some children, fear about being sent to the principal is related to school refusal behavior.

As with other types of assessment, behavioral observation procedures must possess adequate reliability and validity before their routine use can be endorsed. Although early behaviorists tended to accept behavioral observation data on the basis of their deceptively simple face validity, some investigators have enumerated a variety of problems related to their use (e.g.,

TABLE 2-6 • **Sample Items from the Preschool Observation Scale of Anxiety**

1. Physical complaint: Child says he or she has a headache, stomachache, or has to go to the bathroom.
2. Expression of fear or worry: Child complains about being afraid of or worried about something; must use the word "afraid," "scared," "worried," or a synonym.
3. Cry: Tears should be visible.
4. Scream
5. Nail biting: Child actually bites his or her nails in the testing room.
6. Lip licking: Tongue should be visible.
7. Trembling lip.
8. Rigid posture: Part of body is held unusually stiff or motionless for an entire 30-second interval.
9. Avoidance of eye contact: Examiner should have clear trouble making eye contact with the child.
10. Fearful facial expression.

Source: Adapted from B. Glennon and J. R. Weisz, "An Observational Approach to the Reassessment of Anxiety in Young Children," *Journal of Consulting and Clinical Psychology, 46,* 1246–1257 (1978).

Johnson & Bolstad, 1973; Kazdin, 1979). Among these issues are the complexity of the observation code, observer bias, observer drift, and the reactive nature of the observation process itself. It is beyond the scope of this chapter to address these issues. However, when these issues are adequately controlled for, direct observation is a welcome complement to behavioral and diagnostic interviews, self-reports, and rating forms. In our work with school-refusing children we have attempted to incorporate all four sources of information: behavioral and diagnostic interviews, self-reports, behavioral ratings, and behavioral observations.

Family Assessment Measures

Thus far our assessment approach has focused primarily on measures of child functioning. However, as noted in Chapter 1, family influences may play a significant role in the etiology and maintenance of school refusal. Therefore, some form of family assessment is necessary in order to obtain detailed information on parent-child relationships and the broader family context in which the school refusal occurs. Given the different theoretical approaches to understanding family functioning—systems/communication theory, psychoanalytic theory, and behavioral theory—family assessment is complex, with a diversity of assessment tools available to clinicians and researchers (see Grotevant & Carlson, 1989; Jacob & Tennenbaum, 1988).

Although there are many family assessment tools available, their direct relevance to school refusal is unclear at this time. However, there are several important factors that should be considered in deciding how and when to assess families of school-refusing children (cf. Kendall et al., 1992). First, what are the main characteristics of school-refusing children, and how might the family be involved in the etiology and maintenance of such characteristics (e.g., separation concerns in leaving home, nervousness with teachers, anxiety about new situations)? Second, since there are many methods of family assessment that are derived from particular theories of family functioning, what is the assessor's theoretical conception of school refusal, and, based on this conception, which instruments should be selected for use? The clinician needs to understand the theoretical rationale underlying the family assessment tool selected and the extent to which the information obtained from that rationale will be useful in treating school-refusing children.

Self-report instruments have been designed to assess different aspects of family functioning, including the Self-Administered Dependency Questionnaire (Berg, 1974) and the Family Assessment Measure (Skinner, Steinhauer, & Santa-Barbara, 1983). Reflecting a more psychoanalytic approach to understanding parent-child relationships, the Self-Administered Dependency Questionnaire (SADQ) assesses child dependency ("actual" scores) and maternal overprotection ("preferred" scores) in four areas: (1) affections (e.g., "Did he/she come close to you for affectionate contact?"), (2) communication (e.g., "Did he/she talk over his/her troubles with you and ask your help about what was going on in the family?"), (3) assistance (e.g., "Did he/she either make his/her own bed or clear up his/her room?"), and (4) travel (e.g., "Did he/she spend time with you at home when he/she could be out?"). Separate forms exist for parents and their children. Limited psychometric data have been reported on the reliability and validity of the SADQ (Berg, 1974), although Last and Strauss (1990) recently reported encouraging findings, which revealed that school refusers requested more assistance from (i.e., were more dependent on) their mothers than did never psychiatrically ill, non–school refusers and that mothers of school refusers preferred more conversation (i.e., were overprotective of) with their children than mothers of nonrefusers. We have found the scale to be particularly useful for those cases of school refusal in which the problems appear to be related to separation anxiety. In other cases the children and parents tend to report rather normal relationships. The SADQ also seems more useful with younger children than with adolescents, although it has been used for both (cf. Last & Strauss, 1990).

A more recent and global instrument compared to the SADQ, the Family Assessment Measure (FAM-III) is based on behavioral systems/communication theory. The FAM-III was developed to identify areas of family strengths and weaknesses, as well as to differentiate families that are coping successfully from those whose coping styles are more dysfunctional. As described by Jacob and Tennenbaum (1988), the FAM-III is a 134-item self-report instrument that mother, father, and all children 10 years of age and older complete (although it is most useful, in our experience, with adolescents). Items are organized around three different response formats: (1) General Scale (50 items focused on the health/pathology of the family as a whole), (2) Dyadic Relationship Scale (42 items for each dyad assessed, focused on relationships between specific members), and (3) Self-Rating Scale (42 items focused on the individual's perception of his or her functioning in the family). Within each response format, scores are obtained on a number of subscales including Task Accomplishment, Role Performance, Communication, Affective Expression, Affective Involvement, Control, and Values/Norms. Although it is a relatively new instrument, the empirical foundations of the FAM have been examined in a number of studies and appear to be acceptable (see Jacob & Tennenbaum, 1988). In two recent studies, Bernstein and her colleagues (Bernstein & Garfinkel, 1988; Bernstein, Svingen, & Garfinkel, 1990) have explored the use of the FAM with school-refusing adolescents and identified specific dysfunction in the areas of role performance and values and norms. Specifically, they found that the boundaries between parent and child roles were poorly demarcated in such families, resulting in parents who were not effective in their roles to facilitate return to school. Moreover, they suggested that the dysfunction in the arena of values and norms reflected a lack of consistency between explicit and implicit family rules. Parents, they suggested, may give contradictory messages about school attendance, independence, separation from one another, and response to somatization. Although these global patterns were obtained, the authors also noted that their families were highly diverse, reflecting the heterogeneity frequently seen in school-refusing adolescents and their families.

From a behavioral family systems perspective, an example of a potentially useful self-report instrument is the Family Beliefs Inventory (FBI) developed by Roehling and Robin (1986). The FBI was designed to measure unrealistic beliefs about parent-adolescent relationships. Parallel versions of the instruments have been constructed for parents and adolescents. For parents the FBI assesses six distorted beliefs: (1) Ruination, the belief that with too much freedom teenagers will ruin their futures; (2) Obedience, the belief that parents deserve absolute respect and obedience as the ultimate authority from teenagers; (3) Perfectionism, the belief that teenagers should instinctively behave without flaw; (4) Malicious Intent, the belief that adolescents intentionally misbehave to hurt their parents; (5) Self-Blame, the belief that parents are at fault for adolescents' misbehavior; and (6) Approval, the belief that adolescent disapproval of parents' childrearing actions will be catastrophic. FBI scales for adolescents include: (1) Ruination, the belief that parental rules and restrictions will ruin the teenage years; (2) Unfairness, the belief that it is catastrophic when parents treat teenagers unfairly; (3) Autonomy, the belief that parents should give adolescents complete freedom to make decisions concerning rules and responsibilities, and (4) Approval, the belief that it is catastrophic if parents become angry with adolescents. Each belief is assessed via 10 items linked to vignettes depicting frequent sources of conflict between parents and adolescents such as choice of friends and curfew. Its internal consistency and criterion-related validity have been substantiated (Roehling & Robin, 1986).

In recent work in our clinics the Approval Scale of both the parent and adolescent forms has been found to be particularly useful. Frequently we see parents and adolescents who dread lack of approval with one another, resulting in inconsistent and tentative interactions. Fathers have been particularly concerned about their teenagers' misperception of their parenting practices and have, as a result, tended to withdraw from assisting the mother in "tough" decisions such as return to school. Elizur (1986) noted a similar pattern in fathers' coping strategies with school-refusing adolescents.

In sum, family assessment measures provide yet another critical piece of information in the school refusal puzzle. Although variable, many parents are characterized by overindulgence, overprotectiveness, and inconsistent parenting practices, especially related to role performance. Children and adolescents themselves are frequently characterized by dependency and a high need for approval from their parents. The exact relationships between these family measures and the subgroups of school refusal remain to be determined. Based on our review and clinical experiences, however, it is probable that the relationships are complex and not straightforward. Once again, we are mindful of the fact that school refusal is not a unitary syndrome and that it presents itself in various forms.

SUMMARY

Although child behavioral assessment strategies have been slow to evolve, the gap between effective therapeutic techniques and psychometrically sound and developmentally sensitive assessment procedures has been narrowed. The growing sophistication of child behavioral assessment procedures is evidenced by the appearances of behavioral and diagnostic interviews, as well as self- and other-report instruments, that take into consideration developmental, social, and cultural influences as well as cognitive and affective mediators of behavior. Even though direct behavioral observation remains the hallmark of child behavioral assessment, information from these other sources is considered not only valuable but integral in the understanding and subsequent treatment of child behavior disorders.

These advances are clearly evident in the assessment of school refusal behavior. Sophisticated behavioral and diagnostic interviews have been developed, psychometrically sound self-report questionnaires and behavioral rating scales have been put into use, and highly detailed self-monitoring and behavioral observation systems are available. Moreover, these various assessment procedures and devices are, for the most part, developmentally sensitive. Finally, they are empirically validated and lead to individualized and prescriptive treatment strategies, as described in the next chapter. In brief, significant advances have occurred in the past 10 to 15 years.

Behavioral Treatment Strategies

INTRODUCTION

Despite fundamental theoretical differences, both psychodynamic and behavioral approaches to school refusal place emphasis on the child's return to school as the primary criterion of successful intervention (e.g., Ayllon, Smith, & Rogers, 1970; Eisenberg, 1958). As noted by the psychodynamically oriented Eisenberg (1958), it is

> essential that the paralyzing force of the school phobia on the child's whole life be recognized. The symptom itself serves to isolate him from normal experience and makes further psychological growth almost impossible. If we do no more than check this central symptom, we have nonetheless done a great deal. (p. 718)

While behaviorally oriented clinicians might disagree with Eisenberg's labeling of school refusal as a *symptom* (an overt expression of some underlying conflict), they would hardly disagree with his conclusion. In this chapter behaviorally based strategies that are commonly used in achieving this goal will be described and evaluated.

Several clinical management issues need to be addressed prior to a discussion of behavioral treatment procedures:

1. *Parental psychopathology.* When children with school attendance difficulties are referred to clinical services, it is frequently assumed that any

psychopathology that is present resides solely in the child. However, it is not unusual for the parents (especially the mother) to be highly anxious and over-protective and to exhibit dependency on the child. As noted earlier, research-ers have found various forms of "neurotic" disturbance and other psychiatric illness in the parents of school-refusing children (Berg, Butler, & Pritchard, 1974; Lang, 1982; Last et al., 1987). Indeed, parental psychopathology may be so extreme that treatment should really begin with the parents, as has occurred in a number of cases seen in our clinics. The following advice as-sumes that parental psychopathology is not a major or primary factor in school attendance difficulties.

2. *Medical investigation.* Viral infection or other illness often contributes to the development of school refusal. Therefore, close liaison with the family doctor is recommended in order to determine whether the child has any cur-rent physical illness that may preclude school return. In our experience, medical investigation usually reveals that the child is healthy and should be attending school, something we emphasize to the child and parents. For children with chronic medical conditions such as asthma, the family doctor or medical specialist may still recommend school return, but possibly with some pre-cautions. For example, we offered behavioral treatment to a young school refuser who was able to self-administer an inhalant spray (Ventolin) to con-trol his asthma on return to school. On advice from the doctor, he also saw the school nurse each day. The nurse monitored his breathing (airways resis-tance) and provided any additional treatment that was necessary. Consequently, the child was able to participate in all aspects of the behavioral program.

3. *School arrangements.* An important practical question is whether the child should return to his or her current school or attend a new school. In general, it is desirable that the child resumes attendance at his or her current school. However, the perceptions of all parties (child, parents, and teachers) need to be considered before a confirmation of school placement is made. Sometimes a change of school is recommended, as the child's educational needs might be better served at another school. Also, the relationship be-tween family and school may have deteriorated to the point where planning a constructive program for school return is impossible. The convenience of the school and having teachers who are known to the family are important prac-tical advantages associated with the child remaining at his or her current school. So, too, are the child's friends at the current school.

4. *Communication between professionals.* Frequently several professionals are involved in the management of school refusal. It is imperative, therefore, that consistent advice on school return be given to the family and teachers. There are instances in which communication breakdowns have produced disastrous results.

To illustrate, on the advice of a psychologist a mother got her child to school for one lesson as part of a desensitization program. The child had been absent from school for several weeks due to excessive anxiety about school. Unfortunately, they were confronted by an unknown teacher who was antagonistic toward the child and mother. Consequently, the child and mother felt let down by the school and psychologist and nearly withdrew from treatment. We attempt to facilitate communication through regular meetings with teachers and the family and through written guidelines on the treatment program.

5. *Functional analysis.* Given the heterogeneity of school refusal, it is essential to provide individualized behavioral treatment. This can only be achieved by undertaking a careful assessment and formulating a specific hypothesis concerning maintenance variables. As noted in our previous chapter, Kearney and Silverman (1990) have developed a useful functional model for the assessment and treatment of school refusal. This model incorporates both acute and chronic cases of school refusal, as well as other types of school refusal identified in diagnostic classification systems—separation-anxious, phobic, and anxious/depressed. Consistent with their objective of providing a useful functional model for assessment and treatment, Kearney and Silverman outline four categories of maintenance variables, each having its own unique treatment prescription: Category 1 is avoidance of a specific stimulus in the school setting. Given the extensive clinical work and research on the treatment of children's phobias, the treatment plan for such children should include relaxation training and imaginal or *in vivo* desensitization. Category 2 is unsatisfying peer relationships or high social anxiety in an evaluative setting. For children experiencing difficulties in peer relationships, behavior rehearsal and modeling should help improve social skills. Cognitive procedures would be warranted if the child also makes negative self-statements about peer relationships. Category 3 is attention-getting behavior designed to stay at home with a specific caregiver. Working with caregivers should be an important consideration in the treatment plan for these cases. Typically an extinction (ignoring) procedure is used to reduce problems such as tantrums and somatic complaints. A shaping procedure would be helpful in obtaining a gradual school return for those children with severe school refusal. Category 4 is tangible reinforcement for staying at home such as watching television or visiting friends. For children of this category, contingency management is a recommended treatment. This involves negotiating specific positive and negative consequences for appropriate and inappropriate behaviors ("contingency contracting"). Of course, it is possible that more than one category of maintenance variables applies in school refusal, thus calling for comprehensive behavioral treatment.

BEHAVIORAL TREATMENT STRATEGIES

Conceptually, behavioral treatment strategies used in the treatment of school refusal are derived from the principles of classical, vicarious, and operant conditioning. In this section we focus on behavioral treatment strategies that are consistent with a functional model of assessment and treatment for school refusal (Kearney & Silverman, 1990). These behavioral procedures include relaxation training, systematic desensitization and emotive imagery (relevant to Kearney and Silverman's Category 1), modeling and cognitive restructuring (Category 2), and shaping and contingency management (Categories 3 and 4). These treatment strategies are pragmatic and action-oriented and entail exposure to anxiety-provoking stimuli. As Marks (1975) noted, "An important mechanism shared by all of these methods is exposure of the frightened subject to a frightening situation until he acclimatizes" (p. 67). In working with children, we have also found that the use of behavioral procedures invariably requires considerable flexibility and creativity. Thus, as with our assessment procedures, treatment should be developmentally sensitive to ensure the understanding and cooperation of the child (King, Hamilton, & Ollendick, 1988; Morris & Kratochwill, 1983).

Relaxation Training

Relaxation training is frequently a component of behavioral programs for children with school attendance difficulties (e.g., O'Farrell, Hedlund, & Cutter, 1981). Although there are many types of relaxation training, progressive muscle relaxation training is often preferred by clinicians. In this method the individual works on the major muscle groups of the body, engaging in systematic tension-release exercises. Most relaxation training scripts incorporating progressive relaxation have been written for adults (e.g., Bernstein & Borkovec, 1973; Rimm & Masters, 1974). Usually adolescents are able to profit sufficiently from adult scripts. However, children often find the instructions difficult to comprehend or are bored by the lengthy tension-release routine.

In recent years, relaxation training formats for children have been developed. Cautela and Groden (1978) have written a manual on relaxation training for use with children. An important feature of their manual is the relaxation readiness pretest (see Table 3-1), which is designed to assess the child's suitability (compliance with basic instructions) for training in relaxation. We have found this readiness test to be especially useful with young children. A relaxation training script for use with young children has been developed by

TABLE 3-1 • **Pretest to Determine Readiness for Relaxation Training**

The following pretest should be administered to the child. Give three trials for each response.

Name of Child: _____   CODE: ✓ = Correct
Date: _____   X = Incorrect
                                                        NR = No Response

	Trial 1	Trial 2	Trial 3
Phase I. Basic Skills			
1. Ask the child to sit quietly in a chair for 5 seconds, feet still, back straight, head up, without moving or vocalizing. Repeat 2 more times,			
2. Say "Look at me," and ask the child to maintain eye contact for 3 seconds. Child must respond within 5 seconds. Repeat 2 more times.			
Phase II. Imitative Skills			
4. Say "Do this," and raise your hand above your head. Child should imitate this response correctly within 5 seconds. Repeat 2 more times.			
4. Say "Do this," and you tap the table. Child should be able to imitate this response correctly by tapping the table. Repeat 2 more times.			
5. Say "Do this," and you tap your chest. Child should be able to imitate correctly by tapping his chest. Repeat 2 more times.			
Phase III. Following Simple Instructions			
6. Say "Stand up." Child should stand up in front of his chair within 5 seconds. Repeat this instruction 2 more times.			
7. Say "Sit down." Child should sit down in his chair within 5 seconds. Repeat this instruction 2 more times.			
8. Stand 6 feet from the child and say "Come here." Child should stand up and walk toward you without inappropriate movements or vocalizations. Repeat 2 more times.			

Source: J. R. Cautela and J. Groden, *Relaxation: A Comprehensive Manual for Adults, Children, and Children with Special Needs* (Champaign, IL: Research Press, 1978). Copyright 1978 by the authors. Reprinted by permission.

Koeppen (1974). She incorporated fantasy into the muscle tension-release exercises in order to elicit and maintain the child's interest. Koeppen's relaxation training script follows:

Hands and Arms

Pretend you have a whole lemon in your left hand. Now squeeze it hard. Try to squeeze all the juice out. Feel the tightness in your hand and arm as you squeeze. Now drop the lemon. Notice how your muscles feel when they are relaxed. Take another lemon and squeeze it. Try to squeeze this one harder than you did the first one. That's right. Really hard. Now drop your lemon and relax. See how much better your hand and arm feel when they are relaxed. Once again, take a lemon in your left hand and squeeze all the juice out. Don't leave a single drop. Squeeze hard. Good. Now relax and let the lemon fall from your hand. (Repeat the process for the right hand and arm.)

Arms and Shoulders

Pretend you are a furry, lazy cat. You want to stretch. Stretch your arms out in front of you. Raise them up high over your head. Way back. Feel the pull in your shoulders. Stretch higher. Now just let your arms drop back to your side. Okay, kitten, stretch again. Stretch your arms out in front of you. Raise them over your head. Pull them back, way back. Pull hard. Now let them drop quickly. Good. Notice how your shoulders feel more relaxed. This time let's have a great big stretch. Try to touch the ceiling. Stretch your arms way out in front of you. Raise them way up high over your head. Push them way, way back. Notice the tension and pull in your arms and shoulders. Hold tight, now. Great. Let them drop very quickly and feel how good it is to be relaxed. It feels good and warm and lazy.

Shoulders and Neck

Now pretend you are a turtle. You're sitting out on a rock by a nice, peaceful pond, just relaxing in the warm sun. It feels nice and warm and safe here. Oh-oh! You sense danger. Pull your head into your house. Try to pull your shoulders up to your ears and push your head down into your shoulders. Hold in tight. It isn't easy to be a turtle in a shell. The danger is past now. You can come out into the warm sunshine, and, once again, you can relax and feel the warm sunshine. Watch out now! More danger. Hurry, pull you head back into your house and hold it tight. One more time, now. Danger! Pull you head in. Push your shoulders way up to your ears and hold tight. Don't let even a tiny piece of your head show outside your shell. Hold it.

Feel the tenseness in your neck and shoulders. Okay. You can come out now. It's safe again. Relax and feel comfortable in your safety. There's no more danger. Nothing to worry about. Nothing to be afraid of. You feel good.

Jaw

You have a giant jawbreaker bubble-gum in your mouth. It's very hard to chew. Bite down on it. Hard! Let your neck muscles help you. Now relax. Just let your jaw hang loose. Notice how good it feels just to let your jaw drop. Okay, let's tackle that jawbreaker again now. Bite down. Hard! Try to squeeze it out between your teeth. That's good. You're really tearing that gum up. Now relax again. Just let your jaw drop off your face. It feels so good just to let go and not have to fight that bubble gum. Okay, one more time. We're really going to tear it up this time. Bite down. Hard as you can. Harder. Oh, you're really working hard. Good. Now relax. Try to relax your whole body. You've beaten the bubble gum. Let yourself go as loose as you can.

Face and Nose

Here comes a pesky old fly. He has landed on your nose. Try to get him off without using your hands. That's right, wrinkle up your nose. Make as many wrinkles in your nose as you can. Scrunch your nose up real hard. Good. You've chased him away. Now you can relax your nose. Oops, here he comes back again. Shoo him off. Wrinkle it up hard. Hold it just as tight as you can. Okay, he flew away. You can relax your face. Notice that when you scrunch up your nose that your cheeks and your mouth and your forehead and your eyes all help you, and, they get tight, too. So when you relax your nose, your whole face relaxes too, and that feels good. Oh-oh. This time that old fly has come back, but this time he's on your forehead. Make lots of wrinkles. Try to catch him between all those wrinkles. Hold it tight, now. Okay, you can let go. He's gone for good. Now you can just relax. Let your face go smooth, no wrinkles anywhere. Your face feels nice and smooth and relaxed.

Stomach

Hey! Here comes a cute baby elephant. But he's not watching where he's going. He doesn't see you lying there in the grass, and he's about to step on your stomach. Don't move. You don't have time to get out of the way. Just get ready for him. Make your stomach very hard. Tighten up your stomach muscles real tight. Hold it. It looks like he is going the other way. You can relax now. Let your stomach go soft. Let it be as relaxed as you can. That feels so much better. Oops, he's coming this way again. Get ready. Tighten up your stomach. Real hard. If he steps on you when your stomach is hard, it won't hurt. Make your stomach into a rock. Okay, he's moving away again. You can relax now. Kind of settle down, get comfortable, and relax. Notice the difference between a tight stomach and a relaxed one. That's how we want it to feel—nice and loose and relaxed. You won't believe this, but this time he's really coming your way and no turning around. He's headed straight for you. Tighten up. Tighten hard. Here he comes. This is really it. You've got to hold on tight. He's stepping on you. He's stepped over you. Now he's gone for good. You can relax completely. You're safe. Everything is okay, and you can feel nice and relaxed.

This time imagine that you want to squeeze through a narrow fence and the boards have splinters on them. You'll have to make yourself very skinny if you're going to make it through. Suck your stomach in. Try to squeeze it up against your backbone. Try to be as skinny as you can. You've got to get through. Now relax. You don't have to be skinny now. Just relax and feel your stomach being warm and loose. Okay, let's try to get through that fence now. Squeeze up your stomach. Make it touch your backbone. Get it real small and tight. Get as skinny as you can. Hold tight now. You've got to squeeze through. You got through that skinny little fence and no splinters. You can relax now. Settle back and let your stomach come back out where it belongs. You can feel really good now. You've done fine.

Legs and Feet

Now pretend that you are standing barefoot in a big, fat, mud puddle. Squish your toes down deep into the mud. Try to get your feet down to the bottom of the mud puddle. You'll probably need your legs to help you push. Push down, spread your toes apart, and feel the mud squish up between your toes. Now step out of the mud puddle. Relax your feet. Let your toes go loose and feel how nice that is. It feels good to be relaxed. Back into the mud puddle. Squish your toes down. Let your leg muscles help you push your feet down. Push your feet.

Hard. Try to squeeze that mud puddle dry. Okay. Come back out now. Relax your feet, relax your legs, release your toes. It feels so good to be relaxed. No tenseness anywhere. You feel kind of warm and tingly.

Koeppen (1974) suggests that 15-minute training sessions be adopted, with no more than three muscle groups being introduced per session. Two or three sessions per week are recommended for rapid learning of the relaxation skills. On the grounds that some children become overly involved in the fantasy, Ollendick and Cerny (1981) developed a relaxation script without reference to fantasy. This particular relaxation training script is more appropriate for older children:

Hands and Arms

Make a fist with your left hand. Squeeze it hard. Feel the tightness in your hand and arm as you squeeze. Now let your hand go and relax. See how much better your hand and arm feel when they are relaxed. Once again, make a fist with your left hand and squeeze hard. Good. Now relax and let your hand go. (Repeat the process for the right hand and arm.)

Arms and Shoulders

Stretch your arms out in front of you. Raise them high up over your head. Way back. Feel the pull in your shoulders. Stretch higher. Now just let your arms drop back to your side. Okay, let's stretch again. Stretch your arms out in front of you. Raise them over your head. Pull them back, way back. Pull hard. Now let them drop quickly. Good. Notice how your shoulders feel more relaxed. This time let's have a great big stretch. Try to touch the ceiling. Stretch your arms way out in front of you. Raise them way up high over your head. Push them way, way back. Notice the tension and pull in your arms and shoulders. Hold tight, now. Great. Let them drop very quickly and feel how good it is to be relaxed. It feels good and warm and lazy.

Shoulders and Neck

Try to pull your shoulders up to your ears and push your head down into your shoulders. Hold in tight. Okay, now relax and feel the warmth. Again, pull your shoulders up to your ears and push your head down into your shoulders. Do it tightly. Okay, you can relax now. Bring your head out and let your shoulders relax. Notice how much better it feels to be relaxed than to be all tight. One more time now. Push your head down and your shoulders way up to your ears. Hold it. Feel the tenseness in your neck and shoulders. Okay. You can relax now and feel comfortable. You feel good.

Jaw

Put your teeth together real hard. Let your neck muscles help you. Now relax. Just let your jaw hang loose. Notice how good it feels just to let your jaw drop. OK, bite down again hard. That's good. Now relax again. Just let your jaw drop. It feels so good just to let go. OK, one more time. Bite down. Hard as you can. Harder. Oh, you're really working hard. Good. Now relax. Try to relax your whole body. Let yourself go as loose as you can.

Face and Nose

Wrinkle up your nose. Make as many wrinkles in your nose as you can. Scrunch your nose up real hard. Good. Now you can relax your nose. Now wrinkle up your nose again. Wrinkle it up hard. Hold it just as tight as you can. Okay. You can relax your face. Notice that when you scrunch up your nose your cheeks and your mouth and your forehead all help you and they get tight, too. So when you relax your nose, your whole face relaxes too, and that feels good. Now make lots of wrinkles on your forehead. Hold it tight, now. Okay, you can let go. Now you can just relax. Let your face go smooth. No wrinkles anywhere. Your face feels nice and smooth and relaxed.

Stomach

Now tighten up your stomach muscles real tight. Make your stomach real hard. Don't move. Hold it. You can relax now. Let your stomach go soft. Let it be as relaxed as you can. That feels so much better. Okay, again. Tighten your stomach real hard. Good. You can relax now. Kind of settle down, get comfortable, and relax. Notice the difference between a tight stomach and a relaxed one. That's how we want it to feel. Nice and loose and relaxed. Okay. Once more. Tighten up. Tighten hard. Good. Now you can relax completely. You can feel nice and relaxed.

This time, try to pull your stomach in. Try to squeeze it against your backbone. Try to be as skinny as you can. Now relax. You don't have to be skinny now. Just relax and feel your stomach being warm and loose. Okay, squeeze in your stomach again. Make it touch your backbone. Get it real small and tight. Get as skinny as you can. Hold tight now. You can relax now. Settle back and let your stomach come back out where it belongs. You can really feel good now. You've done fine.

Legs and Feet

Push your toes down on the floor really hard. You'll probably need your legs to help you push. Push down, spread your toes apart. Now relax your feet. Let your toes go loose and feel how nice that is. It feels good to be relaxed. Okay. Now push your toes down. Let your leg muscles help you push your feet down. Push your feet. Hard. Okay. Relax your feet, relax your legs, relax your toes. It feels so good to be relaxed. No tenseness anywhere. You feel kind of warm and tingly.

Conclusion

Stay as relaxed as you can. Let your whole body go limp and feel all your muscles relaxed. In a few minutes I will ask you to open your eyes and that will be the end of the session. Today is a good day, and you are ready to go back to class feeling very relaxed. You've worked hard in here and it feels good to work hard. Shake your arms. Now shake your legs. Move your head around. Slowly open your eyes. Very good. You've done a good job. You're going to be a super relaxer.

Ollendick and Cerny (1981) also suggest 15- to 20-minute training sessions and that no more than three muscle groups be introduced in any one training session. The level of relaxation attained by the child is inferred by the therapist from observations of the child during the training sessions and the child's subjective report. Physiological measures (e.g., heart rate) may be possible depending upon resources, although we rarely employ physiological recording. Of course, the introduction of equipment and electrodes would have to be done carefully so as not to frighten the child. Giggling and laughter, persistent shuffling and fidgeting, excessive eyelid movements, and facial tension and grimacing all indicate that the child is experiencing difficulties with the procedure. Relaxation training is usually taught as a coping skill and provides the child with a means of combating feelings of discomfort in stressful situations at home or school. Rarely, however, would it be used as the sole treatment of choice. Several reviews have been written on the usefulness of relaxation training for children in clinic and school settings (e.g., Luiselli, 1980; Richter, 1984).

Systematic Desensitization

The frequently cited pioneering work of Mary Cover Jones in 1924 is a nice illustration of the essence of desensitization. Jones successfully overcame a young boy's (Peter) fear of a rabbit using a series of "toleration steps" requiring closer contact with the rabbit until he was finally able to let the rabbit nibble from his fingers. An important aspect of treatment involved exposing Peter to the feared rabbit in the presence of food, a stimulus that elicited a positive response. Wolpe (1958) refined this approach with the introduction of systematic desensitization. Customarily three steps are involved in systematic desensitization: teaching the child progressive relaxation, constructing a stimulus hierarchy of anxiety-evoking situations ("anxiety hierarchy"), and counterimposing the anxiety scenes with relaxation (see also King, Hamilton, & Ollendick, 1988; Masters et al., 1987; Morris & Kratochwill, 1983; Ollendick & Cerny, 1981).

The first stage of systematic desensitization involves teaching the child how to relax. We have already detailed progressive relaxation procedures that have been modified for use with children. Three or more sessions may have to be devoted to training in relaxation (accompanied by practice in relaxation at home). As even modified relaxation training procedures may prove unsuitable for certain children—especially very young children—other forms of anxiety inhibitors may have to be considered, such as interpersonal relationships, games, or edibles. The choice of anxiety inhibitor needs to be determined by the therapist in consultation with the child's parents (King, Hamilton, & Ollendick, 1988; Morris & Kratochwill, 1983).

The second stage of systematic desensitization entails the construction of the anxiety hierarchy (Masters et al., 1987; Morris & Kratochwill, 1983). Typically this begins while the child is undergoing relaxation training. The anxiety hierarchy consists of a series of anxiety-provoking scenes related to the problem fear, ranging from least anxiety-provoking to most anxiety-provoking. The child is usually given 3×5 inch index cards and asked to write down on each card a brief description of different situations regarding the fear. To obtain a smooth gradation of anxiety-provoking situations, the client is asked to rate the level of fear produced by each of the situations. Typically this involves a 1–10 scale (1 = little or no anxiety; 10 = extreme anxiety). The cards are then placed in order of the amount of anxiety they elicit to form the anxiety hierarchy. Further cards may be added should it seem necessary. The clinician must identify the critical antecedents of the fear reaction and ensure that the appropriate stimulus dimensions run through the anxiety hierarchy.

Older children and adolescents usually show a good understanding of what is required and are able to participate in the construction of the anxiety hierarchy. For young children, however, the clinician tends to rely upon caregivers for information about antecedent stimuli, choice of items, and the appropriate sequencing of items in the anxiety hierarchy. Most anxiety hierarchies consist of between 10 and 20 scenes, although the number of scenes depends upon the individual case. Of course, there are many different types of anxiety hierarchies. Table 3-2 presents several examples of anxiety hierarchies, drawing on cases seen in our clinics. Paul (1969) has distinguished between *thematic* hierarchies, referring to hierarchies in which items are related to the same basic theme, and *spatio-temporal* hierarchies, in which the individual fears a specific situation or event and where the items are graded according to how close they are in space or time to the target situation. Paul (1969) would refer to the hierarchies in Table 3-2 as *combined* hierarchies since they are both thematic and spatial.

During the third stage (sometimes referred to as "systematic desensitization proper") the child is given several minutes to reach a state of deep relaxation. The child is then asked to imagine being in the least anxiety-provoking scene of the hierarchy. The therapist describes the situation and asks the child to imagine being in the scene and then to stop imagining the scene after about 5 to 10 seconds. The child is instructed to signal to the therapist any excessive anxiety that may be experienced during the presentation of the scene. Whereas adolescents are usually able to signal anxiety by raising their finger or hand, children tend to prefer raising their arm. When the scene being presented no longer evokes anxiety, the next scene on the anxiety hierarchy is introduced. The procedure is followed until the most anxiety-provoking item can be imagined as the child continues to relax. The number of sessions to complete systematic desensitization proper varies considerably depending upon how may items there are in the hierarchy and what problems are encountered (see Morris & Kratochwill, 1983).

While imaginal desensitization has been used routinely with children and adolescents, we tend to rely more heavily on real-life desensitization (also labeled *in vivo* desensitization). However, many practical issues need to

TABLE 3-2 • **Examples of Anxiety Hierarchies**

Fear of Going to School

Being driven to school
Sitting in car outside school
Walking onto the school grounds
Entering the main school building
Approaching the classroom via the hall
Being in the classroom
Being in classroom with teacher
Being in classroom with teacher and several classmates
Attending last two classes of the day
Attending school for half a day
Attending school for whole day

Fear of Riding on a School Bus

Looking at school bus parked outside garage
Entering the school bus—no driver or children present
Sitting in the school bus—no driver or children present
Sitting in the school bus with driver present
Sitting in the school bus with driver and several children
Riding the bus to school with several children present
Riding the bus to school with regular load of children
(Sitting toward front of bus)
Riding the bus to school with regular load of children
(Sitting about midway of bus)
Riding the bus to school with regular load of children
(Sitting toward rear of bus)

Test Anxiety

Attending a regular class
Attending class/teacher announces major test
Studying at home several nights before the test
Studying at home the night before the test
Morning of the test/talking to other students about the test
Sitting at desk/waiting for test materials
Looking through test materials
Hearing the teacher say, "You may begin now"
Starting work on the test
Coming to a difficult question/problem
Hearing the teacher say, "Five minutes remaining"

be considered for *in vivo* desensitization to be successful. For example, the frequency and location of the exposures may need clarification with the child. Similarly to imaginal desensitization, we ask the child to confront the anxiety-provoking situation several times before progressing to the next level of the hierarchy. Particular attention is given to physiological and overt indices of anxiety (e.g., trembling hands and hesitation) as well as what the child actually reports (e.g., "I still feel upset"). Finally, the role of parents and teachers during *in vivo* desensitization needs to be addressed. Caregivers are advised to be supportive and encourage the child to persist with the desensitization treatment.

The early clinical literature contains many case reports of systematic desensitization being used in the treatment of school-refusing children. For example, Lazarus (1960) successfully applied systematic desensitization to a girl experiencing school attendance difficulties. The girl developed multiple symptoms following three traumatic experiences of death (a school friend drowned, a playmate died suddenly, and she witnessed a man killed in a motorbike accident). She was afraid of being separated from her mother, had nightmares, and was enuretic. Using a seven-item hierarchy of fears relating to separation from the mother, the child underwent imaginal desensitization over five treatment sessions, which resulted in school return. Lazarus, Davison, & Polefka (1965) employed systematic desensitization as the principal therapeutic strategy with a 9-year-old boy experiencing separation anxiety and school refusal. Initially imaginal desensitization was tried and abandoned due to the boy's "inarticulateness and acquiescent response tending" (he seemed more concerned with earning therapist approval than with describing his true feelings). Therefore, *in vivo* desensitization was implemented, which eventually resulted in school return. However, various anxiety inhibitors had to be introduced during the course of treatment (see Table 3-3).

At this time, systematic desensitization is still used in the treatment of school refusal, although clinicians and researchers are increasingly flexible in its application. For example, O'Reilly (1971) treated a 6-year-old girl (Andrea) with a simple phobia using systematic desensitization. Andrea had developed a phobic reaction toward the school fire alarm. This phobic behavior was distressing to several of her classmates, who also developed neurotic-type reactions to the fire alarm. Therefore, Andrea and her classmates were exposed to progressively longer presentations of the fire alarm in the context of a pleasure-producing auditory stimulus (tape recordings of children's stories and songs). Bornstein and Knapp (1981) applied self-control desensitization to a 12-year-old boy with multiple phobias and school refusal. In this particular variant of systematic desensitization, relaxation and desensitization were presented within a coping framework (e.g., "Relaxation is a skill *you* acquire and *you* apply") (see Goldfried, 1971, for details on the principles of self-control desensitization). This variant of systematic desensitization produced marked improvements that were maintained at one-year follow-up. More recently, McNamara (1988) reported the use of a behavioral

TABLE 3-3 • Steps in the Treatment of a School-Refusing Boy

1. On a Sunday afternoon, accompanied by the therapists, he walked from his house to the school. The therapists were able to allay Paul's anxiety by means of distraction and humor, so that his initial exposure was relatively pleasant.

2. On the next two days at 8:30 A.M., accompanied by one of the therapists, he walked from his house into the schoolyard. Again, Paul's feelings of anxiety were reduced by means of coaxing, encouragement, relaxation, and the use of "emotive imagery" (i.e., the deliberate picturing of subjectively pleasant images such as Christmas and a visit to Disneyland, while relating them to the school situation). Approximately 15 minutes were spent roaming around the school grounds, after which Paul returned home.

3. After school was over for the day, the therapist was able to persuade the boy to enter the classroom and sit down at his desk. Part of the normal school routine was then playfully enacted.

4. On the following three mornings, the therapist accompanied the boy into the classroom with the other children. They chatted with the teacher and left immediately after the opening exercises.

5. A week after beginning this program, Paul spent the entire morning in class. The therapist sat in the classroom and smiled approvingly at Paul whenever he interacted with his classmates or the teacher. After eating his lunch he participated in an active ball game and returned to his house with the therapist at 12:30. (Since parent-teacher conferences were held during that entire week, afternoon classes were discontinued.)

6. Two days later when Paul and the therapist arrived at school, the boy lined up with the other children and allowed the therapist to wait for him inside the classroom. This was the first time that Paul had not insisted on having the therapist in constant view.

7. Thereafter, the therapist sat in the school library adjoining the classroom.

8. It was then agreed that the therapist would leave at 2:30 P.M. while Paul remained for the last hour of school.

9. On the following day, Paul remained alone at school from 1:45 P.M. until 2:45 P.M. (Earlier that day, the therapist had unsuccessfully attempted to leave the boy alone from 10 until noon.)

10. Instead of fetching the boy at his home, the therapist arranged to meet him at the school gate at 8:30 A.M. Paul also agreed to remain alone at school from 10:45 A.M. until noon, provided that the therapist returned to eat lunch with him. At 1:45 P.M. the therapist left again with the promise that if the boy remained until school ended (3:30 P.M.), he would visit Paul that evening and play the guitar for him.

11. Occasional setbacks made it necessary to instruct the lad's mother not to allow the boy into the house during school hours. In addition, the teacher was asked to provide special jobs for the boy to increase his active participation and make school more attractive.

12. The family doctor was asked to prescribe a mild tranquilizer for the boy to take on awakening to reduce his anticipatory anxieties.

13. After meeting the boy in the mornings, the therapist gradually left him alone at school for progressively longer periods of time. After six days of this procedure, the therapist was able to leave at 10 A.M.

(Continued)

TABLE 3-3 • *(Continued)*

---

14. The boy was assured that the therapist would be in the faculty room until 10 A.M., if needed. Thus, he came to school knowing the therapist was present, but not actually seeing him.

15. With Paul's consent the therapist arrived at school shortly after the boy entered the classroom at 8:40 A.M.

16. School attendance independent of the therapist's presence was achieved by specific rewards (a comic book and variously colored tokens that would eventually procure a baseball glove) contingent upon his entering school and remaining there alone.

17. Because the therapist's presence seemed to have at least as much reward value as the comic books and tokens, it was necessary to enlist the mother's cooperation to effect the therapist's final withdrawal.

18. Approximately three weeks later, Paul had accumulated enough tokens to procure his baseball glove. He then agreed with his parents that rewards of this kind were no longer necessary.

Source: A. A. Lazarus, G. C. Davison, and D. A. Polefka, "Classical and Operant Factors in the Treatment of School Phobia," *Journal of Abnormal Psychology, 70:* 225–229 (1965). Copyright 1965 by the American Psychological Association. Reprinted by permission.

self-management program for a female adolescent (Anne) with severe school attendance difficulties. Although school return was accomplished almost immediately, it became apparent that Anne was unable to attend normal lessons because of her high level of anxiety. Therefore, *in vivo* desensitization was implemented to help Anne progressively attend lessons until she was following a full timetable. A gradual increase in lesson attendance and self-confidence was reported by Anne (see Figure 3-1). Our own clinical experience confirms that children become more self-confident as they progress through desensitization. In sum, systematic desensitization is an extremely useful procedure in the treatment of school refusal (reviews by Blagg, 1987; King, Hamilton, & Ollendick, 1988; Morris & Kratochwill, 1983). However, we caution that the use of this procedure should be governed by a careful functional analysis of school refusal behavior (Kearney & Silverman, 1990). In our experience, systematic desensitization is well-suited for those phobic reactions involving a high level of physiological reactivity and extreme avoidance. However, it is not the treatment of choice for those anxieties due primarily to a lack of skills, inadvertent reinforcement from significant others, or other maintenance factors.

Emotive Imagery

Emotive imagery is a variant of systematic desensitization and has been used with children experiencing a range of fears and anxieties. Lazarus and

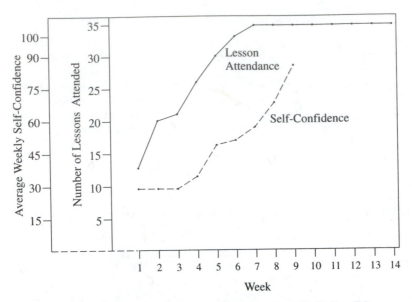

FIGURE 3-1   **Increase in Lesson Attendance and Self-Confidence**

Source: E. McNamara, "The Self-Management of School Phobia: A Case Study," *Behavioral Psycho-therapy, 16,* 217–229 (1988). Used with permission from Academic Press.

Abramovitz (1962) describe emotive imagery as "those classes of imagery which are assumed to arouse feelings of self-assertion, pride, affection, mirth, and similar anxiety-inhibiting responses" (p.191). Rather than muscular relaxation being used as the anxiety inhibitor, feelings of "positive affect" are employed to counter anxiety. An exciting story involving the child's hero images might be told, with fear-related scenes being interwoven at various points in hierarchical order. Of central importance are the child's hero images, usually from television, fiction, or a fantasy from the child's imagination.

The following example of emotive imagery was reported by Lazarus and Abramovitz (1962) in the treatment of a 14-year-old boy who experienced school attendance difficulties due to an intense fear of dogs. After much questioning, the therapist ascertained that the boy had fantasies of racing motor cars. In fact, he had a burning ambition to own a certain Alpha Romeo sports car and race it in the Indianapolis 500. Emotive imagery was induced as follows:

> Close your eyes. I want you to imagine, clearly and vividly, that your wish has come true. The Alfa Romeo is now in your possession. It is your car. It is standing in the street outside your house. You are looking at it now. Notice the beautiful sleek lines. You decide to go

for a drive with some friends of yours. You sit down at the wheel, and you feel a thrill of pride as you realize that you own this magnificent machine. You start up and listen to the wonderful roar of the exhaust. You let the clutch in and the car streaks off. You are out in a clear open road now; the car is performing like a pedigree; the speedometer is climbing into the nineties; you have a wonderful feeling of being in perfect control; you look at trees whizzing by and you see a little dog standing next to one of them. . . . An item fairly high up on the hierarchy was: 'You stop at a cafe in a little town, and dozens of people crowd around to look enviously at this magnificent car and its lucky owner, you swell with pride; and at this moment a large boxer comes up and sniffs at your heels'. . . . (Lazarus & Abramovitz, 1962, p. 192)

Following three sessions of this treatment, the boy reported a marked improvement in his reaction to dogs. Several field assignments involving exposure to dogs were then recommended during the next two sessions, after which therapy was terminated. Twelve months later there was still no trace of his former phobia, according to reports from both the child and his relatives.

Emotive imagery can also be used in the treatment of fears and anxieties that are related to school themes. For example, a young boy with a phobia of his teacher received several sessions of emotive imagery as part of his therapy in one of our clinics. As this particular child was fascinated by Superman, the therapist constructed a fear hierarchy and then asked the child to imagine that he was to join up with Superman on a special mission. An example of the emotive imagery treatment follows:

Superman arrives at your home and explains the nature of the mission, which is to catch people who have stolen equipment from your school. Superman soars through the sky toward school with you secured next to him. You feel strong and confident being with Superman. Now you are at school. Lots of admiring kids crowd around Superman, and you feel especially proud to have been chosen to help. You explain to your friends that Superman is going to try and get back the stolen equipment. There is further excitement and cheers on the part of the children. At this point you notice your teacher . . . she is standing outside the classroom. [Further along the hierarchy.] You and Superman go on a tour of the school looking for clues. Again you feel very proud to be helping Superman. You enter your classroom and find your teacher sitting at her desk.

Rosenstiel and Scott (1977) recommend that, when using imagery techniques with children, imagery scenes should be tailored to the age of the child and treatment ought to incorporate existing fantasies and cognitions. They also point out that nonverbal cues supply important information about the treatment process. For example, changes in muscle tension, alterations in breathing patterns, and changes in facial expressions might be used to assess how well the child is coping with the anxiety-provoking stimuli. In view of the current emphasis on matching therapy with the age-related cognitive and verbal abilities of children, it should be noted that we have found emotive imagery to be especially useful in the treatment of children in primary school grades.

Shaping and Contingency Management

The usefulness of operant-based strategies in the treatment of school-refusing children has been emphasized by numerous clinicians and researchers (e.g., Ayllon, Smith, & Rogers, 1970; Blagg & Yule, 1984; Vaal, 1973). Ollendick and Mayer (1984) have noted the essence of the operant approach. Essentially, strategies based on the operant model attempt to increase the reinforcement value of school attendance (e.g., increased peer acceptance; teacher and parental approval) as well as decrease the reinforcement value of staying at home (e.g., withdrawal of parental attention, prohibiting the watching of television). Until 'natural' consequences (e.g., good grades, improved peer relations) associated with regular school attendance are realized by the school-refusing child, material or social reinforcers in the form of preferred objects and social praise may be required. Thus, an operant-based program should involve both the school and home with respect to the management of contingencies (positive reinforcement and extinction). Following a shaping procedure, full-time school attendance can be established via a series of graduated approximations. Usually the therapist has the child carry out a tolerable school-related morning task (e.g., visit school at normal starting time without going into school) and builds up from this point until satisfactory school attendance is achieved. Alternatively, the therapist can have the child start with a school-related afternoon task (e.g., sitting in on the last class) and work backward in increasing the amount of time spent at school until full-time school attendance occurs.

The now classic study on the operant approach to school refusal is that reported by Ayllon, Smith, and Rogers (1970). The case involved an 8-year-old girl (Valerie) who had gradually stopped attending school in the second grade, with this refusal continuing on into the third grade. Whenever the mother attempted to take her to school, she threw such violent temper tantrums that it was impossible to take her to school. A 10-day baseline was taken in which behavioral observations were made in the child's home and in a neighbor's home. The child's principal and teachers were also interviewed. Table 3-4 shows the procedural and behavioral effects of intervention. Four distinct procedures were used in treatment. The first procedure detailed the prompting-shaping of school attendance. Valerie was taken to school by the therapist's assistant toward the end of the school day. Each day she was taken to school progressively earlier. Although progress was made to the stage where she would remain in school all day without the presence of the assistant, she still refused to get dressed in the morning and walk to school with her three siblings. Thus, the problem was how to provide sufficient motivation to ensure her leaving for school. The second procedure detailed withdrawal of social reinforcers upon failure to leave for school. As Valerie was able to spend one hour with her mother after her siblings had gone to school, the therapist had the mother leave for work at the same time the children left for school. Although the mother left for work at the designated time, Valerie still refused to go to school, and each day she was taken to a neighbor's apartment. Valerie also started to follow her mother to work. The third procedure entailed prompting school attendance combined with a home-based motivational system. This time the mother, rather than the assistant, was responsible for the prompting. A large chart with each child's name and the days of the week was given to the mother. The placement of a star signified one day of going to school on a voluntary basis; five stars indicated perfect attendance for the week and would result in a special treat or outing. Candy was also dispensed for going to school. Under these conditions school attendance improved.

The fourth procedure was designed to prompt voluntary school attendance and introduced a mild aversive element for the mother if Valerie failed to attend school. The mother now left 10 minutes before the children left for school and met the children at school with a reward. If Valerie did not arrive at school with her siblings, the mother had to return home and escort her to school. It was hoped that this inconvenience would prompt the mother into becoming firmer with her child. Only twice was the mother inconvenienced by school refusal under these conditions. The second incident was very significant: "As it was raining, it was a considerable inconvenience for Val's mother to have to go back home. Once she reached home she scolded Val and pushed her out of the house and literally all the way to school. As Val tried to give some explanation the mother hit her with a switch. By the time they arrived at school, both were soaking wet" (Ayllon, Smith, & Rogers, 1970,

TABLE 3-4 • **Procedural and Behavioral Progression During the Treatment of School Refusal**

Temporal Sequence	Procedure	Valerie's Behavior
Baseline Observations Day 1–10	Observations taken at home and and at the neighbor's apartment where Val spent her day.	Valerie stayed at home when siblings left for school. Mother took Val to neighbor's apartment as she left for work.
Behavioral Assessment Day 11–13	Assistant showed school materials to Val and prompted academic work.	Val reacted well to books; she colored pictures and copied numbers and letters.
Behavioral Assessment Day 13	Assistant invited Val for a car ride after completing academic work at neighbor's apartment.	Val readily accepted car ride and on way back to neighbor's apartment she also accepted hamburger offered her.
Procedure 1 Day 14–20	Taken by assistant to school. Assistant stayed with her in classroom. Attendance made progressively earlier while assistant's stay in classroom progressively lessens.	Val attended school with assistant. Performed schoolwork. Left school with siblings at closing time.
Day 21	Assistant did not take Val to school.	Val and siblings attended school on their own.
Procedure 1 Day 22	Val taken by assistant to school.	Val attended school with assistant. Performed schoolwork. Left with siblings at closing time.
Return to Baseline Observations Day 23–27	Observations taken at home.	Val stayed at home when siblings left for school. Mother took Val to neighbor's apartment as she left for work.
Procedure 2 Day 28–29	Mother left for work when children left for school.	Val stayed at home when children left for school. Mother took her to neighbor's apartment as she left for work.
Procedure 3 Day 40–49	Taken by mother to school. Home-based motivational system.	Val stayed at home when siblings left for school. Followed mother quietly when taken to school.
Procedure 4 Day 50–59	On Day 50, mother left for school *before* children left home. Home-based motivational system.	Siblings met mother at school door. Val stayed at home.
	After 15 min. of waiting in school, mother returned home and took Val to school.	Val meekly followed her mother.

(Continued)

TABLE 3-4 • *(Continued)*

Temporal Sequence	Procedure	Valerie's Behavior
Procedure 4 Day 50–59 *(Continued)*	On Day 51, mother left for school *before* children left home.	Val and siblings met mother at school door.
	On Day 52, mother left for school before children left home.	Siblings met mother at school door. Valerie stayed at home.
	After 15 min. of waiting in school, mother returned home and physically hit and dragged Valerie to school.	Valerie cried and pleaded with her mother not to hit her. Cried all the way to school.
	On Day 53–59, mother left for school before children left home.	Val and siblings met mother at school door.
Fading Procedure Day 60–69	Mother discontinued going to school before children. Mother maintained home-based motivational system.	Val and siblings attended school on their own.
Fading Procedure Day 70	Mother discontinued home-based motivational system.	Val and siblings attended school on their own.

Source: T. Ayllon, D. Smith, and M. Rogers, "Behavioral Management of School Phobia," *Journal of Behavior Therapy and Experimental Psychiatry, 1,* 125–138 (1970). Copyright 1970, with kind permission from Elsevier Science Ltd., The Boulevard, Langford Lane, Kidlington 0X5 1GB, UK.

pp. 134–135). The home-based motivational system was withdrawn after one month, with all of the children continuing to attend school. Valerie was successfully treated in 45 days. Academic and social skills improvements were also noted on six-month and nine-month follow-ups.

The treatment strategy described here has several noteworthy strengths. First of all, comprehensive behavioral observations during baseline and treatment were invaluable in selecting and specifying the treatment procedures used. Second, the therapists closely observed Valerie's behavior and were relatively flexible in their approach to treating the problem. Finally, altering the mother's contingencies as well as the child's contingencies proved to be instrumental in improving the child's compliance. However, we hasten to add that we do not suggest nor condone the use of physical punishment (i.e., a switch) in effecting school re-entry. Removal of reinforcers may be as effective. In conclusion, operant-based strategies play a crucial role in our functional analytic approach to the treatment of school-refusing children. Further information on conceptual and practical issues associated with operant-based strategies can be found in other sources (e.g., Martin & Pear, 1988; Masters et al., 1987; Morris & Kratochwill, 1983).

Modeling

Derived from the principles of vicarious conditioning (Bandura, 1968, 1969), modeling involves demonstrating nonfearful behavior in the fear-producing situation and showing the child an appropriate response for handling the feared situation. Thus, anxiety is reduced and appropriate skills are learned by the child. After the demonstration the child is instructed to model or imitate the performance of the model. Following repeated rehearsals of the observed behaviors, the child is given feedback and reinforcement for performance that matches that of the model. Thus, operant principles are used frequently to maintain the desired behaviors once they are acquired via the modeling process (Ollendick & Francis, 1988).

Modeling procedures have much potential in the treatment of school-refusing children. In our own clinics we have found modeling to be very useful in helping children overcome social evaluative anxiety and social skills deficits responsible for school attendance difficulties. To illustrate, we treated a 14-year-old boy with a diagnosis of social phobia. As he had been absent from school for a protracted period, he was particularly anxious about being questioned or teased about school absenteeism on return to school. In the clinic the child observed a peer demonstrate how to respond to this kind of social pressure. Consistent with the research literature (for reviews see King, Hamilton, & Ollendick, 1988; Perry & Furukawa, 1980), we asked the child model to portray a little anxiety at the beginning of the demonstration (known as a "coping model"). Further, we find it useful to draw the child's attention to the salient aspects of the performance. The transcript for part of the session follows:

Therapist: Did you like the way Marc [model] handled that kid?

Child: Yeah . . . he was real good.

Therapist: Marc was a bit nervous at the start . . . that would be a natural thing to happen.

Child: I noticed . . . he didn't give up even though he was a bit nervous.

Therapist: That's right . . . he coped pretty well. Now, what did he actually say when questioned about being away from school?

Child: Something like "Students can miss school for lots of reasons, but now I'm back and looking forward to school. Tell me, what has happened lately?"

Therapist: That's what he said. Well done!

Child: He sounded really convincing the way he said it.

Therapist: I'm glad you noticed that. How you say things can be just as important as what you say. What was it that made it so convincing?

Child: He spoke straight away and didn't get stuck for words.

Therapist: True . . . these things make a big difference. Did you notice how he was standing and the way he looked at the kid?

Child: Yeah . . . it made him look confident.

Subsequent to modeling, we typically ask the child to rehearse assertive responses in the clinic setting. The therapist provides feedback to the child on specific verbal and nonverbal behaviors and may suggest further behavior rehearsal. It should be noted that we allow the child to "experiment" with different kinds of social responses, with guidance from the therapist as to what seems the most appropriate response. However, our clinical experience, as well as that of others (e.g., Kendall et al., 1992), suggests that the child should experience varying degrees of pressure or social threat during the training sessions. This is in keeping with the range of social reactions that can be exhibited by peers and teachers toward that child. It should be emphasized that we adopt a graded approach to stressful social situations, culminating in exposure to high-threat social situations. Although some clinicians may feel apprehensive about putting the child under such pressure, we have found that, provided a graded approach is followed and sufficient rapport has been established with the child, there is no real danger of exacerbating the child's anxiety or school attendance difficulties.

Unfortunately, there have been few reports on the use of modeling procedures in the treatment of school refusal. The most explicit application of modeling was reported by Esveldt-Dawson et al. (1982). Hospitalized in a psychiatric intensive care unit, the subject was a 12-year-old girl with extreme fears of school and unfamiliar males, following alleged sexual molestation by her grandfather. The patient qualified for a *DSM-III* diagnosis of social phobia. Behaviors associated with her presenting problems included avoidance of school and unfamiliar men, diminished ability to interact with peers, and multiple somatic complaints. Treatment focused on decreasing several inappropriate behaviors (stiffness in bodily posture and nervous mannerisms) and the strengthening of appropriate behaviors (eye contact, appropriate affect and gestures). The key aspect of treatment was participant modeling; this involved modeling by the therapist of specific behaviors and subsequent practice by the child. Combined with the use of feedback and social reinforcement, this procedure was applied to a variety of anxiety-provoking situations related to school and unfamiliar males. Marked changes in the target behaviors occurred when treatment was introduced in a multiple-baseline design (see Figure 3-2). Generalization beyond the persons and situations in training were evident from the use of global ratings. Follow-up contacts with the girl suggested that the gains were reflected in school attendance and so-

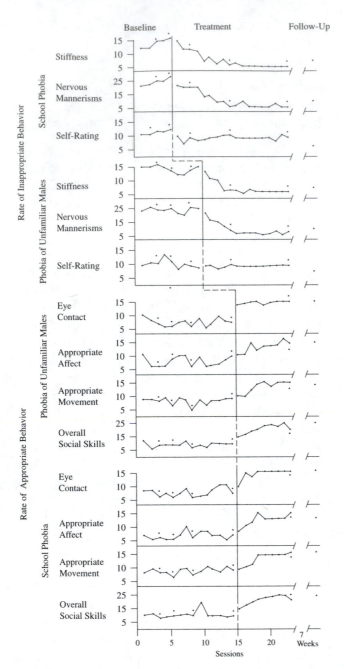

FIGURE 3-2 **Rates of Appropriate and Inappropriate Behaviors Across Experimental Conditions in the Treatment of a Child with Social Phobia**

Source: Reprinted from K. Esveldt-Dawson, K. L. Wisner, A. S. Unis, J. L. Matson, and A. E. Kazdin, "Treatment of Phobias in a Hospitalized Child," *Journal of Behavior Therapy and Experimental Psychiatry, 13,* 77–83 (1988), with kind permission from Elsevier Science Ltd., The Boulevard, Langford Lane, Kidlington OX5 1GB, UK.

TABLE 3-5 • **Factors that Enhance Modeling**

I. Factors Enhancing Acquisition (learning and retention)	II. Factors Enhancing Performance

A. Characteristics of the model
  1. Similarity in sex, age, race, and attitudes
  2. Prestige
  3. Competence
  4. Warmth and nurturance
  5. Reward value
	A. Factors providing incentive for performance
	  1. Vicarious reinforcement (reward to model)
	  2. Vicarious extinction of fear of responding (no negative consequences to model)
	  3. Direct reinforcement
	  4. Imitation of children

B. Characteristics of the observer
  1. Capacity to process and retain information
  2. Uncertainty
  3. Level of anxiety
  4. Other personality factors
	B. Factors affecting quality of performance
	  1. Rehearsal
	  2. Participant modeling

C. Characteristics of the modeling presentation
  1. Live or symbolic model
  2. Multiple models
  3. Slider model
  4. Graduated model procedures
  5. Instructions
  6. Commentary on features and rules
  7. Summarization by observer
  8. Rehearsal
  9. Minimization of distracting stimuli
	C. Transfer and generalization of performance
	  1. Similarity of training setting to everyday environment
	  2. Repeated practice affecting response hierarchy
	  3. Incentives for performance in natural setting
	  4. Learning principles governing a class of behaviors
	  5. Provision of variation in training situations

Source: M. A. Perry and M. J. Furukawa, "Modeling Methods," in F. H. Kanfer and A. P. Goldstein (Eds.), *Helping People Change* (2d ed.). Copyright © 1980 by Allyn and Bacon. Reprinted with permission.

cial interactions in everyday situations. Thus, despite the complexities of the case, participant modeling was very useful in helping the girl overcome her phobias. To conclude, many factors need to be considered for modeling procedures to be effective (Table 3-5 presents a summary list of modeling enhancers). Provided attention is given to these issues (see Perry & Furukawa, 1980), we are optimistic about the potential utility of modeling, especially in view of its effectiveness with other childhood anxieties and phobias (Graziano, De Giovanni, & Garcia, 1979; Ollendick, 1979).

Cognitive Restructuring

A cognitive-based strategy can be defined as a treatment approach that aims at modifying behavior and emotion by changing the individual's pattern of thought (Ledwidge, 1978). In such procedures an attempt is made to alter specific perceptions, images, thoughts, and beliefs through direct manipulation and restructuring of faulty, maladaptive cognitions. Although a variety of procedures have been described, they all share a common focus: the direct modification of faulty cognitions (as assessed through verbal behavior) in order to produce behavior change. Cognitive restructuring is a more recent innovation in the behavioral treatment of school-refusing children. More detailed discussions of cognitive restructuring can be found in other sources (e.g., Bernard & Joyce, 1984; Kendall, 1991; Masters et al., 1987).

As Kendall and his colleagues point out, it is important to provide children with an age-appropriate explanation of cognitive restructuring (Kendall et al., 1991). In their treatment program for children with anxiety disorders (some of whom present with school refusal) they use cartoons with empty thought bubbles to explain the concept of self-talk. Initially the cartoons involve simple, nonthreatening situations in which the character's thoughts are fairly obvious and straightforward. Anxiety-eliciting situations can then be introduced in which the child is encouraged to generate both *anxiety-producing* and *anxiety-reducing* thoughts. Kendall et al. emphasize that the child must realize how these different thoughts are likely to affect feelings and behavior in the actual situation. We have incorporated this approach into our own clinical work with school-refusing children. The following are a 10-year-old boy's responses to a cartoon that portrays an anxiety-provoking situation at school (boy sitting in classroom, teacher asks to see his work):

Therapist: What could he be thinking? What's in his thought bubble?
Child: She won't like his work.
Therapist: How might he feel if he were thinking that?
Child: Not too good . . . nervous.
Therapist: Give me another kind of thought!
Child: I've done my best. I wonder what she will say.
Therapist: That's a good thought. How would it make him feel?
Child: Not as worried.
Therapist: Would it be possible for the boy to ask for help?
Child: Of course. Kids do that in our class.

In general dialogue with the child there are frequent opportunities for the therapist to challenge or dispute irrational beliefs and negative expectations. Of course, this should be done in a gentle and supportive manner. The following transcript illustrates the social evaluative concerns and negative expectations of a 14-year-old boy, along with the disputation of the therapist:

Therapist: [Re going to school] How did you go this morning?

Child: I just didn't want to go to school.

Therapist: What happened this morning, from the moment you woke up?

Child: Mum phoned from work to tell me to get up, then I went back to bed.

Therapist: And what happened next?

Child: I lay there for a bit, and then I thought: I've got to go. Then I had a shower and got dressed.

Therapist: And then . . . ?

Child: Mum phoned again. I packed my bag . . . and I thought: Should I go now or later?

Therapist: What do you think might have kept you from heading off to school once you'd packed your bag?

Child: . . . I was wondering to myself what might happen during the day.

Therapist: What sorts of things did you think could happen today?

Child: . . . I don't know.

Therapist: What about tomorrow? What things would keep you from going to school tomorrow?

Child: Just thinking I wouldn't like being at school.

Therapist: What ended up happening today?

Child: I had a good day.

Therapist: Great. What things did you enjoy about today?

Child: Playing four-square at lunch time.

Therapist: What else?

Child: Doing Infotech [favorite subject].

Therapist: So, how do you think tomorrow might be?

Child: It might be okay.

Therapist: Yeah...that's another way of thinking about school tomorrow. You mightn't know what's going to happen, but you do know that today was okay, even if this morning you weren't sure about how it would be. Okay, what's one thing that could happen tomorrow that you wouldn't like to happen?

Child: . . . I might be asked a question in class.

Therapist: Why wouldn't you like that to happen?

Child: I'd feel awful if I couldn't answer the question.

Therapist: How come not being able to answer the question would make you feel awful?

Child: Because I don't want to seem dumb in front of the class.
Therapist: If someone else couldn't answer one question does that make them dumb?
Child: No, not really.
Therapist: Would it be right for them to think of themselves as dumb?
Child: Probably not.
Therapist: So why should it be different for you?
Child: I don't know really.

Mansdorf and Lukens (1987) have also shown how cognitive restructuring can be used with traditional behavioral procedures in the treatment of school refusal. Two children (a 10-year-old boy and a 12-year-old girl) underwent assessment and treatment. The children had been absent from school for a period of six weeks before referral, and both were "nonresponders" to imipramine therapy. One child was separation-anxious, while the other experienced social evaluation anxiety. A cognitive analysis of the children and parents revealed mediating beliefs and attitudes that were counterproductive to school return (see Table 3-6). The children were then taught how to use coping self-statements to guide positive behavior at school. Parents were also presented with their distorted beliefs about their children and were encouraged to challenge them and use more adaptive cognitions. Following this cognitive preparation, a behavioral program was implemented for the children. This involved graded exposure to the school setting and required parents to be firm about school attendance and ensure that social and activity reinforcers were administered contingently. By the fourth week, regular school attendance had been achieved for both children. A three-month follow-up showed that school attendance had been maintained, with no signs of relapse. In conclusion, while cognitive restructuring is a relatively new development in the treatment of school refusal, it appears to be a useful therapeutic strategy. As with other treatment procedures that have been described, the use of cognitive procedures should be governed by functional analysis.

CASE ILLUSTRATIONS

Furthering our description of the various behavioral treatment strategies that may be used in the management of school-refusing children, we now present two clinical case illustrations. The children concerned were originally referred to our clinics because of severe school attendance difficulties and nega-

TABLE 3-6 • **Analysis of Cognitions and Coping Statements of Parents and Children**

	Child		Parents	
	Analysis	Coping	Analysis	Coping
Subject 1				
	"What will happen when my mother leaves?"	"I'm big enough to care for myself."	"If I push, he'll have a tantrum."	"So what, I'll handle it."
	"I'm scared for my mother when she goes."	"My mother can care for herself well."	"He'll fall apart in school."	"He'll slowly adapt to it."
Subject 2				
	"The kids in school make fun of me."	"That's their problem, not mine."	"My child is sick, I shouldn't push."	"This is the way to help."
	"The teachers might pick on me because of my absences."	"Teachers will understand, they're wise adults."	"Won't it be terrible if she refuses me?"	"No it won't. I'll just do what I should."

Source: I. J. Mansdorf and E. Lukens (1987), "Cognitive-Behavioral Psychotherapy for Separation Anxious Children Exhibiting School Phobia, *Journal of the American Academy of Child and Adolescent Psychiatry, 26,* 222–225. © American Academy of Child and Adolescent Psychiatry, 1987.

tive affectivity. Certainly they meet the criteria for school refusal as set forth by Berg, Nichols, & Pritchard (1969) and elaborated upon in Chapter 1. The cases are described in considerable detail so as to show (1) the interface between assessment and treatment; (2) the use of multicomponent, child-focused therapy; and (3) the need to involve parents and teachers if treatment is to be successful.

Case A

Derrick, a 13-year-old white male in the ninth grade of a local high school, was referred to the Childhood Anxiety Disorders Clinic, Virginia Polytechnic Institute and State University, by school authorities who were concerned about his academic performance in school and his poor attendance record. Although an above-average student, he was in danger of failing ninth grade due to frequent absenteeism, unfinished assignments, and failed course examinations. He was referred eight weeks after the beginning of the school year, following a parent-teacher conference in which his performance and sporadic attendance were discussed. At the time of the conference he had already missed 13 of 40 scheduled physical education classes, 10 of 40 algebra classes, and 6 full days of school. Virginia law permits 20 missed classes per year in a given class before it must be retaken. If more than 20 class periods are missed, the student receives a failing grade for that class (although exceptions to this rule can be made). As Derrick had already missed a number of classes and full school days, he was in danger of failing the entire ninth grade (the school year is approximately 36 weeks long and it was the eighth week of the term).

Additional information from school authorities revealed that Derrick's performance and attendance had deteriorated in the two weeks prior to referral. During that time period he failed to attend school 5 of 10 days. In addition, he missed physical education class (his first scheduled class of the day) on 3 other days (hence, a total of 8 of 10 days in the past two weeks of school) and algebra (the second class of the day) on 1 additional day (a total of 6 of 10 days). Although absenteeism was becoming a definite problem, teachers reported that he was basically a "good" student, one who usually obtained passing grades (i.e., mostly B's and C's) and who was not a discipline problem. They also reported that he had a few friends in school but that he was not particularly well liked. In short, he was described as an "average" student.

Derrick was accompanied to the clinic by his mother, who was seen briefly before Derrick was seen. Background information revealed that Derrick's mother and father had divorced when Derrick was 9 months old and that Derrick and his mother had lived with her parents (Derrick's maternal grandparents) much of the time since the divorce. Derrick's father was described by his mother as an alcoholic, as were his paternal grandfather and paternal uncle. According to Derrick's mother, his maternal grandmother (her mother) had been diagnosed as depressed (subsequently determined to be major depressive disorder). Mother neither reported nor evinced any psychiatric disorders herself. She was, however, quite distraught about her son's problems in school. She stated:

> It's so hard as a single parent . . . what can I do? I leave to go to work in the morning before the school bus arrives, and he just refuses to get on the bus. Nanny [maternal grandmother] can't make him go, neither can Papa [maternal grandfather]. What can I do? I need to work and can't be there in the morning. Sometimes I wonder if he's mad at me and trying to get back at me for something I did. But I don't think so—we really have a good time together. We've been through a lot; we're buddies most of the time.

Mother also indicated that Derrick had a history of being wary in new situations. He had experienced difficulties going to kindergarten and first grade and in transitioning from elementary school to middle school. He also had difficulty meeting new children (for as long as she could remember) and preferred to spend a lot of time by himself. He had, according to his mother, a clear preference for solitary activities. She reported that he did not seem to have problems separating from her or her parents (who handled much of the parenting). Rather, she noted that he just seemed to have difficulty when "anything new comes his way."

In the first session, Derrick presented as a frightened and confused boy who looked somewhat younger than his 13 years. Although of normal height, he was moderately overweight and appeared "podgy." He was reluctant to talk with the examiner initially, looking to his mother to respond for him. Initially, when she failed to answer for him, he looked away from the examiner, avoided eye contact, and looked out the window. With increasing reassurance from the examiner and mother, he started to respond more directly to questions addressed to him. However, when mother was asked to leave the examining room (in order to determine his response), he protested, exclaiming, "Don't go, Mom, stay with me." She was allowed to stay in order to help the examiner develop rapport with Derrick and to help him feel at ease in this "new" situation. This decision proved to be useful as Derrick began to talk more during the latter part of the session.

Using a functional analytic approach, Derrick and his mother were asked to describe a typical school day. Mother indicated that she arose at 6:00 a.m. to get ready for work and to prepare breakfast before leaving the home for work at 7:15 a.m. She reported getting Derrick up at 6:45 a.m. so that he could shower and have breakfast with her (and her parents) before she left for work. Both reported no difficulties with this routine usually; however, mother noted that during the past two weeks Derrick was having trouble waking up and that he was tearful when he came to the breakfast table. He would reportedly state "I don't want to go to school . . . do I have to?" Derrick agreed in the session that he had felt upset about going to school for the past few weeks. He went on to say, "But Mom makes me go. She won't listen to me. I told her that the boys pick on me and call me names. She just makes me go to school." (Later in the session he noted that dressing and undressing for physical education class, teasing by boys who were calling him "queer" names, and having to work on the blackboard in front of the algebra class were the primary reasons for his school refusal.)

Returning to the functional analysis, mother reported that she had to leave for work while Derrick was still upset. Although she requested her mother and father to make sure that Derrick got on the bus to go to school, they were unable to make him do so. He continued to cry and told them he couldn't get on the bus. Although they refused to make him get on the bus, they told him they would take him to school by car if he would be a "big boy" and go after the dreaded classes were over (physical education and algebra). Usually he agreed to do so. At other times he refused to get in the car even though he had promised that he would do so. In the past week he had refused to go four of the five days. Calls to Derrick's mother at her workplace by the grandparents were ineffective in getting Derrick back to school, even though she pleaded with him to do so. On two days during the week prior to referral, mother returned from work (a 21-mile trip one way) to try to get Derrick to go to school. He refused. These events led to the parent-teacher conference and referral to the clinic. Following this first appointment (a Friday afternoon), a second appointment was scheduled for the following Monday morning.

During this session the Anxiety Disorders Interview Schedule for Children (ADIS—C; Silverman & Nelles, 1988) was administered to Derrick, and he completed several self-report instruments, including the Revised Children's Manifest Anxiety Scale (RCMAS; Reynolds & Richmond, 1978), the Children's Fear Survey Schedule—Revised (FSSC—R; Ollendick, 1983), the Children's Depression Inventory (CDI; Kovacs, 1978), and the School Refusal Assessment Scale (SRAS; Kearney & Silverman, 1990). In addition, his mother completed the School Refusal Assessment Scale for parents (SRAS—P; Kearney & Silverman, 1990) and the Revised Behavior Problem Checklist (RBPC; Quay & Peterson, 1983). Copies of the School Refusal Assessment Scale for Teachers (SRAS—T; Kearney & Silverman, 1990) and the Revised Behavior Problem Checklist were forwarded to his physical education and algebra teachers for completion. The assessment process closely followed that described in Chapter 2.

Responses to the ADIS—C revealed that Derrick met diagnostic criteria for avoidant disorder, social phobia, and overanxious disorder. He did not meet criteria for separation anxiety disorder or major depressive disorder. Based on clinical presentation, social phobia was deemed the primary disorder. Derrick obtained a score of 19 on the RCMAS and 174 on the FSSC—R. Both of these scores placed him between one and two standard deviations above the normative means on these instruments. He reported specific fears to a number of items on the "Failure and Criticism" factor of the FSSC—R, including "looking foolish," "being teased," "being criticized by others," and "doing something new." He received a score of 7 on the CDI, a score at the mean for boys his age. On the SRAS he reported elevations on the first two factors: avoidance of fear-producing stimuli in the school setting and escape from aversive social or evaluative situations. For example, to the item "How often do you stay away from school because you feel embarrassed in front of other people at school?" he responded "Almost always." To the item "How often do you have bad feelings about going to school because you are afraid of something related to school (for example, tests, school bus, teacher, fire alarm)?" he stated, "Always." On the SRAS, mother reported very similar responses. However, her responses were somewhat higher on the factor related to avoidance of fear-producing stimuli in the school setting than on the social evaluation factor. On the RBPC she reported elevated scores on the anxiety/withdrawal and attention problems/immaturity factors. Finally, the teachers confirmed problems related to anxiety/withdrawal and attention problems/immaturity on the RBPC. In addition, they noted elevated scores on the motor excess factor of the RBPC and elevated scores on the positive tangible reinforcement factor of the School Refusal Assessment Scale (SRAS). On the SRAS, like Derrick and his mother, they also reported avoidance due to fear-producing stimuli in the school and escape from aversive social or evaluative situations. Thus, Derrick, his mother, and his teachers generally agreed on the nature and function of his problems related to school refusal. However, the teachers suggested a manipulative or controlling quality to this refusal behavior as well. Based on the combined findings, Derrick was viewed as a phobic school refuser rather than a separation-anxious school refuser—a distinction we offered in Chapter 1.

Following the two assessment sessions, Derrick was seen for a total of 10 therapy sessions over a two-month period. The goal, developed with Derrick and his mother, was to have him back in school on a full-time basis as soon as possible, preferably within a two-week period. He was seen twice a week for the first two weeks and once a week for the remaining six weeks. In the first therapy session a plan to have him back in school on a full-time basis within two weeks was agreed upon and a behavioral contract was developed. For the first three days of the two-week period Derrick was to ride to school voluntarily with his grandparents and arrive in time for his third class period. For the next three days of the two-week period he was to arrive in time for his second class period (algebra). Finally, for the next four days he was to arrive on time for his first period. Throughout these two weeks his grandparents were to continue to drive him to school. Completion of the agreed-upon goals was to be reinforced socially by school personnel, the mother, grandparents, and therapist and tangibly reinforced by "outings" with the mother and grandparents. This reinforced return to school was developed as a means to expose Derrick to the fear-producing stimuli in graduated steps. To assist Derrick in reducing and managing his anxiety while undertaking the exposure trials, he was taught muscle relaxation training and a set of coping self-statements to use when he became upset or fearful in the school context. He practiced the exercises in session and role-played various school scenarios. He also practiced specific assertion responses to handle the teases and taunts of his peers.

Derrick was able to accomplish his goals in the first six days. That is, he was able to return to school for his third period, and, after three successful days, to go to school on time for his second period (also for three days). However, on the seventh day he was to return to school in time for his first period class (physical education). He refused to do so. On that day it was necessary for mother to return from work and to accompany him to school (arriving in time for the third period). In the session scheduled for later that day, he reported extreme fear and panic that the students would laugh at him while undressing for physical education class. He practiced responses to their supposed taunts, using the deep-muscle relaxation exercises and self-statements to help him cope. He reported feeling competent at the end of the session and said he thought that he would be able to handle the situation in the morning. In an attempt to provide him with additional support, mother was asked to delay going to work and to drive him to school that morning. Fortunately, he was able to go to school and there was, in fact, little if any teasing during the physical education class. He was also able to go to school for his first period the remaining two days of the second week. Subsequent sessions during the next six weeks were used to bolster and reinforce his new-found skills and to help him ride the bus to school. During that six-week period he rode the bus daily and attended school regularly except for one and a half days in early December. He became sick at school and his grandparents had to come to school to retrieve him. His illness (a type of influenza) lasted the next day as well. However, he returned to school with only minor apprehension the following day. He continued to go to school for the remainder of the six-week period, which coincided with the Christmas holidays.

At that time, eight weeks after the commencement of treatment, he was attending school regularly. The ADIS—C was readministered. He no longer met criteria for social phobia or overanxious disorder; however, he still met criteria for avoidant disorder. He was still wary of meeting new people and of trying new things. Still, his responses on the RCMAS and FSSC—R were in the normative ranges (12 and 142, respectively). Mother still considered him mildly anxious and withdrawn, as did his teachers. His inattention and immaturity "problems," however, were greatly reduced. It appeared, in retrospect, that these problems were due to fidgetiness and overactivity related to his anxieties and fears in the school setting. Although changed in many ways, he was still basically an "inhibited" child (Reznick, 1989).

Following the Christmas break from school (two weeks), four additional sessions were scheduled. One was scheduled the day classes resumed to "check on" his progress. Derrick's mother had requested this session "in case something goes wrong." Derrick was able to go to school that day but did report a return of many of the apprehensive feelings he had reported before treatment began. He was reinforced profusely for his "courage" and his ability to handle his fears rather than have them "control" him. He reported feeling proud of himself and confident that he could continue to attend school the rest of the year. The second post-Christmas session was held two weeks later, followed by a third session one month thereafter, and a final session at the end of the school year. He continued to do well at that time.

Case B

Vicki (a 9-year-old girl) was referred to the Monash Medical Centre School Refusal Clinic by the primary school, at which she was enrolled in the fourth grade. At the time of the referral, Vicki had not attended school for 10 weeks, and her teachers had become very concerned about the effects of such a long period of school absenteeism. The principal reported that he had been in contact with Vicki's parents over this period of time. Initially Vicki had developed a serious viral infection that required medical treatment and rest at home. She missed about two weeks of school because of this illness. After her convalescence, Vicki became quite anxious about returning to school. On school mornings, she would cling to her mother and complain of still feeling unwell. Alarmed at this behavior, the mother took Vicki back to their doctor, who found Vicki to be in good health. According to the principal, it appeared that Vicki's parents had "given up" trying to get her to school. As the father kept long hours in his employment as a machinist, the mother was left with the responsibility of looking after Vicki. It was further reported that the mother had become "too protective" of Vicki, who was the only child in the family.

Two days after the referral, Vicki and her parents were interviewed at the School Refusal Clinic. Initially the therapist spoke to the family about the role of the clinic and then met with the parents and child separately. Similar to the previous case illustration, Vicki was assessed on the Anxiety Disorders Interview Schedule for Children (ADIS—C; Silverman & Nelles, 1988) and a battery of self-report instruments including the Fear Survey Schedule for Children—Revised (FSSC—R; Ollendick, 1983), the Revised Children's Manifest Anxiety Scale (R-CMAS; Reynolds & Richmond, 1978), and the Children's Depression Inventory (CDI; Kovacs, 1978). A Fear Thermometer (FT) was also used to assess her fear of going to school. This was presented in a visual analog format and required a self-rating. The School Refusal Assessment Scale (SRAS; Kearney & Silverman, 1990) was completed by both Vicki and her mother. Finally, both parents completed the Child Behavior Checklist (CBCL; Achenbach & Edelbrock, 1979).

During the administration of the ADIS—C, Vicki was reluctant to leave her parents but seemed reassured when told that they wouldn't be leaving the clinic. Vicki was articulate and cooperative during the interview. Her responses to the ADIS questions indicated a diagnosis of separation anxiety disorder. The first question for this diagnostic category was, "Do you feel really bad or worried when you are away from mum and dad, and do you do whatever you can do to be with them?" Vicki said "yes" and was observed to peep through the door in the direction of her parents! Another question was, "When you have to leave home to go to school or someplace else, do you usually feel sick? For example, do you get stomachaches, headaches, or feel you are going to throw up?" Vicki nodded her head in agreement and acknowledged that she experienced "funny feelings" in her stomach when pressured to go to school. In fact, Vicki answered "yes" to nearly all questions in the separation anxiety disorder category. The administration of the parent version of the diagnostic interview schedule to the mother also produced a diagnosis of separation anxiety disorder. Apparently Vicki had a long history of separation anxiety that could be traced back to a critical event involving the hospitalization of her mother. Vicki was placed in the care of her grandparents, and, never given an appropriate explanation as to what had happened to her mother, she became terrified about her mother's plight. The interview also focused on events over a typical day of the school week, which was revealing in many ways. In particular, since the onset of her school attendance difficulties, Vicki had the close attention of her mother throughout the school day. She was also given the responsibility of looking after the family pets, which she adored. Furthermore, Vicki was able to watch television, play games, and phone her grandparents. Clearly, Vicki's school-refusing behavior was being reinforced in the home environment.

Results for the SRAS confirmed that Vicki's school attendance difficulties were a function of separation anxiety and tangible reinforcers. The subscale that assesses separation anxiety/tangible reinforcers received by far the highest ranking on both child and parent versions of the SRAS. On the Fear Thermometer, Vicki's self-rating was 8. Such a rating indicates an extreme fear of going to school. On the FSSC—R, Vicki also indicated that she experienced "a lot" of fear to items reflective of separation anxiety such as "having to go to the hospital," "death or dead people," and "getting lost in a strange place." Vicki obtained an overall total fear score of 183 (outside the normal range for her age and gender). Vicki's scores for the RCMAS and CDI (18 and 8, respectively) suggested that she experienced a high level of general anxiety but not depression. Regarding the CBCL, mother and father ratings placed Vicki in the clinical range for the Internalizing Scale, but not the Externalizing Scale or Total Problem score.

As part of the assessment the therapist visited the school to discuss Vicki's situation. For ethical reasons and to maintain the cooperation of the family, consent was obtained from Vicki and her parents for the school visit. The therapist was greeted positively by the principal and his deputy and then shown the school attendance record. The record of attendance corroborated previous information given to the therapist; Vicki had been marked absent by her teacher every day since her initial illness. The therapist also observed from the school attendance record that nearly all of the other children in Vicki's class had 100% school attendance for the same period. Vicki's teacher was pleasant and cooperative and had gathered copies of previous school reports and samples of Vicki's work for the therapist. Vicki's grades were about average. The teacher believed that Vicki was "a bit anxious" when at school but stressed that she was not a problem in class. As far as the teacher knew, Vicki had never been teased or bullied at school. However, the teacher indicated that Vicki had not gone away on any school excursions or camps and was always the first child to see her mother after school. The latter observations are consistent with the behavior of separation-anxious school refusers. Finally, the teacher agreed to complete the CBCL. Teacher ratings confirmed the picture of a child experiencing emotional distress, with Vicki being scored in the clinical range on the Internalizing Scale. Overall, our assessment and functional analysis produced a clear and converging picture concerning Vicki's school refusal behavior. (Also, there was no evidence of parental psychopathology or history of school refusal in the parents.)

The goal of behavioral treatment for Vicki was voluntary school attendance. From our functional assessment it was evident that two factors had to be addressed if we were to accomplish this goal. First, we had to deal with the extreme anxiety she experienced upon actual or anticipated separation from her mother. Second, it had become evident that staying at home through the day had become very rewarding for Vicki. In addition to the attention she received from her mother, she had access to television, games, and other activities. The first maintenance factor was addressed through *in vivo* desensitization. Consistent with our earlier discussion, the steps in this program were carefully negotiated with Vicki and her parents and the school. After considering various options for the first step in school return, Vicki selected attending her art class, something that had given her much enjoyment in the past. Her art classes were scheduled for the last two lessons of the day. It was agreed that mother would wait in her car parked near the school, and that she would not enter the school grounds or classroom. Although these arrangements were followed, Vicki was observed to look out of the window for her mother on several occasions. She asked her teacher, "Is Mum still there? Is she okay?" Vicki confirmed that she felt a bit anxious but pleased that she stuck it out and didn't run away from school. After another two days of attending school under these arrangements, Vicki appeared less anxious or worried during class.

The next step of *in vivo* desensitization entailed Vicki being at school for one or two classes while her mother was at home. Mother would still drive Vicki to school and collect her after her classes. (It was about a 10-minute drive from home to school.) Vicki became a little upset as these plans were explained to her, but she agreed that this new step would be a good test of whether she could cope being away from her mother. To her own surprise, Vicki coped very well at school. Although on one occasion she said she felt unwell and wanted to phone her mother (ignored by the teacher), Vicki's overall behavior was described as "fairly normal" and "well adjusted." Vicki's stay at school was then extended to a half-day (mother staying at home). Vicki attended school on a half-day basis for just under two weeks and was able to tolerate separation from her mother. Consequently, the therapist recommended that Vicki attend school for the whole day. Vicki seemed to welcome this change, as she now wished to be like her classmates. (A little social embarrassment had been experienced as a result of her "special arrangements" with the school.) During the desensitization program, Vicki was encouraged to try different strategies for coping with her separation anxiety at each of the exposures. Although relaxation training was attempted with Vicki, she had no interest in this particular coping strategy. Instead, she preferred to rely on thinking about how her superheroes would handle themselves in stressful situations. She applied many anxiety-reducing self-statements such as, "Stop thinking silly thoughts . . . be positive." The classroom activities themselves also served to distract Vicki from any feelings of discomfort. Interestingly, those occasions when Vicki was by herself were the most stressful and involved thoughts of running home to mother. However, Vicki managed to deal with her anxieties and resisted any temptation to run away from school.

As already noted, a significant maintenance variable in Vicki's school refusal behavior concerned events at home. In essence, Vicki enjoyed a range of tangible and social reinforcers for staying at home. Therefore, several sessions with the parents were directed at the importance of appropriate contingency management. Attention from mother, play activities, and telephone calls were kept to a minimum through the school day. Several days later, Vicki was heard to say, "It's no longer fun around here." Parents were also encouraged to ignore somatic complaints and negative remarks about school. The mother became very skilled at the implementation of this strategy by walking away or changing the topic of conversation whenever Vicki made inappropriate comments. The mother was surprised at how quickly these inappropriate behaviors were brought under control. In our clinical experience, the behavior of parents at times of separation has a strong influence on the child's emotional reaction. Therefore, the therapist emphasized the need for the mother and father to be "good coping models" and to make their farewells brief and positive when leaving Vicki at school and other places. Although the mother found this difficult initially, she managed to become more positive and confident. Finally, the parents were encouraged to "recognize" positive changes in Vicki. This was achieved through verbal praise and spending more time with Vicki after school and on weekends. Treatment occurred over a 10-week period, with the family being seen weekly.

Post-treatment assessment showed marked improvements in Vicki. She now attended school on a completely voluntary basis and had not missed a day since full-time school return. Vicki and her mother were reinterviewed on the ADIS—C/P, and it was found that Vicki no longer met criteria for separation anxiety disorder. Vicki was now planning on staying overnight with friends and going to school camps, things she had never done before. When readministered the Fear Thermometer, Vicki looked somewhat amazed that anyone could be afraid of going to school! She pointed to the zero and said, "That's not a problem anymore." The FSSC—R and R—CMAS were also readministered to Vicki while her parents and teacher were readministered the CBCL. Again Vicki's scores for all measures were in the normative range, confirming that she had overcome her emotional distress. Six months later Vicki developed an illness that kept her away from school for three days. On this occasion she returned to school with no signs of relapse, to the delight of her parents and teachers.

RESEARCH SUPPORT

Thus far we have provided an account of behavioral treatment strategies that may be used in the management of school-refusing children, drawing on our own experience as well as the clinical literature. Although suggestive of the efficacy of behavioral treatments, this case material is largely anecdotal or uncontrolled from a scientific viewpoint. We now review the research support for the efficacy of behavioral treatment strategies. Given the difficulties in accessing clinical services and the ethical problems associated with control conditions, research advances in the behavioral treatment of school refusal have proceeded fairly slowly. However, some support can be marshaled for the efficacy of behavioral treatment strategies.

Illustratively, Kearney and Silverman (1990) have reported a study on the behavioral treatment of seven school-refusing children and adolescents who qualified for various diagnoses on psychological evaluation. Most of the children met the criteria for an anxiety disorder diagnosis, and several children received multiple diagnoses. On the basis of how the child scored on the School Refusal Assessment Scale, he or she was assigned to one of four functional categories. These categories describe the motivating conditions for school refusal and determine the kind of prescriptive treatment provided to the child. The first category consisted of those children ($n = 1$) who were fearful of a specific stimulus or experienced symptoms of overanxiousness in the school setting (category labeled *specific fearfulness/general overanxiousness*). Treatment included relaxation training and systematic desensitization. In the second category were the children ($n = 4$) with unsatisfying peer relationships or high social anxiety in an evaluative setting *(escape from aversive social situations)*. Cognitive intervention and/or modeling procedures were applied for these children to increase social skills proficiency. The third category included children ($n = 1$) who engaged in tantrums and other behaviors in order to stay at home with their mother or another caregiver *(attention getting/separation-anxious)*. Shaping and the differential reinforcement of other behavior formed the treatment. The fourth category included those children ($n = 1$) who wished to remain at home for tangible reasons such as watching television or visiting friends *(tangible reinforcement)*. Children in this category were treated via contingency contracting procedures. The treatment sessions were conducted over three to nine weeks. Full-time school attendance was achieved by six of the seven children and was maintained at six-month follow-up. All reported moderate improvements in daily levels of anxiety, depression, and/or global distress. One of the subjects in the second category did not return to school and began work instead. This study illustrates the value of functional analysis and the need for individualized treatment when dealing with a problem as heterogeneous as school refusal. In the absence of control conditions, however, it is not possible to argue that the interventions alone were responsible for therapeutic changes.

An early investigation reported by Miller and his colleagues is of particular interest as it evaluated the relative efficacies of systematic desensitization and traditional psychotherapy compared to a waiting-list control condition (Miller, Barrett, & Hampe, 1972). The target phobias were mainly school phobia (69 percent) and fear of storms, the dark, and domestic animals. Limited data reported on the school refusers suggest they consisted of separation-anxious children and children with phobic reactions toward school events or situations. Both systematic desensitization and psychotherapy groups received 24 sessions of individual treatment over a three-month period. Muscle relaxation training and construction of fear hierarchies were completed during the first four sessions of the systematic desensitization group. In the following sessions the child was instructed to imagine progressively greater fear-eliciting stimuli while remaining relaxed, and when all items of the hierarchy could be imagined without fear, an *in vivo* assessment was scheduled. If the results of this assessment were negative, imaginal desensitization was resumed. In the psychotherapy group, young children were seen for play therapy, while older children were seen for interview therapy. Both older and younger children were encouraged to explore their hopes, fears, and dependency needs. Additionally, the children were "encouraged to examine and formulate both behavioral strategies for coping with stress and the affect accompanying these efforts" (p. 271). Further, intervention with families of children in this group was essentially the same as for children in the systematic desensitization group: "Where parent-child interaction patterns appeared to reinforce fear behavior, behavior therapy principles were employed to restructure contingency schedules, for example, eliminating television during school hours for a school phobic who stayed home" (p. 271). Thus, the "psychotherapy" treatment contained many factors of "behavioral" treatment, even though children did not specifically undergo systematic desensitization.

The children's phobias were assessed on two parent-completed instruments: the Louisville Behavior Checklist (Miller et al., 1971) and the Louisville Fear Survey for Children (Miller et al., 1972). The evaluations were completed prior to treatment, following treatment, and at a five-week follow-up. Parents of children in the two treatment groups reported a greater reduction in fear in their children than did parents in the waiting-list group; the two treatment groups did not differ, however. In an examination of age differences in treatment outcome, it is noteworthy that the younger children (ages 6 to 10 years) were more responsive to treatment than were the older children (ages 11 to 15 years). This pattern occurred for both systematic desensitization and psychotherapy. Unfortunately, no specific information is reported on school attendance or other behavioral indices of school refusal. Overall, the findings of the investigation fail to provide adequate empirical support for the efficacy of systematic desensitization, which is not surprising given our earlier discussion on the need for individual functional analysis and treatment.

In contrast to a graduated approach to school return, some clinicians and researchers recommend that behavioral principles be utilized to facilitate *immediate* school return (Blagg & Yule, 1984; Kennedy, 1965). The belief that school-refusing children should undergo a rapid re-entry to school, using force if necessary, is by no means a recent innovation. In fact, this approach was first reported by psychoanalytic workers (Glaser, 1959; Rodriguez, Rodriguez, & Eisenberg, 1959). Recognizing the advantages of an early re-turn to school, Kennedy (1965) developed a simple and pragmatic program for school-refusing children couched in learning theory terms. According to Kennedy (1965): "The treatment involved the application of broad learning theory concepts by blocking the escape of the child and preventing secondary gains from occurring. In addition, the child was reinforced for going to school without complaint" (pp. 286–287). Kennedy's rapid treatment program for school refusal involves six essential components: good professional public relations, avoidance of emphasis on somatic complaints, forced school atten-dance, structured interview with parents, brief interview with child, and fol-low-ups. Of these, the critical feature was suggested to be forced school at-tendance (cf. *in vivo* flooding). It was advocated that the father take the child to school, where the principal or other staff take an active part in keeping the child in the classroom. However, it appears that there was little necessity for actual physical force in getting children back to school. In all cases, having the parents come to a firm decision about school return was generally enough.

Kennedy (1965) carried out his rapid treatment program with 50 school refusal cases over an eight-year period. The age range of the children was 4 to 16 years, although only 10 children were older than 12 years, and the onset of their school refusal was abrupt and of short duration. Of the school refusal cases, Kennedy reports that five might be considered semicontrols. They were untreated cases of considerable duration of school absenteeism or cases that had been unsuccessfully treated elsewhere. All of the 50 cases responded to the rapid treatment program with a complete remission of school refusal symptoms. The families were followed up two weeks and six weeks after intervention and then on an annual basis for two to eight years. In discussing these results, which are quite outstanding, Kennedy commented that these children may have represented a type of school phobia that "is not really a severe phobic attack at all, but border on malingering of a transient nature which would spontaneously remit in a few days anyway" (p. 289). Taking into account these considerations, Kennedy concludes that the treatment pro-gram may facilitate a remission of what is a serious problem despite its possible transient nature. In the absence of nontreatment controls, however, it is difficult to gauge the effectiveness of Kennedy's rapid treatment program. It should also be noted that these children and their families were more responsive to treatment than those evincing more chronic and persistent refusal.

A more detailed account of the rapid treatment of school-refusing children has been reported by Blagg (1977, 1987). This particular treatment plan stresses early return to school and incorporates:

1. Desensitization of the stimulus through humor and emotive imagery
2. Blocking the avoidance response through forced school attendance
3. Maximizing positive reinforcement for school attendance both at home and at school
4. Extinction of protests, fear reactions, and psychosomatic complaints through contingency management

In addition to providing comprehensive guidelines on the behavioral management of school refusal, Blagg and Yule (1984) have evaluated the effectiveness of their behavioral prescription. The behavioral treatment approach (BTA) was systematically applied to a series of 30 school refusal cases referred over a three-year period. These 30 cases were compared with 16 hospitalized school refusers (HU) and 20 school refusers who received home instruction and psychotherapy (HT). The 66 cases involved in the study met diagnostic criteria of school refusal similar to those proposed by Berg, Nichols, and Pritchard (1969). Although there was no random allocation to treatment groups, the groups were systematically compared on a range of variables. Most of the children were in the 11- to 16-year age range. There were no statistically significant differences on sex, social class distribution, intelligence, or reading age. They were very similar with respect to associated symptoms, school- and home-related anxieties, family size, parent attitudes, and employment. Applying Kennedy's criteria, half of the children in the BTA group, three-quarters of the HU group, and one-quarter of the HT group were classified as chronic school refusers. Thus, the three groups were reasonably similar in the clinical presentation of school refusal.

Operational criteria were employed to compare treatment results in this investigation. A child was judged a treatment "success" if he or she returned to full-time schooling without any further problems. One attendance breakdown was allowed, provided that the child quickly responded to "booster" treatment. A child was classified as a "partial success" if he or she returned to school for at least one year but then had attendance breakdowns culminating in school refusal. A child was judged a treatment "failure" if he or she did not return to normal schooling or returned for less than three months and was unresponsive to further treatment. After one year of treatment, 93.3 percent of the BTA group were judged to be successful compared with 37.5 percent of the HU group and 10 percent of the HT group. Attendance rates were also compared for the year prior to follow-up. While 83 percent of the BTA group were attending school on more than 80 percent of occasions, this occurred for only 31 percent of the HU group and for none of the HT group. Five girls in the BTA group did not meet the criterion attendance rate between the end of treatment and follow-up. The girls concerned were over 13 years of age, had low scores on the WISC—R (Verbal), and were chronic in their attendance patterns. Four of these girls had siblings who also had attendance problems, as well as parents who were far from cooperative during treatment.

In addition to being effective, behavioral treatment was the most economical form of intervention. The average length of behavioral treatment was 2.53 weeks, compared with 45.3 weeks of hospitalization and 72.1 weeks for home instruction and individual psychotherapy. As noted by the researchers, salary costs would be extremely high for those cases involving hospitalization. Of course, the study is by no means immune to criticism. Although quite understandable in terms of obligation to provide a clinical service, a no-treatment control condition was not included. Thus, the extent to which spontaneous remission accounts for the results can be queried. Given the duration of the pretreatment school refusal and the differences in outcome between the three groups, however, it does not seem likely that spontaneous remission is the operative variable as far as behavioral treatment is concerned. Another possible criticism is that subjects were not randomly allocated to the treatment conditions. Thus, it can be argued that easier cases were dealt with using behavioral treatment. This does not appear to be so in view of the fact that no significant differences were found among the groups on major subject characteristics.

Finally, as Wolf (1978) and others have noted, the nature of behavioral goals, interventions, and outcomes is in need of "social validation." From an ethical stance, the acceptability of the behavioral approach to the treatment of school refusal is an important issue. Also, it should be recognized that acceptability has implications for client cooperation during treatment. Gullone and King (1991) had high school students, parents, and professionals rate the acceptability of various treatments that were described in relation to a case of school refusal. The treatments included: (1) home tuition and psychotherapy, (2) hospitalization, (3) medication, and (4) behavior management. Behavior management and home tuition/psychotherapy received higher ratings on acceptability than did hospitalization or medication (see Figure 3-3). In fact,

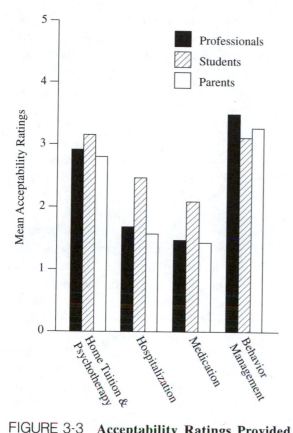

FIGURE 3-3 **Acceptability Ratings Provided by Students, Parents, and Professionals Regarding Treatment Options for School Refusal**

Source: Data from E. Gullone and N. J. King, "Acceptability of Alternative Treatments for School Refusal. Evaluations by Students, Caregivers and Professionals," *British Journal of Educational Psychology, 61,* 346–354 (1991).

behavior management was the most acceptable of all the treatment options. Interestingly, students were more accepting than were parents or professionals of the hospitalization and medication conditions. Why behavior management was the preferred option is unknown, although it may be hypothesized that it is seen as the closest of the options to everyday child-rearing practices. Although these findings are encouraging in terms of the acceptability of behavioral treatment on the part of the community, we must emphasize that there has been insufficient research on the actual efficacy of behavioral interventions for school-refusing children. In our review we also noted major methodological limitations—for example, lack of appropriate controls and inadequate measures—in the studies concerned. Therefore, further research of a higher scientific standard is urgently required on the behavioral treatment of school refusal.

SUMMARY

In this chapter we noted that many issues need to be considered by clinicians in the behavioral treatment of school-refusing children. Above all, treatment should be based upon a thorough assessment and functional analysis. This individualized approach to treatment is particularly important in view of the complexity and heterogeneity of school refusal. Also, medical investigation may be necessary in order to determine the child's current state of health and readiness for school return. Although the behavioral treatment of the school-refusing child reflects well-established conditioning and information-processing principles, considerable flexibility and creativity are often required by the therapist in meeting the age-related cognitive and verbal skills of the child. We described a number of behavioral treatment strategies that may be used with school-refusing children, including relaxation training, systematic desensitization, emotive imagery, contingency management procedures, modeling, and cognitive restructuring. These strategies are useful in helping the child overcome his or her fears and anxieties, hence facilitating school return. As attested to by a vast clinical literature, behavioral treatment strategies appear to be highly effective with school-refusing children. However, too few controlled studies have been conducted on the efficacy of behavioral treatment strategies for us to draw confident conclusions about their scientific status.

▶ 4

Pharmacotherapy

INTRODUCTION

Pharmacotherapy has an established place in the treatment of school refusal. However, prior to consideration of specific psychotropic medications that might be used with school refusal, a general overview of pharmacological treatments in children will be provided. In the history of the treatment of psychopathological disorders, drugs have been used to treat symptoms. Psychotropic drugs act on the brain by blocking or enhancing the action of neurotransmitters, which are the chemicals in the brain that conduct messages between the nerve cells. These drugs are used because, apart from their general action on the brain, they have specific effects on those parts of the brain that modulate feelings (e.g., the limbic and thalamic system) and arousal (e.g., the reticular activating system) (Briant, 1978). Thus, psychotropic drugs may stimulate or sedate, alter the emotional experience of anxiety or panic, and influence mood and concentration. Therefore, psychopharmacological treatments are used for the modification of emotional and behavioral symptoms (White, 1980).

At times the symptoms treated may equate with a specific diagnosis such as attention deficit hyperactivity disorder (stimulant medication) or tic disorder (where haloperidol, a butyrophenone neuroleptic drug, might be prescribed). More frequently the symptom treated by the drug may relate to a number of possible diagnoses. For example, the symptomatic relief by drugs of anxiety, panic, and depression in children with school refusal might occur in children with a range of diagnoses such as major depression, dysthymia, separation anxiety disorder, or overanxious disorder. It is worth emphasizing that in all branches of medical practice, drugs are used to modify and ameliorate symptoms. These symptoms might relate to a specific diagnosis. However, drug treatment alone usually does not cure a disease but produces effects that help or allow the body's natural healing or repair processes to occur or relieves symptoms and thus prevents or modifies the deleterious consequences of the symptoms. In the case of some disorders such as depression and schizophrenia, effective drug treatment has been associated with an increased understanding of possible biological etiology. Psychopathology has complex biopsychosocial determinants; therefore, psychopharmacological agents, at best, have a modulating effect that can facilitate change in psychological function and social relationships (Carr, 1983).

Indications for Drug Use

Before using psychotropic medication in children, the following indications should be met.

1. Identification of specific symptoms and behaviors that are known to be modified by psychopharmacological agents
2. A comprehensive psychiatric assessment that allows these symptoms and behaviors to be incorporated into a diagnostic framework such as the *DSM* or *ICD*
3. The placement of these symptoms and behaviors and diagnosis in the context of social, family, psychological, and biological contributing factors
4. A determination that the symptoms and behavior are causing definite distress to the child and are of such severity or persistence that there is a definite impairment in social and mental functioning and school performance
5. The fact that available safer and less invasive treatments, such as behavior therapy, have been considered or tried and found to be ineffective or only partially effective
6. The selection, where possible, of a single drug for the task that has the fewest side effects and lowest possible toxicity
7. Explanation of the purpose, action and side effects of the drug to the parents and if possible the child
8. Ascertainment that the family has access to a physician or clinic that can regularly follow up the child to monitor progress, check for side effects, and supervise cessation of treatment at the appropriate time.

Action of Drugs

Except for emergency treatment, children are usually given drugs by mouth. The medication is absorbed into the bloodstream from the stomach or small intestine and then passes through the liver, where enzymes often alter, or metabolize, the compounds. This initial filtering by the liver leaves some of the drug intact and produces a number of metabolites. Most of these metabolites are not pharmacologically active, but the few that are, together with what remains of the drug, enter the bloodstream where they become available to produce a clinical effect. The degree to which a drug is metabolized by the liver varies between individuals and is part of the reason for wide variations in the amount of active drug found in the blood of different persons taking the same amount of medication. It also accounts for wide variations in the therapeutic dose of a drug required between individuals (the therapeutic range).

Drugs enter the bloodstream from the liver and most of the drug becomes bound to plasma protein. Only the smaller fraction of the drug that remains unbound is available to produce a pharmacological effect. The brain comprises a large amount of lipids or fats, and for a drug to be effectively absorbed into the brain from the bloodstream, it should be lipid-soluble. Most psychotropic drugs are highly lipid-soluble, which means they readily dissolve into the fatty brain cell membranes and thus pass across the "blood brain barrier" into the brain to produce their pharmacological action (Gittelman & Kanner, 1986).

Drugs are eliminated from the body by repeated metabolism in the liver and excretion through the bile into the feces, or into urine from the kidneys. The length of time taken for the elimination of drugs from the body varies widely between different types of drugs and is referred to as the *half-life* of the drug. This is the time taken for 50 percent of the medication to be eliminated from the blood or saliva where its concentration is measured. Drugs such as the stimulant methylphenidate have short half-lives of several hours (Waters, 1990). Other drugs such as the phenothiazines have long half-lives of 20–40 hours and remain in the body for days (Gilman et al., 1985; Waters, 1990). In general, children can tolerate relatively higher doses of medication than can adults, because their hepatic metabolism and renal excretion of drugs are more efficient. This, together with a reduced capacity for protein binding of drugs in the blood, means that levels of drugs such as the tricyclic antidepressants rise faster and their half life is shorter in children than in adults (Simeon & Ferguson, 1985).

The amount of drug in the blood (serum level) does not necessarily reflect the amount of drug available in the body because some drugs, like diazepam (Valium), are stored and metabolized in other tissues, such as the gut wall (Gittelman & Kanner, 1986).

Once in the brain, most psychoactive drugs produce their effects by interacting with neurotransmitters. These are chemicals released by nerves into the gap or synapse between nerves, to act on receptors of the next nerve. The most well understood neurotransmitters are acetylcholine (ACH), dopamine (DA), serotonin (5HT), noradrenaline (NA), and gamma amino butyric acid (GABA). There are many more neurotransmitters, and new ones are continually being identified. Drugs act on a variety of neurotransmitters in different ways. For example, cyclic antidepressants enhance the action of neurotransmitters by blocking their re-uptake and activating post-synaptic receptors. Other drugs, such as the neuroleptics, block the receptors for DA, NA, and ACH (Waters, 1990).

Drug Safety and Side Effects

Drugs can have potent general or systematic effects on the body, as well as more specific effects on the brain. Many of these effects are referred to as "side effects," although they are an integral part of the range of pharmacological effects of the drug. Most side effects are dose-dependent, with higher doses producing an increase in the number and severity of side effects. The therapeutic range is the dose required to produce clinical benefit and an acceptable, tolerable level of side effects. Once the dose exceeds this range, most drugs become toxic, producing increasingly serious side effects including death in some instances. Some side effects are dependent on time: Short-term side effects are more noticeable at the beginning of treatment; long-term effects emerge as treatment continues; and withdrawal side effects occur following cessation of treatment or reduction in dose (Gittelman & Kanner, 1986).

Sensitivity to drugs varies widely in children as a function of their size and the maturity of their metabolic systems such as the liver. Therefore, a dose that produces benefit in one child may produce unbearable side effects in another. Sensitivity to certain drugs may be familial or due to acquired allergic reactions to the drug. Children are more likely than adults to experience paradoxical side effects with behavior that is opposite to that which is expected. For example, the use of benzodiazepines in children can make them disinhibited, restless, and overexcited (Waters, 1990).

A comprehensive assessment of side effects is required from controlled clinical trials of a drug before it is released for general use. Continuing evaluation of drugs, along with mechanisms for reporting side effects, is an essential component of medical practice and governmental regulation of the pharmaceutical industry. The reliable assessment of drugs for side effects should involve the use of standardized checklists and behavioral scales; laboratory monitoring; physical and neurological examination; and, where necessary, use of special investigations, such as psychological tests of cognitive functioning and electroencephalographic (EEG) monitoring (Campbell, Green, & Deutsch, 1985). A comprehensive review of side effects provided by Campbell, Green, and Deutsch is summarized in Table 4-1.

A child's response to psychoactive medication may vary if the child is unwell with a fever or other illness. Psychotropic medication may also interact to either potentiate or negate the effects of another drug. Care should always be exercised if a child is taking more than one drug to ensure that drug interactions are understood and serious ones avoided. For example, tricyclic antidepressants such as imipramine may antagonize the effect of drugs used to treat hypertension, or they can act to lower the threshold for epileptic fits thus reducing the effectiveness of anticonvulsant drugs. The tricyclic antidepressants also potentiate the action of drugs such as alcohol that depress brain function. Therefore, if taken together, drowsiness and impaired coordination and concentration are likely to readily occur.

Administration of Medication

The prescription of medication should only occur after parents have been informed of the diagnosis and treatment plan and the expected benefits and possible side effects of the medication. The child should be involved in this discussion as appropriate to his or her developmental and cognitive level. In general, it is best to begin with a low dose that might not even be therapeutic, gradually raising the dose until the therapeutic effect is achieved or until side effects become intolerable. This process of *dose titration* should include regular meetings with the parents and child. A record of the child's behavior should be obtained from the parents and teacher, and for some disorders standardized self-reports and parent or teacher questionnaires are useful. For example, response to drug treatment of school refusal based on separation anxiety might be evaluated by child self-reports, using the Revised Fear Survey Schedule for Children (FSSC—R; Ollendick, 1983) and parent reports such as the Louisville Fear Survey (Miller et al., 1971).

Compliance is better with a once-per-day dose, which is possible with most psychotropic medication. The dose given should reach the known therapeutic range of the drug, and this may require occasional measurement of

TABLE 4-1 • **Possible Psychotropic Drug Side Effects**

1. **Behavioral Toxicity.** Deleterious alterations in behavior, psychomotor and cognitive performance, personality, mood, and interpersonal relationships.
2. **Behavioral and Other Withdrawal Effects.** New symptoms such as anxiety, insomnia, restlessness, irritability, nausea, vomiting, weight loss, and worsening of pre-existing symptoms (rebound phenomena).
3. **Central Nervous System Side Effects.** Extra pyramidal effects (acute dystonic reactions, i.e., spasms of muscles including the tongue and eyes, dyskinesias, parkinsonian reactions, akathisia, i.e., motor restlessness, and rabbit syndrome, i.e., rapid chewing movements), tardive and withdrawal dyskinesias (involuntary slow and rhythmical movements of muscle group, such as the face and arms, which is usually a long-term and irreversible side effect of neuroleptic medication), epilepsy (usually from lowering of epileptic threshold).
4. **Supersensitivity Psychosis.** Usually transient worsening of psychotic features on withdrawal of neuroleptic medication.
5. **Electrophysiological Effects.** Electroencephalogram (EEG) recordings may show an increased number of abnormalities in response to psychotropic medication.
6. **Autonomic Nervous System Effects.** Dry mouth, blurred vision, urinary retention, sweating, nausea and constipation, may occur with drugs such as tricyclic antidepressants.
7. **Cardiovascular Side Effects.** Faintness or syncopy, changes in blood pressure and pulse, and heart conduction changes seen in the electrocardiogram (ECG) may occur, particularly with tricyclic antidepressants.
8. **Abnormal Laboratory Findings.** Particularly related to blood chemistry, liver, and renal function.
9. **Endocrine and Metabolic Side Effects.** Alteration or cessation of menstrual periods, breast enlargement, hormone changes (such as thyroid, growth hormone, cortisol and prolactin), blood sugar changes, weight gain with neuroleptics and tricyclic antidepressants, and decreased appetite and weight loss with stimulant medication.
10. **Adverse Effects on Cognition.** Changes in performance on psychological tests and a reduction in IQ can occur.
11. **Adverse Effects on Linear Growth and Maturation.** May occur with stimulant medication use over the time of puberty.

Source: Adapted from M. Campbell, W. H. Green, and S. I. Deutsch, *Child and Adolescent Psychopharmacology* (Beverly Hills, CA: Sage Publications, 1985).

plasma concentration. If side effects prevent the therapeutic range from being achieved and there is no measurable improvement, then the drug should be discontinued. Medication should be prescribed for as short a time as possible. For those children who take medication over a more prolonged period, such as stimulant medication, occasional days or weekends off the medication ("drug holidays") should occur. When it is time to finish treatment with medication, the dose should be *gradually* withdrawn. Drug tapering is necessary with most psychotropic medications because of the risk of rebound symptoms and, in the case of benzodiazepines, epileptic fits and other emotional and behavioral manifestations of drug withdrawal (Waters, 1990).

A child rarely has full responsibility for taking medication. Usually parents are asked to remind the child when it is medicine time and to give him or her the prescribed dose. Medication can easily be forgotten in the busy activity of family life, or it may become a focus for pre-existing conflict and oppositional behavior from children toward their parents. Parents may be apprehensive about possible side effects and readily stop the medication the moment their child makes any complaint even if this is not drug-related. Despite verbal advice from the physician and printed instructions on the medication packet regarding the dose regime, parents may also stop the drug as soon as the child shows some improvement or may only give the drug when there is a crisis. In one study of stimulant medication treatment for attention deficit disorder, nearly half of the families did not persist with the drug treatment as recommended (Sleator, 1985).

Compliance becomes even more difficult with adolescents, who are much more sensitive to issues of independence. They are more likely to resent instructions from their parents about taking medication and resist taking medication that they fear might have an effect on their thinking and self-control. For example, one study found that only about a third of adolescents with acute leukemia reliably took their medication even though their illness was life-threatening (Smith et al., 1979). The most serious potential problem with compliance is the overuse or abuse of medication by parents either through the mistaken belief that more medication than prescribed will help the child recover more quickly or in an attempt to sedate or control the child by giving extra medication. This can become even more problematic and potentially dangerous should they decide to also give their child some of their own medication, leading to a risk of drug interaction. Compliance is likely to be improved if the physician takes time and care to explain all aspects of the use of the drug to both parents, preferably together with the child, and to also elicit the cooperation of the child or adolescent in an individual interview. Careful labeling of the medication container, frequent review of the child's progress, and having parents telephone the clinic to discuss drug issues can help further improve compliance.

Drugs are often referred to by their generic name, which is the name of the specific chemical compound. The brand name or trade name is a trademarked name carefully chosen for commercial and advertising purposes by the pharmaceutical company that produces the drug. There may be a number of trade names for the same drug, and trade names often vary between countries. A trade name begins with a capital letter, but generic names are presented in lowercase letters. For example, imipramine, a tricyclic antidepressant that may be used in the treatment of school refusal, is manufactured by several different pharmaceutical companies and carries a number of different trade names such as Tofranil, Imiprin, and Melipramine. Generic drug names will be used in this chapter.

PHARMACOTHERAPY OF SCHOOL REFUSAL

The treatment of school refusal usually involves a coordinated multimodal approach, including behavioral treatment and school consultation. Medication may also be prescribed as part of the general treatment approach, with the aim of returning the child to school as soon as possible (Bernstein, 1990). Psychotropic medication frequently has a role as an additional complementary treatment of severe cases of school refusal, particularly those due to separation anxiety and/or depression. Psychopharmacological treatment aims to reduce psychological symptoms and improve behavior, but it also more generally influences central and peripheral nervous system function and can produce a number of side effects such as tremors, sedation, and inhibition of learning or, more rarely, other potentially dangerous complications such as changes in heart muscle conduction (Waters, 1990). Therefore, the use of psychotropic medication for the treatment of school refusal should be based on a thorough assessment that reveals that the severity of symptoms and lack of response to psychological treatments warrant the use of these agents.

A range of different medications has been tried in children with school refusal, including antidepressants, anxiolytics, neuroleptics, and stimulants. Although beta-adrenergic blocking agents such as propranolol and nadolol have been used as a treatment for anxiety disorders in adults because they reduce the physiological manifestations of anxiety (Ballenger, 1986; Desai, Taylor-Davies, & Barnett, 1983), they have not yet been tested systematically in children with anxiety disorders. The efficacy and role of specific groups of medications and their indications for use in the treatment of school refusal will be examined in the following sections of this chapter.

Antidepressants

There are two major groups of antidepressants, the monoamino oxidase inhibitors (MAOI) and the cyclic antidepressants. The MAOI antidepressants have been used only rarely in children and do not have an established place as a treatment for childhood psychiatric disorders (Waters, 1990). They have the dangerous potential to raise blood pressure when combined with tyramine, which occurs in fermented foods such as cheese and pickles. Compliance with a special diet that avoids tyramine-containing food is difficult to achieve with children.

A new type of MAOI, called moclobemide and described as a reversible inhibitor of monoamine oxidase A (RIMA), has been recently introduced. It is reported to be effective and remarkably free of side effects in adults (Tiller, Maguire, & Davies, 1990; Versiani et al., 1989), including no report to date of adverse cardiovascular system side effects. Moclobemide may have great potential but has not yet been used in any properly controlled trial for the treatment of clearly defined anxiety or depressive disorders in children.

The cyclic antidepressants comprise tricyclic compounds, such as imipramine and amitriptyline and related derivatives. Their mode of action is thought to be via the activation of post-synaptic monoamine receptors and the blocking of pre-synaptic monoamine re-uptake (Waters, 1990). Their psychotropic effects are probably due to a combination of antidepressant tranquilizer and anticholinergic actions (Carr, 1983).

The use of tricyclic antidepressants for the treatment of children with anxiety disorder, especially school refusal, has a long history. One school of thought, particularly from Great Britain, argues that these medications are effective because they treat the depression associated with the anxiety and school refusal (Frommer, 1967; Hersov, 1977). Others have argued that the therapeutic effect of imipramine in the treatment of school refusal is achieved not via a nonspecific improvement of mood but due to a reduction in the anxiety and panic engendered by separation from parents (Gittelman-Klein & Klein, 1971).

Despite the continuing clinical use of tricyclic antidepressants in the treatment of school refusal, unequivocal evidence that these medications are more effective than placebo is lacking (Puig-Antich et al., 1987). The landmark study by Gittelman-Klein and Klein (1971, 1973, 1980) reported that imipramine was beneficial in the treatment of school refusal and separation anxiety. They conducted a double-blind placebo controlled study on the efficacy of imipramine in the treatment of school-refusing children. The children, aged 6 to 15 years, had been absent from school for at least two weeks or were intermittently attending in great distress. Initially 42 children were randomly assigned to either an imipramine group or placebo group for a six-week period. Seven children were lost to the study, leaving 16 in the imipramine group and 19 in the placebo group. Medication was administered in the morning and evening; the dosage was fixed for the first two weeks, then adjusted weekly to a maximum of 200 mg per day. The mean dose was around 150 mg per day with a range from 100 mg to 200 mg per day. During the course of treatment the child and family were seen weekly, and these sessions included behavioral psychotherapy. The families were instructed to maintain a firm attitude with respect to school attendance, and in most cases a parent was encouraged to accompany the child to school if need be. These interventions varied according to the severity of the child's anticipatory anxiety and the mother's ability to set and enforce limits. After six weeks of treatment, 47 percent of the placebo group and 81 percent of the imipramine group were attending school regularly. Self-ratings of improvement were much higher for the children on imipramine than the placebo-treated children. The researchers claimed that children responded to the medication regardless of whether depression was initially present or not, although for those who were depressed, their depressive symptoms also improved. There was one case of orthostatic hypotension, which is a significant fall in blood pressure on standing that causes faintness and dizziness. Other reported side effects, such as dry mouth, were all mild and transient and disappeared without dose alteration.

Unfortunately, these striking findings have not been replicated. A study by Berney and colleagues failed to demonstrate any therapeutic effects over a 12-week double-blind placebo controlled trial of clomipramine in doses of 40–75 mg per day in children with school refusal (Berney et al., 1981). At the end of this study, most of the children were still suffering from separation anxiety, and over 40 percent of both placebo and medication groups were not attending school. This study used less than half the amount of medication, which is of similar potency to imipramine, compared to that used in the Gittelman-Klein and Klein (1971) study. Gittelman-Klein (1975a) has reported that no child in their study improved on less than 75 mg of imipramine per day.

The study by Berney et al. (1981) also used individual psychotherapy and parent counselling instead of adjunctive behavioral treatment. This difference may have contributed to the discrepancy between the two studies, although it should be noted that the rates of improvement in the control groups were similar. Another possible explanation of the different results between these two studies is that clomipramine probably has some different central nervous system actions compared with imipramine in that it is a serotonergic tricyclic antidepressant that is specifically effective in the treatment of obsessive compulsive disorder (Flament et al., 1985). In addition, children in the Berney et al. (1981) study were on average several years older and also appeared to have more depressive symptoms than did the Gittelman-Klein and Klein (1971) group, although the oldest child in both groups was 14.

In a study conducted by Bernstein and her colleagues, 24 children with school refusal were treated in a double-blind placebo controlled study comparing the anxiolytic drug alprazolam with imipramine (Bernstein, Garfinkel, & Borchardt, 1990). Ten of these 24 children had a depressive disorder, 10 had a combined anxiety and depressive disorder, and only 4 had a discrete anxiety disorder. The children were older than those in the two studies previously mentioned (Gittelman-Klein & Klein, 1971; Berney et al., 1981), with an average age of 14 years (7–17 years). All medication or placebo subjects were involved in an educational support and consultation program to facilitate school re-entry and received weekly individual psychotherapy. Alprazolam dosages ranged from 1.0 to 3.0 mg per day and imipramine doses from 150 to 200 mg per day (measurement of plasma levels range 125–250 ng per ml). This study failed to find any significant changes in anxiety and depression scale scores between the alprazolam, imipramine, and placebo treatment groups, when pretreatment scores were used as covariates. However, the active medication groups tended to show the most improvement. There were five dropouts from this study (alprazolam group = 1, imipramine group = 3, and placebo group = 1), and one child was excluded from data analysis due to a high lie score on the Revised Children's Manifest Anxiety Scale (Reynolds & Richmond, 1978), indicating a marked underreporting of symptoms. This left six children in each of the treatment groups. All children in the treatment groups showed improved school attendance, but most placebo control children also exhibited an improvement on this measure.

More recently, Klein and her coworkers have attempted to build on their earlier work by studying the efficacy of imipramine in a double-blind randomized six-week trial in 21 children age 6 to 15 years with separation anxiety disorder (Klein, Koplewicz, & Kanner, 1992). A total of 45 children of normal intelligence who presented to their clinic with a separation anxiety disorder were initially treated with a four-week program of behavioral and family management. More than half of these children significantly improved during the four weeks of behavioral-family treatment, confirming that this approach to treatment should be the first that is tried. At the end of the four-week behavioral program, 21 children still met the *DSM-III* criteria for separation anxiety disorder, and they entered a six-week imipramine-placebo double-blind treatment trial and continued to receive behavioral treatment. Imipramine dose increased over a period of more than seven days of treatment to a maximum of 5 mg per kg per day. Of the 21 children who entered the drug trial, 15 had symptoms of school refusal, secondary to their separation anxiety disorder. Only 2 of the children had a concurrent diagnosis of major depressive disorder. At the end of the six-week drug trial, a range of assessments and ratings completed by the child and other informants showed the same degree of improvement in both imipramine and placebo groups. The researchers do not report on return to school as an outcome variable in those of the sample who had school refusal.

Moreover, the children receiving imipramine had significantly more complaints of side effects, including irritability and angry outbursts. Only 3 of the 11 children receiving imipramine, compared to 7 of the 9 children taking placebo, reported no side effects. Twelve complaints of side effects in the imipramine group were rated as moderate to severe, but in no child did treatment need to be stopped or dose reduced because of side effects. Electrocardiograph (ECG) findings of delays in electrical conduction through the heart (shown by increases in the P-R interval and the QRS, which are separate elements of the ECG recording) were associated with imipramine treatment, but in no instance did the delay pass the standard established as the upper limit for safe pharmacological intervention (Elliott & Popper, 1991). The researchers found that the efficacy of imipramine was less satisfactory than in their previous study and from the point of view of side effects the drug was less well tolerated. They were unable to explain why this might be so, apart from a suggestion that the rating scales used may have lacked descriptive validity by not documenting the high levels of anxiety experienced by the children at the time of referral. However, they still concluded that "imipramine need not be precluded from consideration in the management of separation anxiety disorder, but that a good drug effect cannot be expected with the regularity that could be anticipated based on previous results" (Klein, Koplewicz, & Kanner, 1992, p. 26). The confidence that tricyclic antidepressant medication is an effective treatment of school refusal, engendered by the single earlier study of Gittelman-Klein and Klein (1971), has not been sustained by these two latest studies (Bernstein, Garfinkle, & Borchardt, 1990; Klein, Koplewicz, & Kanner, 1992). However, further studies are required before abandoning this treatment approach altogether.

Side Effects.   Tricyclic antidepressants have a range of side effects that are most commonly minor, but rare and serious side effects such as cardiotoxicity, seizures, and death have been reported (Waters, 1990). The most common side effects are mediated via the autonomic nervous system with symptoms of dry mouth, constipation, nausea, anorexia, and weight loss. Dizziness, insomnia, drowsiness, and a fine tremor may also be troublesome (Waters, 1990). Although these side effects are relatively minor and transient or disappear with reduction of dose, they can distress the child and are a major factor in noncompliance. Allergic skin reactions and thrombocytopaenia, which is a decrease in the number of blood platelets below normal that leads to easy bruising and bleeding, have also been described following the prolonged use of imipramine for more than six months. Tricyclic antidepressants may also produce paradoxical effects on behavior leading to agitation, confusion, excitement, and irritability.

The most serious potential side effect that places a significant caution on the use of these medications in children relates to cardiotoxicity. ECG changes and the development of heart block in adults taking tricyclic antidepressants have been recognized for more than a decade (Glassman & Bigger, 1981). ECG changes include delay in electrical conduction (prolongation of the P-R interval) and arrhythmias. A study by Bartels and colleagues of 39 children taking imipramine or desipramine showed an average increase in P-R interval of 0.01 seconds (Bartels et al., 1991). Eleven of the subjects (28 percent) developed P-R interval prolongation of 0.02 seconds or greater and a new first degree atrio-ventricular (A-V) block developed in two subjects. These cardiac changes were not related to the dosage (0.44–5.71 mg per kg per day), the plasma concentration, or the choice between imipramine or desipramine. The children with increased P-R intervals of 0.02 seconds or more were more likely to have an abnormality in their ECG identified prior to treatment. Children with baseline conduction and non-conduction abnormalities recorded the larger P-R interval increases after treatment. None of the children in this study developed any clinical abnormalities, and the researchers concluded that tricyclic antidepressants were relatively safe to use in the treatment of children who had normal baseline ECGs. However, they advocate caution in the prescription of tricyclic medication for children with a history of cardiac disorder or pretreatment ECG abnormality. These cautions are further highlighted in a review of three reported cases of sudden death in children receiving desipramine (Riddle et al., 1991). As desipramine could be implicated in the cause of death, these authors argue for increased caution in the use of this drug, and perhaps other tricyclic antidepressants, in children. In particular, they urge that an ECG and rhythm strip be done prior to treatment, during the period of increase in medication up to therapeutic dosage, and then from time to time during the course of treatment. They recommend that medication be discontinued in any child whose Q-T interval, corrected for heart rate, exceeds 0.425 seconds. Children with a positive family history of heart conduction problems and sudden death should have a comprehensive cardiac assessment prior to commencement on tricyclic antidepressant medication. The measurement of plasma drug levels during treatment would limit the possibility of unexpectedly high drug levels. It would also be prudent to review the child's pulse during the course of treatment.

There is no doubt that more research is needed on the effects of tricyclic antidepressants on cardiac function in children in order to determine more clearly the relative and definite contraindications to their use. The potential hazards of these drugs also highlight the need to adequately assess children for the possibility of pre-existing heart disease and to undertake physical and ECG examination prior to the initiation of drug treatment.

Anxiolytics

These drugs are also called minor tranquilizers, probably a misnomer in children because of their tendency to produce disinhibition, restlessness, and excitation (Waters, 1990). There are two classes of drugs in this group, the barbiturates and the benzodiazepines. The barbiturates are an older class of drugs with known tranquilizing and anti-anxiety properties in adults. Their use in children is not recommended because of their addictive properties and their tendency to produce restless excitation and disinhibition in children.

The role of benzodiazepines in the treatment of childhood anxiety disorders and school refusal has yet to be established. Some early studies indicated that the benzodiazepine chlordiazepoxide may have a role in the treatment of school refusal (D'Amato, 1962; Kraft et al., 1965; Frommer, 1967). The studies by D'Amato (1962) and Kraft et al. (1965) were not double-blind studies with a control group. Nonetheless, strong effects were obtained. In the study by D'Amato (1962), eight of nine school-refusing children treated with 10–30 mg of chlordiazepoxide per day were attending school after two weeks. Kraft et al. (1965) used higher doses of chlordiazepoxide (30–130 mg per day) to treat children with a range of psychiatric disorders. Their best results were with 18 children with school refusal (14 responded and were able to return to school). The study by Frommer (1967) was better designed, employing a double-blind crossover design. It compared the effectiveness of the monoaminoxidase inhibitor phenelzine, taken together with chlordiazepoxide, to the use of phenobarbital alone in 15 school-refusing children. The combined medication was reported to be more effective than the barbiturate, although details of treatment outcome and follow-up were notably lacking. In addition, the diagnostic status of children in this study was imprecise and it could not be determined if the therapeutic benefit was due to the benzodiazepine alone or a combination of drugs.

The study by Bernstein, Garfinkel, and Borchardt (1990), reviewed earlier in this chapter, attempted in a more methodologically sound way to document the usefulness of the benzodiazepines in the treatment of school refusal. These authors used a double-blind placebo controlled study of the benzodiazepine alprazolam compared with imipramine in the treatment of school refusal. Alprazolam has been widely studied and shown to be effective in the treatment of adults with panic disorders (Sheehan et al., 1984). The study sample was mostly young adolescents (7–17 years). Ten of the 24 children had a depressive disorder; only 4 had an anxiety disorder alone, but a further 10 had a combination of anxiety and depressive disorder. The maximum dose range for the alprazolam group was 1 to 3 mg per day (0.02 to 0.03 mg per kg per day). All subjects in both medication or placebo groups participated in a school return program and received weekly individual psychotherapy. All of the children, with one exception in the placebo group, had returned to school with improved attendance at the end of eight weeks. Children in both medication groups showed significant improvements in anxiety and depression rating scale scores compared to placebo, but these results must be treated with caution because there were significant pretreatment differences in anxiety symptoms and when pretreatment scores were used as covariates there were no significant differences between the groups on change in rating scale scores after treatment. The trends to greater improvement, particularly in the alprazolam and to a lesser extent imipramine treatment groups compared with the placebo group, might have been due to the effects of the medication but could also be due to pretreatment differences in the rating scale scores.

The side effects of alprazolam were reported as mild, with symptoms such as headache and abdominal pain. As these symptoms were also reported by the placebo group, they probably represented somatic symptoms associated with school refusal anxiety. Blurred vision, constipation, dry mouth, dizziness, and drowsiness were also reported by some children taking alprazolam. There were no withdrawal symptoms reported, although the researchers took care to taper off treatment.

A recent study by Simeon and colleagues on the use of alprazolam in the treatment of children with overanxious and avoidant disorders also failed to demonstrate a significant difference between alprazolam and placebo in a double-blind trial of 30 outpatient children (Simeon et al., 1992). They found a strong treatment effect in both medication and placebo groups. There were only a few mild side effects to alprazolam treatment and, after gradual drug withdrawal, there were no rebound or withdrawal symptoms observed. However, there were no children with school refusal reported in this study. In contrast to studies reported with adults this study demonstrated that alprazolam is no more effective than placebo in the treatment of anxiety disorders in children and adolescents.

The benzodiazepines are routinely used as premedication for anesthesia and surgery in the belief that they reduce acute situational anxiety; however, there is no research evidence that they are more effective than placebo in the treatment of school refusal. Further, there is no clear evidence that the use of benzodiazepines complements or improves the response to behavioral management. Despite this lack of evidence and the predilection of benzodiazepines to paradoxical side effects and dependency, a Canadian study indicated that they were the most widely used psychotropic medication in children (Quinn, 1986). This was particularly true for the long-term treatment of anxiety disorders, fears, insomnia, and nightmares, with a prevalence of usage from 0.12 percent in children under four years to 0.43 percent in youth 15 to 19 years of age.

Neuroleptics

Thirty to 40 years ago, neuroleptics such as chlorpromazine and thioridazine were regarded as having an antipsychotic action due to their ability to reduce anxiety. A number of placebo control studies using neuroleptics to treat a range of psychiatric disorders in children found no significant change in reported levels of anxiety (Garfield et al., 1962; Lucas & Pasley, 1969). Further, neuroleptic drugs may cause a range of serious side effects such as tardive dyskinesia, which may be irreversible (Waters, 1990). The use of neuroleptic medication can no longer be justified as a treatment for school refusal unless the refusal is an associated symptom of a psychotic disorder such as schizophrenia or, where the occasion briefly demands, for several days at most, a high level of sedation.

Stimulants

There is no evidence that stimulants have any role to play in the treatment of school refusal that is based on an anxiety or depressive disorder. In fact, stimulant medication may worsen anxiety disorders (Waters, 1990). Aman and Werry (1982) provide evidence that anxious hyperactive children showed a deterioration in cognitive performance when given methylphenidate (0.35 mg per kg). Children with attention deficit hyperactivity disorder frequently have a range of learning and school adjustment problems and may be truant, but it would be rare for them to present with school refusal (Klein, Koplewicz, & Kanner, 1992). Only in the very unlikely case of school refusal being associated with attention deficit hyperactivity disorder would treatment with stimulant medication such as dextroamphetamine or methylphenidate have any part to play in the management.

Cautions

Focusing on the "symptom" of school refusal in treatment is taking an empirical approach (Achenbach, 1985) rather than a categorical diagnostic approach. Psychotropic drugs have tended to be used in children to treat a symptom or presenting problem rather than a specific disorder specified in a diagnostic category such as the *DSM* or *ICD*. The time has come to assess the use of drugs more specifically with larger trials that either target discrete diagnostic categories such as separation anxiety disorder (building on studies such as that by Klein, Koplewicz, & Kanner, 1992), or that target a symptom such as school refusal but study differential responses by children with discrete diagnostic disorders (following on from smaller studies such as Bernstein, Garfinkel, and Borchardt, 1990). These studies are necessary to determine if there is any more precise diagnostic indication for medication rather than a general symptomatic drug effect regardless of diagnosis. Such studies would also help to advance our knowledge of the taxonomies of child psychopathology and explore the interaction between symptoms such as school refusal and the development and course of different disorders such as separation anxiety disorder and depression. The large number of patients required for these studies to have sufficient statistical power would probably necessitate multicenter cooperative research.

Children with school refusal are unlikely to seek treatment for themselves, and, although it should happen, they may not be involved in the discussion and decision to prescribe drug treatment. Parents may be ambivalent or uneasy about medication. The child's symptoms may also be serving some wider purpose in the family such as being at home to comfort a depressed parent. These and other factors, such as the frequency of taking the medication and the development of even minor side effects, make noncompliance with treatment a significant issue. In a study of the efficacy of stimulant medication for the treatment of attention deficit hyperactivity disorder, nearly half of the children and their families failed to comply with the treatment (Sleator, 1985). There was a dropout noncompliance of 21 percent (5 of 24 subjects) in the comparative placebo controlled study of imipramine and alprazolam as treatments for school refusal conducted by Bernstein, Garfinkel, and Borchardt (1990).

Compliance can be improved by involving the child, as well as the parents, in the decision to use medication and by frequently reviewing progress and assessing any side effects that might develop. Research investigations on the effectiveness of medication should also include, if possible, other measures of compliance such as counting the tablets and urine or serum testings for the drug and its metabolites. The dose of medication should be gradually increased to the therapeutic range but should still be the lowest dose possible to achieve the therapeutic effect. Medication may have a role in the treatment of severe cases of school refusal but should be used within the context of the concurrent provision of behavioral, educational, and family treatments.

CASE ILLUSTRATION

Peter, age 9, was adopted from infancy and had mild mental retardation but was integrated into a normal school setting with remedial education assistance. No details were known about his biological parents, although his birth and the antenatal period were reported to have been normal. He lived in a middle-class home with his father (45 years), mother (41 years), and two sisters (19, 16 years). He was reported to have always been a rather shy and clinging child, who initially had difficulty separating from his mother to go to school and was not adventurous. He was referred following a six-month period of increasing distress and difficulty attending school. He complained of stomachaches and would become anxious to the point of vomiting on many school days. He was frightened that his parents would be injured or killed in an accident and often woke at night in distress following bad dreams and would then insist on sleeping in his parents' bed. Other presenting symptoms included poor appetite with some weight loss, moodiness and irritability, unhappiness and tearfulness, self-deprecatory statements and low self-esteem, poor concentration, and deteriorating school performance. Assessment revealed that Peter presented with a mixed separation anxiety disorder and depression. With some difficulty he revealed that his emotional disturbance had been occasioned by bullying and teasing in the school playground and on his way home from school by an older boy. There were sexual overtones to this bullying because the boy had also tried to grab Peter's genitals. Peter had not been able to tell his parents or the teacher about these episodes for fear of retaliation from the boy. However, other factors contributed to his difficulties as well. Peter had a new teacher who was not as sensitive and friendly as his previous teacher. There were also some family tensions. His oldest sister was tense and stressed by the pressure of her final year at secondary school and there was some minor marital conflict related to the father's work demands.

A behavioral program was developed for Peter, aimed at school return and reduced emotional distress. Peter underwent relaxation training and *in vivo* desensitization, while his parents received training in child behavior management skills. However, this program was unsuccessful in returning Peter to school. After four weeks, Peter's somatic symptoms had increased and he was overwhelmed with panic during the *in vivo* desensitization program (especially when his father attempted to get him in their car to go to school). He was eating very little and had become withdrawn and depressed. Therefore, a decision was made to prescribe an antidepressant. The suggestion of medication was initially resisted by the mother but then reluctantly accepted when her son told her he wanted to take the tablets to help him "get better." The purpose of the medication and the possible side effects were discussed with Peter in a session where he also talked at length about the distress his symptoms were causing. The parents were also encouraged to continue using behavioral strategies (e.g., praise for school attendance) while Peter was on medication.

A full physical examination prior to commencement of the medication was normal, including a normal ECG tracing and normal blood count and liver function tests. His pulse was regular and of normal rate. Peter weighed just under 25 kg. Imipramine (25 mg tablet) was administered with the dose being increased over a three-week period to 75 mg per day (3 mg per kg) as shown in Table 4-2. Peter was given a holiday from school in week 1 on the understanding that he was returning to school in week 2. With regard to side effects, he experienced a dry mouth, but this did not bother him. Although he may have had more frequent nightmares during the first week, he reported an

TABLE 4-2 • **Imipramine Dose Schedule and Side Effects for School-Refusing Child of Case Illustration**

Week	Morning	Night Time	Daily Dose	Side Effects
1	—	25 mg	1 mg/kg	? stomach pain ? nightmares dry mouth
2	—	50 mg	2 mg/kg	
3	25 mg	50 mg	3 mg/kg	
Continuing to 16	25 mg	50 mg	3 mg/kg	fine tremor (5–11)
17	—	50 mg	2 mg/kg	
18		25 mg	1 mg/kg	
19	NIL	NIL	NIL	NIL

overall improvement in sleep. In week 2 his father took him to school, and Peter reported anxiety and distress and complained of abdominal pain. His mother was convinced that the abdominal pain was a drug side effect even though he had experienced these pains before commencement of medication. By week 4 he was feeling more confident about going to school and was no longer complaining of abdominal pains or symptoms of panic. By week 6 he was no longer moody and irritable and there was a noticeable improvement in his self-esteem as witnessed by the general positive nature of his comments and behavior. He was again walking to school with some other children. The teacher reported that his concentration had improved and that he was fully able to participate in his educational program. The school was providing some unobtrusive playground supervision and teachers were convinced that bullying was no longer a problem.

Although Peter was much better, he wished to continue to take the tablets because he felt they "still helped" him and his parents agreed with this decision. The medication was tapered off over a 3-week period (16 weeks after its commencement). At that stage, which was just before the end of the school year, Peter had no symptoms of anxiety or depression, was happily attending school, and was fully participating in his education and social life within the limits of his mild degree of mental retardation. A follow-up ECG was done at week 7. This remained normal, although there was a slight increase of less than 0.01 secs in the P-R interval, which was still within clinically safe and acceptable limits (Glassman & Bigger, 1981; Bartels et al., 1991; Elliot & Popper, 1991). His pulse remained regular and of normal rate. The drug side effect of a slight dry mouth persisted throughout the treatment. Peter developed a mild fine intention tremor in concentrating on fine motor work such as writing and drawing, which persisted from about week 5 to week 11 and then disappeared (see Table 4-1). There were no symptoms reported on withdrawal of the medication, and Peter remained well and free of symptoms of psychopathology during the long summer vacation and into the next school year at the follow-up review some four months after stopping the medication.

SUMMARY

Pharmacotherapy can play an important adjunctive role in the treatment of school-refusing children, particularly when the child has a separation anxiety disorder and/or major depressive disorder. Initially we examined several fundamental issues in drug therapy, including mode of action, side effects, and administration of drugs. While cyclic antidepressants such as imipramine are often preferred in the drug treatment of school refusal, there is debate about the rationale for their usage. Side effects range from minor to serious, the latter including cardiotoxicity, seizures, and death. The potential hazard of these drugs highlights the need to assess children for the possibility of pre-existing heart disease and undertake physical and ECG examination prior to the initiation of drug treatment. Moreover, recent research findings raise doubts about the efficacy of antidepressants in the treatment of school refusal. Anxiolytics (mainly the benzodiazepines) have also been used in the drug treatment of school refusal. Again, the efficacy and safety of these drugs have been questioned. Finally, we emphasized that for those school refusal cases in which drug therapy appears warranted, noncompliance can be a serious obstacle to treatment. Clearly, drug treatment should be approached with caution.

▶ 5

Epilogue

CONCLUDING REMARKS

Thus far, we have described the diagnosis, assessment, and treatment of school-refusing children in some detail. As we have noted, these children and their families are highly complex and, in most instances, highly variable in their presentation. Each child and her or his family is different, and each requires an individual functional analysis to determine the nature of the school refusal, its antecedents, its consequents, and its correlates. Clinical work with these children is difficult and frequently fraught with significant challenges. As a result, a number of issues characterize the clinical treatment of these children.

For example, engaging these children in discussion about the nature of their school-related problems and their reactions to and "ownership" of these problems is not always easy or straightforward. Many of these children view the locus of their school refusal outside of themselves; that is, they blame others (e.g., parents, teachers, peers) or medical illnesses (e.g., headaches, stomachaches) for their problems. Others acknowledge broad fears or worries about separation from their parents or about some aspect of the school setting but are seemingly unable to identify particular events, thoughts, or feelings.

Similarly, many parents and teachers present obstacles to the effective treatment of these children. Stresses in the family may cloud the family's ability to deal clearly and effectively with school return; in other instances, parental psychopathology or limited resources may interfere. In a similar vein, some teachers and school principals appear unable or unwilling to work toward effective return and follow through on necessary accommodations and actions. For some, philosophical differences are evident: they disagree with our basic premise that early return is essential for both short-term and long-term success.

In this final chapter we shall briefly discuss some of the issues that make the assessment and treatment of school-refusing children difficult and less than straightforward. From our vantage point, challenges are evident at three distinct levels: the individual child level, the family level, and the school or system level.

Moreover, successful therapy in the short term provides no guarantee that treatment gains will be maintained in the long term, particularly for the child who continues to experience major stress at home or in school. Thus, planning for the maintenance of gains is an important element in the overall treatment program for these children. We shall comment on this issue as well in this final chapter.

THE SCHOOL-REFUSING CHILD IN TREATMENT

Prior to referral for treatment, many school-refusing children are subjected to incessant questioning by their teachers and parents about why they do not want to go to school. Frequently this questioning takes the form of "What is wrong with you" and "What can be so scary about the school" or "What could possibly happen to your parents" that would warrant such concerns. Implicit in much of this questioning is the notion that the child really has nothing to be afraid of or concerned about and that she or he is being "silly" or even "stupid" in having such worries. In addition, many parents and teachers automatically assume that many of these children are simply negativistic, noncompliant, or "willful" in an attempt to stay home from school and to get out of schoolwork. They tend to discount what the child views as legitimate and "real" concerns. Although some school-refusing children may avoid school because of these factors, many do not. For those who have legitimate worries or concerns, this type of questioning and attitude about school attendance is usually counterproductive, leading the child to be more withdrawn and inhibited about disclosing the reasons for school refusal. Even for those whose school refusal is related to secondary gain and the reinforcements that occur while away from school, such attitudes serve to strengthen their resolve and increase their noncompliance and oppositional behavior. In our experience, such questioning is rarely constructive and infrequently leads to desired behavior change.

Given this history of aversive questioning and "blaming," it is important that the therapist listen to the child's account of what occasions the refusal before automatically accepting or believing the views presented by parents or teachers. As noted in Chapter 2, we frequently see the child with his or her parents and then see the child alone to ensure that we obtain as much information as possible. Such a meeting is followed by a visit to the school to obtain additional detail as needed. The important point here is that the child must be listened to and given the opportunity to present his or her perspective on the school refusal. While this suggestion might seem obvious, it is imperative that it be followed for effective treatment to result.

In the initial session it is also critical that the therapist develop rapport with the child before proceeding directly to a functional analysis of the school refusal. Considerable clinical skill is required in establishing and then maintaining a working relationship with the child throughout this and subsequent sessions. In addition to traditional therapist qualities such as empathy and warmth, we encourage our therapists to be cheerful and positive in their interactions with the child. It is important for the therapist to listen to what the child has to offer, accept it, and use it (in some form) in problem formulation and treatment. A good sense of humor is useful in this regard and can be remarkably effective in obtaining the child's participation and cooperation. Of course, positive reinforcement for talking about specific concerns is a must.

Successful engagement of the child in therapy also requires identification and clarification of treatment goals. Initially we give the child the opportunity to discuss the advantages and disadvantages of the current situation regarding school attendance. Most are able to identify both. Frequently cited advantages include "having more time with Mom," "avoiding bullies at school," "not having to do math problems," "not having to get up in front of class," and "not being embarrassed." Disadvantages include "missing out on what my friends are doing," "having to stay in my room while I am home from school," "having my parents mad at me," and "being bored at home." Of course, the specific advantages and disadvantages are idiosyncratic to each case and fully understood only through a thorough functional analysis. Regardless of specific reasons, the initial comments of the child are useful in building rapport and in formulating initial treatment goals. Building on what the child reports, the therapist might say, for example:

There are many boys like you who fear going to school because of other boys who bully them. They often feel unsafe and that something might happen to them, like they will be beat up in the restroom or someplace else in school. As a result, they want to stay home where it is safe and the bullies can't get them. That's understandable, isn't it? I would be afraid too if I thought someone might beat me up at work. It wouldn't be fun going to work each day if I worried about that, would it. Boys like you who have been away from school for a while also frequently worry what it will be like going back to school. I realize that school return will be difficult, and that even talking about it can make you nervous or upset. My approach in working with kids who have trouble going to school is to teach them ways to cope with the situations at school or home that cause them difficulty. I will be helping you learn specific things you can do to make you feel less afraid and to help you handle the problems you are having better. It won't be easy, but together we can do it. Do you have any questions about what our goal will be?

From our perspective, it is critical that the child (and the parents) understand from the onset that the goal of treatment is school return. Still, we desire the child's input and we make him or her an active collaborator in the process.

However, proceeding with therapy assumes that the child recognizes that school refusal is a problem (i.e., it has disadvantages) and that she or he is aware of the thoughts and feelings that accompany school refusal. Some school-refusing children seem to have difficulty in acknowledging that school refusal is a problem and in recognizing the anxiety or fear associated with refusal. Kendall et al. (1992) have labeled this "denial of anxiety." We view the problem somewhat differently. We believe that many of these children are not "denying" their anxiety, but, rather, they have just not had the opportunity, or taken the opportunity, to identify the specific thoughts and feelings associated with their school refusal. Once they do so, they frequently identify disadvantages and the anxiety associated with the reasons for refusal. Shaping and positive reinforcement are useful in eliciting this information.

This approach was nicely illustrated in an early case study reported by Perkins and colleagues (Perkins, Rowe, & Farmer, 1973). They found that they needed to help their adolescent chronic school refuser develop awareness of his social anxiety and emotional reactions related to school attendance. Pocket money was used to reinforce the adolescent's spontaneous talk and opinions about positive and negative affect. As he progressed, he was required to closely observe his own behavior, thoughts, and feelings, particularly his thoughts and feelings about anxiety in social situations. It then became possible to conduct an intensive functional analysis of his social anxiety and school refusal behavior. In our own work we have rarely found it necessary to use monetary reinforcement to meet this goal; social reinforcements and behavioral contracts have sufficed.

Of course, many other issues arise in clinical work with school-refusing children. The problems are undoubtedly as diverse as the heterogeneity of school refusal itself, and not all can be mentioned or commented upon here. Before leaving this topic, however, we would like to illustrate how something as seemingly unimportant as the sex of the therapist might be an important factor in efficacious treatment.

Case Illustration

Angela was referred because of recent-onset school refusal behavior and peer relationship difficulties. Although anxiety was a strong feature in her clinical presentation, she did not meet criteria for any of the anxiety disorders. Angela was 12 years old and in her first year of junior high school. During the initial interview with Angela and her parents her mother said that she had only recently discovered that Angela was going through puberty and that she was anxious about menstruation. It was apparent that Angela was very embarrassed about this discussion and that she did not wish to talk about this with the male therapist. This was acknowledged and Angela was asked if she would be more comfortable with a female therapist. She indicated that she would be, and appropriate arrangements were made after the first session. During the assessment sessions that followed, Angela reported that she was very worried and embarrassed about what was happening to her. She further noted that she had not had the opportunity to get advice regarding menstruation from her mother (who it turns out did not realize that her 12-year-old was beginning her menses) and that she thought that something was terribly wrong with her and that she could not possibly share this information with her mother (due to her embarrassment). Angela also revealed that some boys at school had teased her about menstruation, something that produced absolute panic and seemingly precipitated the school refusal.

The therapist provided Angela factual information about menstruation and puberty and made some appropriate disclosure about her own experiences and how she managed to cope with her own concerns about menstruation in school. Using cognitive and behavioral procedures described in Chapter 3, the therapist helped Angela learn various ways of coping with peer teasing and arranged for her and her mother to have discussions about menstruation and pubertal development. School return was imminent. Although we do not have evidence that a male therapist would not have been effective with Angela, we respected Angela's wishes, and school return was effected.

This case illustrates the subtle nuances of treatment and the diversity of issues that can arise with school-refusing children. We did not anticipate menstruation concerns nor the need for a female therapist upon referral; yet, referring her to a female therapist and addressing specific issues related to teasing and embarrassment (via cognitive-behavioral procedures) appeared useful in achieving a successful outcome. More systematic study would be needed to determine which aspects of our intervention proved critical.

THE FAMILY CONTEXT

As noted earlier, the family is an important contextual factor that may affect both the development and expression of school refusal. In fact, there is some evidence that school refusal "tends to run in families," most probably due to a combination of genetic and learning-based factors. For example, in an early study, Berg (1976) found that 14 percent of children in a large sample of agoraphobic women suffered from school refusal. Inasmuch as school refusal is reported to occur in about 1 percent to 5 percent of children in general (see Chapter 1), an association between maternal agoraphobia and school refusal is suggested by these findings. In another early work, Gittelman-Klein (1975b) showed that 19 percent of the mothers of school-refusing children in their study were diagnosed with a major anxiety or depressive disorder, compared with 2 percent of mothers in a clinical control group (mothers of children with hyperactive disorder). Thus, as can be seen, an association between the type of childhood disorder (school refusal versus hyperactivity) and the type of parental psychopathology is probable.

More recently Bernstein and Garfinkel (1988) have demonstrated similar familial relationships. They compared the family pedigrees of six children with severe school refusal with those of a matched sample of children with attention deficit and oppositional defiant disorder. Structured diagnostic interviews, combined with blind and independent family histories, revealed that in four of the six families of children with school refusal, major anxiety or major depressive disorders were present in both the mothers and fathers, as well as in three generations of relatives. Such familial histories were not found in the clinical control group of children. Again, a relationship between child and parent psychopathology is suggested.

Certain patterns of family functioning may also be related to the type of school refusal that is observed. Lang (1982), for example, suggested that a hostile, dependent, and enmeshed parent-child relationship exists in families in which school refusal is primarily due to separation anxiety. In these instances, he argued, excessive dependency between the parent (usually the mother) and the child exists. In fact, it is frequently noted that such dependency is actively encouraged and reinforced by the parent. In support of this view, Berg and McGuire (1974) found mothers of school-refusing children to be overly protective, overly controlling, and, at the same time, ambivalent in their parenting style. They attempted to control their children by making them dependent on them; however, they simultaneously expressed ambivalence about this control and were inconsistent in their parenting practices.

Bernstein and her colleagues have recently affirmed these patterns for school-refusing children. In an early study, Bernstein and Garfinkel (1988) showed that the parents of these children reported more disturbance on a family assessment measure than did the parents of a comparison group of attention deficit and oppositional defiant disorder children. In particular, the mothers of school refusers reported more concerns about control and dependency. In a subsequent investigation of 76 school-refusing children, Bernstein, Svingen, and Garfinkel (1990) showed that these effects were more pronounced in the mothers of school-refusing children who were primarily separation-anxious. Mothers of school-refusing children who were also characterized by attentional and conduct problems were less likely to report dependency concerns. However, the mothers of these comorbid children were more likely to report other concerns—namely, disciplinary concerns related to acting out and noncompliant behaviors.

In our own clinical work with these children we have noted similar issues. Frequently mothers of separation-anxious refusers are overly dependent on their children and seem to lack effective parenting strategies. As noted in the early literature (see Chapter 1), many of the fathers we see are passive and uninvolved in parenting activities or report being ineffective in their attempts to manage their children. They report feeling helpless and feeling extremely angry at their children (and, in some instances, at their wives, whom they view as contributing to their child's refusal). Not knowing what to do, they frequently report disengaging from parenting activities.

Such parental dysfunction can markedly affect the assessment and treatment process. Frequently such parents do not work together as a team; often, they allow their own problems to interfere with the successful school return of their child. Although it is highly probable that such parents would benefit from conjoint marital therapy, we attempt to bypass such issues by working with them on becoming effective parents and behavior change agents for their child. More specifically, we teach them effective parenting skills and teach them how to be our "assistants" in effecting the necessary change.

Many of these parents lack the requisite skills to issue effective directions to their children and to consequate their behavior consistently. For example, they might say, "John, would you like to get up and go to school this morning?" rather than, "John, it's time to get up and get ready for school." Or, in response to some complaint about school, they might say, "That's really terrible, Mr. Jones should not treat you like that. It really is unfair. He has no right to treat you like that. I will go and talk to his supervisor." A more appropriate response might be: "I hear what you are saying. It really sounds like he's picking on you and you don't like it. I wonder what you could do to make the situation better?" As can be seen from these brief examples, dysfunctional parents tend to give nonspecific directions, phrasing their instructions more like requests (e.g., "Would you like to get up?") or pleas ("Please won't you get up when I call?"). They also "collude" with their child, frequently assuming responsibility for and "ownership" of their child's concerns. Both of these strategies are ineffective and serve to reinforce school refusal.

In addition, parents of school-refusing children tend to consequate behavior inconsistently—inadequately at some times and lavishly at other times. They may tend to ignore appropriate behaviors (such as getting up on time, preparing for school, and good behavior reports from teachers); at other times, they may reinforce lavishly by purchasing exorbitant gifts for the child (one of our parents offered to buy her 13-year-old son a new bicycle if he went to school for one day); at still other times they reinforce inadequately (one of our children was offered a new computer game if he went to school for the remainder of the year, a little over 3 months).

Clearly, in these instances, parent training becomes an integral part of treatment. In fact, if our functional analysis reveals a relative absence of significant anxiety in the child, parent training might be the sole treatment. However, we have rarely found parent training alone to be sufficient. More frequently we find parental dysfunction accompanied by significant anxiety in the child. In our experience, poor parenting practices are often a factor regardless of whether the child's school refusal is related primarily to separation anxiety or to some phobic aspect of the school situation itself. The role of the family (and, in this case, the extended family) is evident in the brief case study that follows.

Case Illustration

Family issues emerged in the assessment of Emily, a 9-year-old girl presenting with school attendance difficulties. At the initial interview, Emily and her parents reported that they were a "happy" family. Observations during the interview seemed to support this conclusion. However, toward the end of the interview it became clear that Emily's maternal grandparents were a "big part" of the family and the "problem." Although the grandparents were described as "very loving toward the family" and "generous in their financial support," they also tended to interfere in many aspects of family life. Specifically, "Nana" and Emily had developed a very close relationship over the years (Emily, it was learned, was her favorite grandchild—she was also the oldest grandchild). Both parents worked; the grandparents lived nearby. Upon return from school, Emily would routinely go to her grandparents' home, where she would be lavishly showered with treats and affection. Frequently she would spend Saturday evenings at her grandparents' home. Although Emily's parents had some concern about the amount of time their daughter was spending at her grandparents', they were not overly concerned since "Mom had done the same thing when she was a child."

Whenever Emily was sick during the week, she would spend the school day at her grandparents' home. Initially this had not been a major problem, as she had missed only a few days of school each year due to illness. However, in this school year (eight weeks into the school term) she had already missed 14 days of school. Her parents became concerned about the number of days missed and the possibility that Emily was missing school to be with her grandparents. Their concerns were partially justified. Life at Nana's house was good: Emily was allowed to watch TV with Nana, play games with "Papa," and have relatively free access to snacks, sodas, and other treats. Afternoons were spent on excursions to the market and other "fun" places. She was their "Little Princess" who was the center of attention and who could do no wrong.

Emily, however, also reported major concerns about "speaking in front of the class" and "being called on by the teacher." On the diagnostic interview she met criteria for social phobia, although this had not been acknowledged or recognized properly by her parents or teacher. She was petrified by such occurrences and reported panic-like symptoms. Thus, our analysis revealed a social phobia that was likely negatively reinforced by school avoidance and positively reinforced by well-intentioned but overly doting grandparents. A type of dependency was clearly developing between Emily and her grandmother. Coincidentally, Emily's mother reported a similar relationship with her own grandmother.

The grandparents became very upset when told by their daughter that Emily had been referred to the clinic. They firmly believed that Emily had an illness (the flu) and that, if anything, she should be taken to a medical doctor, not a psychologist. When informed that Emily had recently been taken to the family doctor and found to be a healthy child, they were not placated. When told that she had specific fears about speaking in front of her class and reciting things in class and that these fears were contributing to her school refusal, they were not appeased. They truly felt she was ill and that she needed their assistance.

Treatment initially consisted of instructing Emily's parents in assertion skills in order to deal more effectively with her grandparents. Further, if Emily were "sick," Emily's parents were instructed to take turns staying home with her. Visits to the grandparents were permitted only if Emily had attended school that day, and on Saturday evening only if Emily had attended school every day that week. Concurrent with this contingency program, Emily's social phobia was treated with the cognitive-behavioral procedures outlined in Chapter 3. During the first few weeks of treatment, sessions were scheduled twice a week so that Emily could master relaxation and self-instruction skills. Further, exposure trials were used in the session by having Emily practice speaking in front of others (imagining herself doing so) and raising her hand and being called on by the therapist (teacher). Treatment progress was swift: Within four weeks she was attending school on a regular basis. A key to the success of the program in this instance appeared to be the full cooperation of the grandparents. Once confronted by Emily's parents, they agreed to participate in the program fully (and reported being embarrassed about their potential role in her school refusal).

Of course, such cooperation is not always forthcoming from immediate or extended family members. In the absence of such active collaboration, at least for those cases that involve family dysfunction, treatment usually takes longer and may not be effective initially. At such times we re-double our efforts to get the significant parties involved. When family dysfunction is not present, treatment is usually more direct and efficacious.

SCHOOL CONSULTANCY

In our experience, most teachers and school principals attribute school refusal to anxiety within the child or to home-based problems between the parent and child. That is, they tend to view the refusal as due to insecurity or inadequacy in the child or to a "symbiotic" relationship between child and parent, with dependency at the core. Rarely do they see the school itself and, in particular, their own classroom or teaching style as contributing to school refusal. For children who are separation-anxious and school-refusing, their assumptions about causal factors may be largely correct. Yet even for these children, teachers' responses to the "whiny," clinging, and dependent behavior they see in their classroom may be critical in the maintenance of these behaviors. The responses of principals, school nurses, and other school staff might also serve a maintaining function. In cases of separation-anxious school refusers, teachers and other staff must be recruited to assist with the school return program, just as parents must be. They need to be enlisted as behavior change agents who will enact the re-entry program (Blagg, 1987; King & Ollendick, 1989; Ollendick & King, 1990).

School personnel need to be instructed, coached, and reinforced on providing conditions that will serve as effective antecedents to reduce home-based "dependency-related" behaviors. Welcoming the child as she or he exits from the bus (or parent's car), walking the child into the school and classroom, enlisting the child in early morning special duties as "teacher's assistant," and restructuring aspects of the school day to accommodate the anxious child are some of the many activities we have found useful. In effect, we attempt to transfer some of the "dependency" from the parent onto the school personnel, at least initially. We also recruit school personnel to assist in re-entry by teaching them (and reinforcing them) to ignore negative behaviors such as crying, whining, and illness-related statements or actions and to reinforce positive behaviors such as arriving at school, contributing to class activities, and remaining at school.

The importance of school personnel in enacting successful re-entry of the separation-anxious school refuser cannot be underestimated. Nor can their importance be minimized with children whose school refusal is related to specific aspects of the school itself such as speaking in front of class, dressing for physical education classes, or being bullied by peers. Although their clinical presentation is different from separation-anxious children, these children also require antecedent and consequent conditions that favor successful re-entry. They need to know that they will not be ridiculed, embarrassed, or taken advantage of by their peers or, in some cases, by the school personnel themselves. At times, classes and teachers may need to be changed; at other times, a change in school may be necessary. Generally, however, "fine-tuning" is all that is necessary to support successful re-entry. Frequently, for example, an assistant principal or teacher may be unaware of how his or her interaction style affects children and might be viewed as overly intimidating or caustic to some children. We have seen this to be so particularly in children progressing from one grade to another in the same school or from one school to another (e.g., elementary school to middle school), as well as in children transferring from one school to another (due to family relocation).

Similarly, there may well be conditions in the classroom or the transition from one classroom to another that can be changed to reduce anxiety. For example, one 11-year-old girl was particularly anxious about dressing for physical education class at the same time as some of her 13-year-old schoolmates; a 7-year-old boy was terrified of riding to school on a bus that went through a certain neighborhood where he had been attacked two weeks earlier; a 13-year-old boy was worried about speaking in front of class since he had observed his teacher ridicule (in his view) another child; a 10-year-old girl was terrified of being called to the principal's office for fear of being reprimanded; and a 14-year-old boy dreaded the transition from one class to another because he had to go to his locker to get his supplies and was picked on by the school bullies. Although cognitive-behavioral anxiety-reducing strategies (see Chapter 3) were used in the treatment of each of these children, environmental or contextual changes were also enacted. Of course, teachers and other school personnel were critical in effecting these changes.

Not all school personnel are receptive to our ventures. Many continue to indicate that the "real" problem resides in the child or in the parent-child relationship and disown any role in the etiology or maintenance of the school refusal. They actively refuse to participate in its treatment. Such cases are extremely difficult to treat and are frequently fraught with setbacks and failure. Although we attempt to confront these issues and to address them with the school personnel as best we can, as a last resort we occasionally recommend school transfer. It should be clear, however, that this strategy should not be viewed as the best solution. Sometimes, in our experience, it is the only solution.

Hersov (1985) and Blagg (1987) have identified the following patterns in a school that point to the likelihood that return to school will be difficult and that often signal a setting that occasions school refusal:

- **A.** Relatively high absenteeism rates for students, which may be matched by high absenteeism rates among staff
- **B.** A relatively large group of low-achieving students in the older age group, where attendance is not closely monitored or seen as a concern by the school
- **C.** Large class sizes that make it difficult for teachers to take a close interest in the individual child
- **D.** A high level of disruptive behavior and disciplinary problems in the children, associated frequently with low staff morale

We would add three other observations to this profile:

- **E.** An authoritarian system, characterized by "top-down" management that is bound by strict rules and regulations with little autonomy afforded individual teachers
- **F.** Teachers and other staff who are overly rigid and authoritarian themselves and who are unable or unwilling to accommodate the needs of individual children
- **G.** School personnel who are overly anxious themselves and overly dependent upon the children for approval and acceptance

These problems, as well as others, make it essential to work closely with the school. Starting at the "top" of the school hierarchy often pays dividends in obtaining cooperation of teachers and other staff. This is especially important if a change in the child's class schedule or class placement is to be considered. These changes may result in considerable conflict, however. Teachers may feel threatened—i.e., that they have failed. As a result, such changes in schedules need to be raised sensitively and responsively. So, too, do issues of teacher style and teacher effectiveness. As noted earlier, most teachers tend to view the refusal as residing in the child or parent-child relationship, not in their teaching style. We use the "goodness-of-fit" notion to help teachers understand and accept our analysis. That is, we do not "blame" them for the child's problem so much as we try to help them see that some children learn and respond better under certain conditions than other ones. Although it is not an easy concept, most learn to accept and appreciate it.

School personnel attitudes about behavioral treatment strategies can also be a deterrent to successful programming. Whereas evidence favors the acceptability of behavioral approaches to school refusal (Gullone & King, 1991), other research suggests that teachers may be somewhat negative in their reactions to behavioral interventions, particularly when couched in excessive jargon (Elliot, 1988; Woolfolk, Woolfolk, & Wilson, 1977). Care should be taken to present the program in a straightforward, jargon-free, and collaborative manner; respect for school personnel and their profession should be paramount.

Some of the issues involved in school consultancy are highlighted in the case that follows.

Case Illustration

As part of the assessment of a 15-year-old boy, John, the school was visited by the therapist. After meeting with the principal and being assured of the school's full cooperation, the therapist was referred to the guidance counselor at the school, who was to serve as the primary facilitator of school re-entry. After the therapist explained that the cooperation of the entire school staff would be needed and devised a collaborative re-entry plan with the counselor, the counselor indicated that some of the teachers would likely be resistant to the program. She noted that some of the teachers felt that John was a "spoiled" child. They described him as a "Mommy's boy," as someone who just needed to be treated with firmness and "made to come to school." "No nonsense" should be tolerated. Although the counselor recognized that John was fearful of being bullied and that he dreaded being embarrassed in classes, some of the teachers felt that he just "needed to grow up." After all, he was 15 years old. Other teachers recognized his concerns and were more understanding of them. They also thought that some of his worries were exacerbated by events at school. Thus, a conflict about how to conceptualize John's problems among John's teachers was evident.

The therapist met with the teachers and explored their attitudes about John. Differences of opinion were indeed evident, and not easily resolved. The therapist requested each of the teachers to complete a checklist on John (Achenbach's Child Behavior Checklist) so that he could get a better "picture" of John and his problems in school. Some of the teachers complied; others did not. Those who felt his problems were insignificant tended not to complete the checklist, while those who viewed his problems as important did so. Only after another meeting did all teachers complete (reluctantly) the forms. Differences remained. Eventually it was decided to implement the re-entry program in the morning only (four teachers agreed to "give the program a try"), and to restructure John's school day such that he had the four classes of these teachers in the morning. This phase of the program lasted for four weeks, during which John was also trained in relaxation, self-instruction, and self-control. Following successful attendance in the mornings, the program was extended systematically to the afternoon. Two of the three remaining teachers then agreed (somewhat reluctantly) to try the program; it became necessary to effect a change in the remaining class. Within 10 weeks, John was attending school on a regular basis.

This case represents a number of issues related to school consultancy, especially for older school refusers who are enrolled in high schools. School personnel did not agree on the reasons for refusal or on recommended treatment strategies. In our experience, collaboration with school personnel is key; compromise and creativity are frequently needed for successful school re-entry.

MAINTAINING TREATMENT GAINS

Successful treatment requires the therapist to be cognizant of issues at three major levels: the individual child, the family, and the school. We have attempted to elucidate many of these issues in the earlier parts of this chapter. Successful re-entry, however, does not guarantee long-term success. The maintenance of treatment gains is critical in establishing the long-term efficacy of these procedures.

For some children, reduction in anxiety and successful re-entry into school are highly reinforcing. They return to school with relative ease, almost as if they had never been absent. They are delighted to be back with their friends and to be challenged again by academic rigors. In our experience, however, this represents a minority of school-refusing children. Most school-refusing children return to school under duress and find it an unpleasant and unrewarding experience. Their friends wonder where they have been and what was "wrong with them"; they have not kept up with their schoolwork and have fallen behind; and their teachers seem to lack understanding and insist that they make up exams *today,* complete projects *tomorrow,* and "pick up where they left off," lest they get further behind. Such stressors greatly complicate the likelihood of return to school that is persistent and durable.

Such stressors in the school setting can be dealt with directly by preparing the child's peers and teachers (and other school staff) for his or her return. If the return program is graduated, such stressors are minimized. Both teachers and peers anticipate gradual return in such programs, and the child has been completing school assignments (it is hoped) on a prearranged basis. When return is more abrupt, following a complete and prolonged absence, however, these problems may be accentuated. That is, the child has been away from school for a prolonged period of time, perhaps for as much as six weeks or four months, and the teachers and peers have advanced considerably during the child's absence. In these instances we have found it useful to go to the school and talk with the child's teachers about things they can do to make the child welcome upon his or her return (a "welcome back" banner can be prepared, the children in the class can be informed of the impending return and be asked to prepare a special reception, and favorite cookies or cakes can be prepared). Sometimes we have gone to the classroom itself and talked with the students about "Jimmy's" return and how helpful they can be in making him feel welcome and good about returning to school. These activities are especially useful in elementary schools. In secondary schools we have found it useful to recruit the child's best friends (with the school-refusing child's permission) and favorite teachers to assist with return. In our experience, it is important to activate a support system prior to re-entry.

Still, stressors may persist at home and in school. Family conflict, bereavement over a personal loss, being teased or rejected at school, and being ridiculed in the classroom are representative stressors that many of these children continue to experience after successful re-entry. Clearly, the child must be assisted to understand that such stressful events are likely to be encountered and that they need not automatically result in school avoidance and refusal. Various scenarios or vignettes can be presented to the child that call for the identification of the problem and the generation of effective coping strategies. Such "problem-solving" strategies and "innoculation" training are consistent with the cognitive-behavioral procedures detailed in Chapter 3. Of course, many other steps can be taken to facilitate the maintenance of therapy gains, including consultation with parents and teachers regarding the application of child management strategies (see also Kendall et al., 1992; Ollendick & Cerny, 1981).

We also recommend "booster" sessions as a useful means of maintaining treatment gains. Kendall and his colleagues have distinguished between two major types of booster sessions (Kendall & Braswell, 1985; Kendall et al., 1992). The first type of booster session is useful when the child has encountered a particularly difficult situation that has resulted in marked distress. These sessions are usually unplanned and are scheduled on an as-needed basis. As one example, a socially phobic child might have returned to school successfully and three weeks later an unexpected event occurs that serves to "recondition" specific fears related to speaking in front of the class. The child might have stuttered in front of others or the teacher might have provided constructive criticism that was interpreted negatively, for example. A couple of sessions might be necessary to help the child deal with this temporary setback.

The second type of booster session is more proactive and preventive. For example, booster sessions might be scheduled when stressful problems are about to be encountered by the child or family, such as examinations at the end of the academic term, moving to a new school, or an impending separation or divorce in the family. These sessions help prepare the child through practice and refinement of problem-solving and coping skills. Behavior rehearsal strategies are particularly effective in practicing anticipated solutions and outcomes.

In keeping with our treatment framework, both types of booster sessions involve a wide variety of behavioral and cognitive strategies, and, in some instances, pharmacotherapy might also be considered. Medications might be administered on a temporary basis to enhance the effects of the cognitive-behavioral treatments. Consistent with our previous comments, involvement of parents and school personnel is seen as a positive step toward the likely efficacy of booster sessions, as seen in the following case study.

Case Illustration

Therapy for Ian, a 13-year-old boy with intermittent school attendance problems, consisted of helping him cope with excessive social anxiety. Social interactions with peers and teachers were extremely anxiety-provoking, mainly because of his lack of social skills (e.g., insufficient eye contact, stooped posture, and unassertive responding). Tests and essays also caused extreme anxiety and worry. Even relatively minor evaluative tasks such as cleaning the blackboard elicited intense fear of "being shown up in front of others." Accordingly, he made excuses to avoid social interactions and feigned illness in times of evaluation. Social skills training (Matson & Ollendick, 1988) consisting of instruction, modeling, role play, and reinforcement resulted in marked improvements in his interactional style. Also, with the help of his teachers it was possible to implement an *in vivo* desensitization program for his evaluative fears. Relaxation training was undertaken and provided him with a "physical means" of coping with his heightened physiological arousal at times of actual or anticipated social evaluative stress. Cognitive therapy was also necessary to address his negative expectations of failure. After six weeks of therapy, Ian managed 100 percent school attendance for two straight weeks. However, the therapist emphasized to Ian that he should continue to apply his coping skills in stressful situations.

Three months later, Ian was scheduled for a follow-up session at the clinic. He presented in an agitated state, avoiding eye contact with the therapist and mumbling in a low, unclear voice. Ian reported that he had been doing "pretty well" at school, up until the last week. The turning point was having to take two major tests and submit three major written assignments all within the same week. He felt overwhelmed by the pressure and "scared to death that he was going to fail once again" and that he would be "humiliated in front of the world." Further inquiry on the part of the therapist revealed that Ian had not missed any school, at least not yet. Furthermore, he reported that he had completed all of the assignments and taken the two tests. At this stage the therapist suggested that it might be helpful for him to think about his achievements:

> Despite a tough time at school, you have stuck it out. . . . You must have wondered if you would survive it all . . . but you know, you did. . . . You took the tests and completed the assignments, something you have not been able to do for a long time. . . . You did it . . . good for you . . . you must feel really good about what you have accomplished.

Although Ian didn't readily accept the therapist's accolades or show appreciation of what he had accomplished, eventually he did so. Two booster sessions were then arranged to help him through the next few weeks, when three more examinations were scheduled and one additional paper was due. The same therapeutic procedures were used, although the focus was tailored to the remaining tests and completion of the term paper. The therapist also provided feedback on Ian's eye contact, tone of voice, and body posture as he verbalized his concerns. He was reinforced with verbal praise for more socially skilled behaviors in the session. Subsequently Ian reported that he benefitted from the booster sessions and "enjoyed" seeing the therapist again. Consultation with parents and school personnel revealed that Ian had good support from family, friends, and school during this stressful time.

SUMMARY

In this final chapter we have addressed several integrative and "nagging" issues in the treatment of children who refuse school. First, we discussed potential difficulties in working with the child that must be acknowledged and addressed by the therapist. For example, difficulty with being able to describe the source of the fear or worry is a problem for some school refusers. This problem can be dealt with by helping the child recreate the situation as vividly as possible and conducting a thorough functional analysis. Second, we discussed problems in working with families. Here it was emphasized that psychological problems in the parents, as well as poor parenting skills, pose serious obstacles to the implementation and evaluation of cognitive-behavioral programs. Active collaboration with parents is critical. Third, at the broader systems level, we also considered the school setting. Attendance rates, staff morale, resources, and the commitment of school personnel all have an influence on the likelihood of successful school return. We stressed the importance of acknowledging the value of the principal, the teachers, and other staff in effecting re-entry. Their full cooperation and active collaboration are also required. We also recognized that the child will likely encounter stressful events that may produce relapse after a successful return to school. Booster sessions were recommended as an effective way of helping the child cope with these situations and facilitate the maintenance of treatment gains. Such procedures, following the use of cognitive-behavioral and pharmacologic strategies as espoused in this book, frequently result in persistent and durable change.

▶ References

Achenbach, T. M. (1978). The Child Behavior Profile: I. Boys aged 6–11. *Journal of Consulting and Clinical Psychology, 46,* 478–488.

Achenbach, T. M. (1985). Assessment of anxiety in children. In A. H. Tuma & J. Maser (Eds.), *Anxiety and the anxiety disorders.* Hillsdale, NJ: Erlbaum.

Achenbach, T. M. (1991). Integrative guide for the 1991 CBCL/4–18, YSR, and TRF profiles. Burlington, VT: University of Vermont Department of Psychiatry.

Achenbach, T. M., & Edelbrock, C. S. (1979). The Child Behavior Profile: II. Boys aged 12–16 and girls aged 6–11 and 12–16. *Journal of Consulting and Clinical Psychology, 47,* 223–233.

Achenbach, T. M., McConaughy, S. H., & Howell, C. T. (1987). Child and adolescent behavioral and emotional problems: Implications of cross-informant correlations for situational specificity. *Psychological Bulletin, 101,* 213–232.

Adams, P. L., McDonald, N. F., & Huey, W. P. (1966). School phobia and bisexual conflict: A report of 21 cases. *American Journal of Psychiatry, 123,* 541–547.

Agras, S. (1959). The relationship of school phobia to childhood depression. *American Journal of Psychiatry, 116,* 533–536.

Aman, M. G., & Werry, J. S. (1982). Methylphenidate and diazepam in severe reading retardation. *Journal of the American Academy of Child Psychiatry, 21,* 31–37.

American Psychiatric Association (1987). *Diagnostic and statistical manual of mental disorders* (3d ed.—revised). Washington, DC: Author.

American Psychiatric Association (1994). *Diagnostic and statistical manual of mental disorders* (4th ed.). Washington, DC: Author.

Angelino, H., Dollins, J., & Mech, E.V. (1956). Trends in the "fears and worries" of school children as related to socio-economic status and age. *Journal of Genetic Psychology, 89,* 263–276.

Atkinson, L., Quarrington, B., & Cyr, J. J. (1985). School refusal: The heterogeneity of a concept. *American Journal of Orthopsychiatry, 55,* 83–101.

Atkinson, L., Quarrington, B., Cyr, J. J., & Atkinson, F. V. (1989). Differential classification in school refusal. *British Journal of Psychiatry, 155,* 191–195.

Ayllon, T., Smith, D., & Rogers, M. (1970). Behavioral management of school phobia. *Journal of Behavior Therapy and Experimental Psychiatry, 1,* 125–138.

Baker, H., & Wills, V. (1978). School phobia: Classification and treatment. *British Journal of Psychiatry, 132,* 492–499.

Ballenger, J. C. (1986). Pharmacotherapy of panic disorders. *Journal of Clinical Psychiatry, 47,* 27–33.

Bandura, A. (1968). Modeling approaches to the modification of phobic disorders. In R. Porter (Ed.), *Ciba Foundation Symposium: The role of learning in psychotherapy.* London: Churchill.

Bandura, A. (1969). *Principles of behavior modification.* New York: Holt, Rinehart, & Winston.

Bartels, M. G., Varley, C. K., Mitchell, M. D., & Stam, S. J. (1991). Pediatric cardiovascular effects of imipramine and desipramine. *Journal of the American Academy of Child and Adolescent Psychiatry, 30,* 100–103.

Bauer, D. (1980). Childhood fears in developmental perspective. In L. Hersov & I. Berg (Eds.), *Out of school. Modern perspectives in truancy and school refusal* (pp. 189–208). Chichester, England: Wiley.

Beck, A. T., & Emery, G. (1985). *Anxiety disorders and phobias. A cognitive perspective.* New York: Basic Books.

Beck, A., Ward, C., Mendelson, M., Mock, J., & Erbaugh, J. (1961). An inventory for measuring depression. *Archives of General Psychiatry, 4,* 561–571.

Beidel, D. (1991). Social phobia and overanxious disorder in school-age children. *Journal of American Academy of Child and Adolescent Psychiatry, 30,* 545–552.

Beidel, D. C., Neal, A. M., & Lederer, A. S. (1991). The feasibility and validity of a daily diary for the assessment of anxiety in children. *Behavior Therapy, 22,* 505–517.

Berg, I. (1974). A Self-Administered Dependency Questionnaire (SADQ) for use with mothers of school children. *British Journal of Psychiatry, 124,* 1–9.

Berg, I. (1976). School phobia in the children of agoraphobic women. *British Journal of Psychiatry, 128,* 86–90.

Berg, I. (1980). School refusal in early adolescence. In L. Hersov & I. Berg (Eds.), *Out of school. Modern perspectives in truancy and school refusal* (pp. 231–249). Chichester, England: Wiley.

Berg, I., Butler, A., & Hall, G. (1976). The outcome of adolescent school phobia. *British Journal of Psychiatry, 121,* 509–514.

Berg, I., Butler, A., & Pritchard, J. (1974). Psychiatric illness in mothers of school-phobic adolescents. *British Journal of Psychiatry, 125,* 466–467.

Berg, I., & Fielding, D. (1978). An evaluation of hospital in-patient treatment in adolescent school phobia. *British Journal of Psychiatry, 132,* 500–505.

Berg, I., & Jackson, A. (1985). Teenage school refusers grow up: A follow-up study of 168 subjects, ten years on average after inpatient treatment. *British Journal of Psychiatry, 119,* 167–168.

Berg, I., Marks, I., McGuire, R., & Lipsedge, M. (1974). School phobia and agoraphobia. *Psychological Medicine, 4,* 428–434.

Berg, I., & McGuire, R. (1971). Are school phobic adolescents overdependent? *British Journal of Psychiatry, 119,* 167–168.

Berg, I., & McGuire, R. (1974). Are mothers of school-phobic adolescents over-protective? *British Journal of Psychiatry, 124,* 10–13.

Berg, I., Nichols, K., & Pritchard, C. (1969). School phobia—its classification and relationship to dependency. *Journal of Child Psychology and Psychiatry, 10,* 123–141.

Berganza, C. E., & Anders, T.F. (1978). An epidemiologic approach to school absenteeism. *Journal of the American Academy of Child Psychiatry, 17,* 117–125.

Bernard, M. E., & Joyce, M. R. (1984). *Rational-emotive therapy with children and adolescents: Theory, treatment strategies, preventative methods.* New York: Wiley.

Berney, T., Kolvin, I., Bhate, S. R., Garside, R. F., Jeans, J., Kay, B., & Scarth, L. (1981). School phobia: A therapeutic trial with clomipramine and short-term outcome. *British Journal of Psychiatry, 138,* 110–118.

Bernstein, D. A., & Borkovec, T. D. (1973). *Progressive relaxation training: A manual for the helping professions.* Champaign, IL: Research Press.

Bernstein, G. (1990). Anxiety disorders. In B. D. Garfinkel, G.A. Carlson, & E. B. Weller (Eds.), *Psychiatric disorders in children and adolescents* (pp. 64–83), Philadelphia: Saunders.

Bernstein, G. A. (1991). Comorbidity and severity of anxiety and depressive disorders in a clinical sample. *Journal of the American Academy of Child and Adolescent Psychiatry, 30,* 43–50.

Bernstein, G. A., & Garfinkel, B. D. (1986). School phobia: The overlap of affective and anxiety disorders. *Journal of the American Academy of Child and Adolescent Psychiatry, 25,* 235–241.

Bernstein, G. A., & Garfinkel, B. D. (1988). Pedigrees, functioning, and psychopathology in families of school phobic children. *American Journal of Psychiatry, 145,* 70–74.

Bernstein, G. A., Garfinkel, B. D., & Borchardt, C. M. (1990). Comparative studies of pharmacotherapy for school refusal. *Journal of the American Academy of Child and Adolescent Psychiatry, 29,* 773–784.

Bernstein, G. A., Svingen, P., & Garfinkel, B. D. (1990). School phobia: Patterns of family functioning. *Journal of the American Academy of Child and Adolescent Psychiatry, 29,* 24–30.

Birleson, P. (1981). The validity of depressive disorder in childhood and the development of a self-rating scale: A research report. *Journal of Child Psychology and Psychiatry, 22,* 73–88.

Blackman, M., & Wheler, G. H. T. (1987). A case of mistaken identity: A fourth ventricular tumor presenting as school phobia in a 12 year old boy. *Canadian Journal of Psychiatry, 32,* 584–587.

Blagg, N. (1977). A detailed strategy for the rapid treatment of school phobics. *Behavioural Psychotherapy, 5,* 70–75.

Blagg, N. (1987). *School phobia and its treatment.* London: Croom Helm.

Blagg, N. R., & Yule, W. (1984). The behavioural treatment of school refusal—a comparative study. *Behaviour Research and Therapy, 22,* 119-127.

Bornstein, P. H., & Knapp, M. (1981). Self-control desensitization with a multiphobic boy: A multiple baseline design. *Journal of Behavior Therapy and Experimental Psychiatry, 12,* 281–285.

Briant, R. (1978). An introduction to clinical pharmacology. In J. Werry (Ed.), *Paediatric pharmacology: The use of behavior modifying drugs in children* (pp. 3–28). New York: Brunner/Mazel.

Broadwin, I. T. (1932). A contribution to the study of truancy. *American Journal of Orthopsychiatry, 2,* 253–259.

Brown, R. E., Copeland, R. E., & Hall, R. V. (1974). School phobia: Effects of behavior modification treatment applied by an elementary school principal. *Child Study Journal, 4,* 125–133.

Burke, A. E., & Silverman, W. (1987). The prescriptive treatment of school refusal. *Clinical Psychology Review, 7,* 353–362.

Burt, C. (1925). *American Journal of the Young Delinquent.* London: University of London Press.

Campbell, S. (1989). Developmental perspectives in child psychopathology. In T. H. Ollendick & M. Hersen (Eds.), *Handbook of child psychopathology* (2d ed., pp. 5–28). New York: Plenum.

Campbell, M., Green, W. H., & Deutsch, S. I. (1985). *Child and adolescent psychopharmacology.* Newbury Park, CA: Sage.

Carlson, G. A., & Cantwell, D. P. (1979). A survey of depressive symptoms in a child and adolescent psychiatric population. *Journal of the American Academy of Child Psychiatry, 18,* 587–599.

Carr, R. (1983). The role of medication in the treatment of the disturbed child. In P. D. Steinhauer & Q. Rae-Grant (Eds.), *Psychological problems of the child in the family* (pp. 635–663). New York: Basic Books.

Casteneda, A., McCandless, B. R., & Palmero, D. S. (1956). The children's form of the Manifest Anxiety Scale. *Child Development, 16,* 317–326.

Cautela, J. R., & Groden, J. (1978). *Relaxation. A comprehensive manual for adults, children, and children with special needs.* Champaign, IL: Research Press.

Chazan, M. (1962). School phobia. *British Journal of Educational Psychology, 32,* 200–217.

Chiles, J. A., Miller, M. L., & Cox, G. B. (1980). Depression in adolescent delinquent population. *Archives of General Psychiatry, 37,* 1179–1184.

Coolidge, J. C., Hahn, P. B., & Peck, A. L. (1957). School phobia: Neurotic crisis or way of life? *American Journal of Orthopsychiatry, 27,* 296–306.

Cone, J. D. (1978). The behavioral assessment grid (BAG): A conceptual framework and taxonomy. *Behavior Therapy, 9,* 882–888.

Cooper, J. A. (1973). Application of the consultant role to parent-teacher management of school avoidance behavior. *Psychology in the Schools, 10,* 259–262.

Costello, A. J., Edelbrock, C. S., Dulcan, M. K., Kalas, R., & Klaric, S. H. (1984). *Report on the NIMH Diagnostic Interview Schedule for Children (DIS-C)*. Washington, DC: NIMH.

D'Amato, G. (1962). Chlordiazepoxide in the treatment of school phobia. *Diseases of the Nervous System, 23,* 292–295.

Desai, N., Taylor-Davies, A., & Barnett, D. (1983). The effects of diazepam and oxpranolol on short term memory in individuals of high and low state anxiety. *British Journal of Clinical Pharmacology, 15,* 197–201.

Di Nardo, P. A., O'Brien, G. T., Barlow, D. H., Waddell, M. T., & Blanchard, E. B. (1983). Reliability of DSM-III anxiety disorder categories using a new structured interview. *Archives of General Psychiatry, 40,* 1070–1079.

Doerfler, L. A., Felner, R. D., Rowlison, R. T., Raley, P. A., & Evans, E. (1988). Depression in children and adolescents: A comparative analysis of the utility and construct validity of two assessment measures. *Journal of Consulting and Clinical Psychology, 56,* 769–772.

Edelbrock, C., & Costello, A. J. (1984). Structured psychiatric interviews for children and adolescents. In G. Goldstein & M. Hersen (Eds.), *Handbook of psychological assessment* (pp. 276–290). Elmsford, NY: Pergamon Press.

Eisenberg, I. (1958). School phobia: A study in the communication of anxiety. *American Journal of Psychiatry, 14,* 712–718.

Elizur, J. (1986). The stress of school entry: Parental coping behaviors and children's adjustment to school. *Journal of Child Psychology and Psychiatry, 27,* 625–638.

Elliot, S. N. (1988). Acceptability of behavioral treatments: Review of variables that influence treatment selection. *Professional Psychology: Research and Practice, 19,* 68–80.

Elliott, G. R., & Popper, C. W. (1991). Tricyclic antidepressants: The QT interval and other cardiovascular parameters. *Journal of Child and Adolescent Psychopharmacology, 1,* 187–189.

Estes, H. R., Haylett, C. H., & Johnson, A. M. (1956). Separation anxiety. *American Journal of Orthopsychiatry, 10,* 682–695.

Esveldt-Dawson, K., Wisner, K. L., Unis, A. S., Matson, J. L., & Kazdin, A. E. (1982). Treatment of phobias in a hospitalized child. *Journal of Behavior Therapy and Experimental Psychiatry, 13,* 77–83.

Evans, I. M., & Nelson, R. O. (1977). Assessment of child behavior problems. In A. R. Ciminero, K. S. Calhoun, & H. E. Adams (Eds.), *Handbook of behavioral assessment* (pp. 603–681). New York: Wiley-Interscience.

Eysenck, H. J. (1968). A theory of the incubation of anxiety/fear responses. *Behaviour Research and Therapy, 6,* 309–321.

Eysenck, H. J. (1979). The conditioning model of neurosis. *Behavioural and Brain Sciences, 2,* 155–199.

Finch, A. J. Jr., & Rogers, T. R. (1984). Self-report instruments. In T. H. Ollendick & M. Hersen (Eds.), *Child behavior assessment: Principles and procedures* (pp. 106–123). Elmsford, NY: Pergamon Press.

Finch, A. J. Jr., Saylor, C. F., & Edwards, G. L. (1985). Children's Depression Inventory: Sex and grade norms for normal children. *Journal of Consulting and Clinical Psychology, 53,* 424–425.

Flakierska, N., Linström, M., & Gillberg, C. (1988). School refusal: A 15–20-year follow-up study of 35 Swedish urban children. *British Journal of Psychiatry, 152,* 834–837.

Flament, M. F., Rapoport, J. L., Berg, C. J., & Kitts, C. (1985). A controlled trial of clomipramine in childhood obsessive compulsive disorder. *Psychopharmacology Bulletin, 21,* 150–152.

Forehand, R. L., & McMahon, R. J. (1981). *Helping the non compliant child: A clinician's guide to parent training.* New York: Guilford Press.

Frommer, E. A. (1967). Treatment of childhood depression with antidepressant drugs. *British Medical Journal, 1,* 729–732.

Garfield, S. L., Helper, M. M., Wilcott, R. C., & Muffly, R. (1962). Effects of clorpromazine on behavior in emotionally disturbed children. *Journal of Nervous and Mental Disease, 135,* 147–154.

Garvey, W. P., & Hegrenes, J. R. (1966). Desensitization techniques in the treatment of school phobia. *American Journal of Orthopsychiatry, 36,* 147–152.

Gilman, A. G., Goodman, L. S., Rall, T. W., & Murad, F. (1985). *Goodman and Gilman's: The pharmacological basis of therapeutics* (7th ed.). New York: Macmillan.

Gittelman, R., & Kanner, A. (1986). Psychopharmacotherapy. In H. C. Quay & J. S. Werry (Eds.), *Psychopathological disorders of childhood* (pp. 455–495). New York: Wiley.

Gittelman-Klein, R. (1975a). Pharmacotherapy and management of pathological separation anxiety. In R. Gittelman (Ed.), *Recent advances in child psychopharmacology* (pp. 255–272). New York: Human Sciences Press.

Gittelman-Klein, R. (1975b). Psychiatric characteristics of the relatives of school-phobic children. In D. V. S. Sankar (Ed.), *Mental health in children* (vol. 1, pp. 325–334). New York: PJD Publications.

Gittelman-Klein, R., & Klein, D. F. (1971). Controlled imipramine treatment of school phobia. *Archives of General Psychiatry, 25,* 204–207.

Gittelman-Klein, R., & Klein, D. F. (1973). School phobia: Diagnostic considerations in the light of imipramine effects. *Journal of Nervous and Mental Disease, 156,* 199–215.

Gittelman-Klein, R., & Klein, D. (1980). Separation anxiety in school refusal and its treatment with drugs. In L. Hersov & I. Berg (Eds.), *Out of school. Modern perspectives in truancy and school refusal* (pp. 321–341). Chichester, England: Wiley.

Glaser, K. (1959). Problems in school attendance: School phobia and related conditions. *Pediatrics, 23,* 371–383.

Glassman, A. H., & Bigger, J. T. (1981). Cardiovascular effects of therapeutic doses of tricyclic antidepressants. *Archives of General Psychiatry, 38,* 815–820.

Glennon, B., & Weisz, J. R. (1978). An observational approach to the reassessment of anxiety in young children. *Journal of Consulting and Clinical Psychology, 46,* 1246–1257.

Goldfried, M. R. (1971). Systematic desensitization as training in self-control. *Journal of Consulting and Clinical Psychology, 37,* 228–234.

Goldfried, M. R., & Kent, R. N. (1972). Traditional versus behavioral personality assessment: A comparison of methodological and theoretical assumptions. *Psychological Bulletin, 77,* 409–420.

Granell de Aldaz, E., Vivas, E., Gelfand, D. M., & Feldman, L. (1984). Estimating the prevalence of school refusal and school-related fears. A Venezuelan sample. *Journal of Nervous and Mental Disease, 172,* 722–729.

Granell de Aldaz, E., Feldman, L., Vivas, E., & Gelfand, D. M. (1987). Characteristics of Venezuelan school refusers: Toward the development of a high-risk profile. *Journal of Nervous and Mental Disease, 175,* 402–407.

Graziano, A. M., De Giovanni, I. S., & Garcia, K. A. (1979). Behavioral treatment of children's fears: A review. *Psychological Bulletin, 6,* 804–830.

Gross, A. M. (1984). Behavioral interviewing. In T. H. Ollendick & M. Hersen (Eds.), *Child behavioral assessment: Principles and procedures* (pp. 61–79). Elmsford, NY: Pergamon Press.

Grotevant, H. D., & Carlson, C. I. (1989). *Family assessment: A guide to methods and measures.* New York: Guilford Press.

Gullone, E., & King, N. J. (1989). Acceptability of behavioral interventions: Child and caregiver perceptions. In M. Hersen, R.M. Eisler, & P. Miller (Eds.), *Progress in behavior modification* (vol. 24, pp. 132–151). Newbury Park, CA: Sage.

Gullone, E., & King, N. J. (1991). Acceptability of alternative treatments for school refusal. Evaluations by students, caregivers, and professionals. *British Journal of Educational Psychology, 61,* 346–354.

Hampe, E., Miller, L., Barrett, C., & Noble, H. (1973). Intelligence and school phobia. *Journal of School Psychology, 11,* 66–70.

Hampe, E., Noble, H., Miller, L. C., & Barrett, C. L. (1973). Phobic children one and two years posttreatment. *Journal of Abnormal Psychology, 82,* 446–453.

Hatzenbuehler, L. C., & Schroeder, H. E. (1978). Desensitization procedures in the treatment of childhood disorders. *Psychological Bulletin, 85,* 831–844.

Hayes, S. C., Nelson, R. O., & Jarrett, R. B. (1987). The treatment utility of assessment: A functional approach to evaluating assessment quality. *American Psychologist, 42,* 963–974.

Healy, W. (1915). *The individual delinquent.* London: Heinemann.

Herjanic, B., & Reich, W. (1982). Development of a structured psychiatric interview agreement between child and parent on individual symptoms. *Journal of Abnormal Child Psychology, 10,* 307–324.

Hersen, M. (1970). Behavior modification approach to a school-phobia case. *Journal of Clinical Psychology, 26,* 128–132.

Hersov, L. A. (1960a). Persistent non-attendance at school. *Journal of Child Psychology and Psychiatry, 1,* 130–136.

Hersov, L. A. (1960b). Refusal to go to school. *Journal of Child Psychology and Psychiatry, 1,* 137–145.

Hersov, L. A. (1977). School refusal. In M. Rutter & L. Hersov (Eds.), *Child psychiatry. Modern approaches* (pp. 455–486). Oxford: Blackwell.

Hersov, L. (1985). School refusal. In M. Rutter & R. Hersov (Eds.), *Child and adolescent psychiatry: Modern approaches* (2d ed., pp. 382–399). Oxford: Blackwell Scientific.

Hirshfeld, D. R., Rosenbaum, J. F., Biederman, J., Bolduc, E. A., Faraone, S. V., Snidman, N., Reznick, J. S., & Kagan, J. (1992). Stable behavioral inhibition and its association with anxiety disorder. *Journal of the American Academy of Child and Adolescent Psychiatry, 31,* 103–111.

Hodges, K. (1978). *Manual for the Child Assessment Schedule* (CAS available from the author). Durham, NC: Duke University Department of Psychiatry.

Hollingshead, A. B., & Redlich, F. (1958). *Social class and mental illness.* New York: Wiley.

Holmes, F. B. (1936). An experimental investigation of a method of overcoming children's fears. *Child Development, 1,* 6–30.

Jacob, T., & Tennenbaum, D. L. (1988). *Family assessment: Rationale, methods and future directons.* New York: Plenum.

Jacobsen, V. (1948). Influential factors in the outcome of treatment of school phobia. *Smith College Studies in Social Work, 18,* 181–202.

Jersild, A. T., Goldman, B., & Loftus, J. J. (1941). Comparative study of the worries of children in two school situations. *Journal of Experimental Education, 9,* 323–326.

Johnson, A. M., Falstein, E. I., Szurek, S. A., & Svendsen, M. (1941). School phobia. *American Journal of Orthopsychiatry, 11,* 702–711.

Johnson, S. M., & Bolstad, O. D. (1973). Methodological issues in naturalistic observation: Some problems and solutions for field research. In L. A. Hamerlynck, L. C. Handy, & E. J. Mash (Eds.), *Behavior change: Methodology, concepts, and practice* (pp. 7–67). Champaign, IL: Research Press.

Jones, M. C. (1924a). The elimination of children's fears. *Journal of Experimental Psychology, 7,* 382–390.

Jones, M. C. (1924b). A laboratory study of fear: The case of Peter. *Journal of Genetic Psychology, 31,* 308–315.

Kagan, J., Reznick, J. S., & Snidman, N. (1987). The physiology and psychology of behavioral inhibition in children. *Child Development, 58,* 1459–1473.

Kazdin, A. E. (1979). Situational specificity: The two-edged sword of behavioral assessment. *Behavioral Assessment, 1,* 57–75.

Kazdin, A. E. (1981). Assessment techniques for childhood depression: A critical appraisal. *Journal of the American Academy of Child Psychiatry, 20,* 358–375.

Kazdin, A. E. (1988). Childhood depression. In E. J. Mash & L. G. Terdal (Eds.), *Behavioral assessment of childhood disorders* (2d ed., pp. 157–195). New York: Guilford Press.

Kazdin, A. E., & Petti, T. A. (1982). Self-report and interview measures of childhood and adolescent depression. *Journal of Child Psychology and Psychiatry, 23,* 437–457.

Kearney, C. A., & Silverman, W. K. (1988). Measuring the function of school refusal behavior: The School Refusal Assessment Scale. Paper presented at the 1988 annual meeting of the Association for Advancement of Behavior Therapy, New York.

Kearney, C. A., & Silverman, W. K. (1990). A preliminary analysis of a functional model of assessment and treatment of school refusal behavior. *Behavior Modification, 14,* 340–366.

Kearney, C. A., & Silverman, W. K. (1993). Measuring the function of school refusal behavior: The School Refusal Assessment Scale. *Journal of Clinical Child Psychology, 22,* 85–96.

Kendall, P. C. (Ed.) (1991). *Child and adolescent therapy. Cognitive-behavioral procedure.* New York: Guilford Press.

Kendall, P. C., & Braswell, L. (1985). *Cognitive-behavioral therapy for impulsive children.* New York: Guilford Press.

Kendall, P. C., Chansky, T. E., Friedman, M., Kim, R., Kortlander, E., Sessa, F. M., & Siqueland, L. (1991). Treating anxiety disorders in children and adolescents. In P. C. Kendall (Ed.), *Child and adolescent therapy. Cognitive-behavioral procedures* (pp. 131–164). New York: Guilford Press.

Kendall, P. C., Ellsas, T. E., Kane, M. T., Kim, R. S., Kortlander, E., Ronan, K. R., Sessa, F. M., & Siqueland, L. (1992). *Anxiety disorders in youth. Cognitive-behavioral interventions.* Boston: Allyn and Bacon.

Kendall, P. C., Howard, B. L., & Epps, J. (1988). The anxious child. Cognitive-behavioral treatment strategies. *Behavior Modification, 12,* 281–310.

Kennedy, W. A. (1965). School phobia: Rapid treatment of fifty cases. *Journal of Abnormal Psychology, 70,* 285–289.

King, N. J., Hamilton, D. I., & Ollendick, T. H. (1988). *Children's phobias: A behavioural perspective.* Chichester, England: Wiley.

King, N. J., & Ollendick, T. H. (1989). School refusal: Graduated and rapid behavioural treatment strategies. *Australian and New Zealand Journal of Psychiatry, 23,* 213–223.

King, N. J., Ollendick, T. H., & Gullone, E. (1990). School related fears of children and adolescents. *Australian Journal of Education, 34,* 99–112.

King, N. J., Ollendick, T. H., & Gullone, E. (1991). Test anxiety in children and adolescents. *Australian Psychologist, 26,* 25–32.

King, N. J., Ollendick, T. H., & Gullone, E. (1992). Negative affectivity in children and adolescents: Relations between anxiety and depression. *Clinical Psychology Review, 11,* 441–459.

King, N. J., Ollier, K., Iaucone, R., Schuster, S., Bays, K., Gullone, E., & Ollendick,T. H. (1989). Fears of children and adolescents: A cross-sectional Australian study using the Revised Fear Survey Schedule for Children. *Journal of Child Psychology and Psychiatry, 30,* 775–784.

Klein, R. G., & Last, C. G. (1989). *Anxiety disorders in children.* Newbury Park, CA: Sage.

Klein, R. G., Koplewicz, H. S., & Kanner, A. (1992). Imipramine treatment of children with separation anxiety disorder. *Journal of the American Academy of Child and Adolescent Psychiatry, 31,* 21–28.

Koeppen, A. S. (1974). Relaxation training for children. *Elementary School Guidance and Counseling, 9,* 14–21.

Kovacs, M. (1978). *Interview schedule for children.* Unpublished manuscript. University of Pittsburgh, PA.

Kovacs, M., & Beck, A. T. (1977). An empirical-clinical approach toward a definition of childhood depression. In J. G. Schulterbrandt & A. Raskin (Eds.), *Depression in childhood: Diagnosis, treatment, and conceptual models* (pp. 1–25). New York: Raven Press.

Kraft, I. A., Ardali, C., Duffy, J. H., Hart, J. T., & Pearce, P. (1965). A clinical study of chlordiazepoxide used in psychiatric disorders of children. *International Journal of Neuropsychiatry, 1,* 433–437.

Kunzelman, H. D. (Ed.) (1970). *Precision teaching.* Seattle, WA: Special Child Publications.

Lang, M. (1982). School refusal: An empirical study and system analysis. *Australian Journal of Family Therapy, 3,* 93–107.

Lang, M., & Tisher, M. (1978). *Children's Depression Scale.* Victoria, Australia: Australian Council for Educational Research.

Lang, P. J., & Cutherbert, B. N. (1984). Affective information processing and the assessment of anxiety. *Journal of Behavioral Assessment, 6,* 376–395.

Lang, P. J., & Lazovik, A. D. (1963). Experimental desensitization of a phobia. *Journal of Abnormal and Social Psychology, 66,* 519–525.

Lapouse, R., & Monk, N. (1959). Fears and worries in a representative sample of children. *American Journal of Orthopsychiatry, 29,* 803–818.

Last, C. G., & Francis, G. (1988). School phobia. In B. B. Lahey & A. E. Kazdin (Eds.), *Advances in clinical child psychology* (vol. 11, pp. 193–222). New York: Plenum.

Last, C. G., Francis, G., Hersen, M., Kazdin, A. E., & Strauss, C. (1987). Separation anxiety and school phobia: A comparison using DSM-III criteria. *American Journal of Psychiatry, 144,* 653–657.

Last, C. G., Francis, G., & Strauss, C. C. (1989). Assessing fears in anxiety-disordered children with the Revised Fear Survey Schedule for Children (FSSC-R). *Journal of Clinical Child Psychology, 18,* 137–141.

Last, C. G., & Strauss, C. C. (1990). School refusal in anxiety-disordered children and adolescents. *Journal of the American Academy of Child and Adolescent Psychiatry, 29,* 31–35.

Lazarus, A. A. (1960). The elimination of children's phobias by deconditioning. In H. J. Eysenck (Ed.), *Behaviour therapy and the neuroses* (pp. 114–122). Oxford: Pergamon Press.

Lazarus, A. A., & Abramovitz, A. (1962). The use of emotive imagery in the treatment of children's phobias. *Journal of Mental Science, 108,* 191–195.

Lazarus, A. A., Davison, G. C., & Polefka, D. A. (1965). Classical and operant factors in the treatment of a school phobia. *Journal of Abnormal Psychology, 70,* 225–229.

Ledwidge, B. (1978). Cognitive behavior modification: A step in the wrong direction? *Psychological Bulletin, 85,* 353–375.

Leton, D. A. (1962). Assessment of school phobia. *Mental Hygiene, 46,* 256–265.

Leventhal, T., & Sills, M. (1964). Self-image in school phobia. *American Journal of Orthopsychiatry, 34,* 685–695.

Lick, J. R., & Katkin, E. S. (1976). Assessment of anxiety and fear. In M. Hersen & A. S. Bellack (Eds.), *Behavioral assessment: A practical handbook* (pp. 175–206). Elmsford, NY: Pergamon Press.

Linehan, M. (1977). Issues in behavioral interviewing. In J. D. Cone & R. P. Hawkins (Eds.), *Behavioral assessment: New directions in clinical psychology* (pp. 30–51). New York: Brunner/Mazel.

Lucas, A. R., & Pasley, F. C. (1969). Psychoactive drugs in the treatment of emotionally disturbed children: Haloperidol and diazepam. *Comprehensive Psychiatry, 10,* 376–386.

Luiselli, J. K. (1980). Relaxation training with the developmentally disabled: A reappraisal. *Behavior Research of Severe Developmental Disabilities, 1,* 191–213.

Malcarne, V. L., & Ingram, R. E. (in press). Cognition and negative affectivity. In T. H. Ollendick & R. M. Prinz (Eds.), *Advances in clinical child psychology.* New York: Plenum.

Mansdorf, I. J., & Lukens, E. (1987). Cognitive-behavioral psychotherapy for separation anxious children exhibiting school phobia. *Journal of the American Academy of Child and Adolescent Psychiatry, 26,* 222–225.

Marks, I. M. (1975). Behavioral treatments of phobic and obsessive-compulsive disorders: A critical appraisal. In M. Hersen, R. M. Eisler, & P. M. Miller (Eds.), *Progress in behavior modification* (vol.1, pp. 65–158). New York: Academic Press.

Martin, G., & Pear, J. (1988). *Behavior modification. What is it and how to do it* (3d ed.). Englewood Cliffs, NJ: Prentice-Hall.

Mash, E. J., & Terdal, L. G. (Eds.) (1981). *Behavioral assessment of childhood disorders.* New York: Guilford Press.

Mash, E. J., & Terdal, L. G. (Eds.) (1988). *Behavioral assessment of childhood disorders* (2d ed.). New York: Guilford Press.

Masters, J. C., Burish, T .G., Hollon, S. D., & Rimm, D. C. (1987). *Behavior therapy. Techniques and empirical findings* (3d ed.). San Diego, CA: Harcourt Brace Jovanovich.

Matson, J. L., & Ollendick, T. H. (1988). *Enhancing children's social skills.* Elmsford, NY: Pergamon Press.

Maziade, M., Capéraà, P., Laplante, B., Boudreault, M., Thivierge, J., Côte, R., & Boutin, P. (1985). Value of difficult temperament among 7-year-olds in the general population for predicting psychiatric diagnosis at age 12. *American Journal of Psychiatry, 142,* 943–946.

McMahon, R. J. (1984). Behavioral checklists and rating forms. In T. H. Ollendick & M. Hersen (Eds.), *Child behavioral assessment: Principles and procedures* (pp. 80–105). Elmsford, NY: Pergamon Press.

McNamara, E. (1988). The self-management of school phobia: A case study. *Behavioural Psychotherapy, 16,* 217–229.

Miller, L. C., Barrett, C. L., & Hampe, E. (1972). Comparison of reciprocal inhibition, psychotherapy and waiting list control for phobic children. *Journal of Abnormal Psychology, 79,* 269–279.

Miller, L. C., Barrett, C. L., & Hampe, E. (1974). Phobias of childhood in a prescientific era. In A. Davids (Ed.), *Child personality and psychopathology: Current topics* (vol.1, pp. 89–134). New York: Wiley.

Miller, L. C., Barrett, C. L., Hampe, E., & Noble, H. (1971). Revised anxiety scales for the Louisville Behavior Check List. *Psychological Reports, 29,* 503-511.

Miller, L. C., Barrett, C. L., Hampe, E., & Noble, H. (1972). Factor structure of childhood fears. *Journal of Consulting and Clinical Psychology, 39,* 264–268.

Mitchell, S., & Shepherd, M. (1967). The child who dislikes going to school. *British Journal of Educational Psychology, 37,* 32–40.

Moore, T. (1966). Difficulties of the ordinary child in adjusting to primary school. *Journal of Child Psychology and Psychiatry, 7,* 17–38.

Morris, R. J., & Kratochwill, T. R. (1983). *Treating children's fears and phobias: A behavioral approach.* Elmsford, NY: Pergamon Press.

Neisworth, J. T., Madle, R. A., & Goeke, K. E. (1975). "Errorless" elimination of separation anxiety: A case study. *Journal of Behavior Therapy and Experimental Psychology, 6,* 79–82.

Nichols, K. A., & Berg, I. (1970). School phobia and self-evaluation. *Journal of Child Psychology and Psychiatry, 11,* 133–141.

O'Farrell, T. J., Hedlund, M. A., & Cutter, H. S. G. (1981). Desensitization for a severe phobia of a fourteen-year-old male. *Child Behavior Therapy, 3,* 67–77.

Ollendick, T. H. (1979). Fear reduction techniques with children. In M. Hersen, R. M. Eisler, & P. M. Miller (Eds.), *Progress in behavior modification* (vol.8, pp. 127–168). New York: Academic Press.

Ollendick, T. H. (1983). Reliability and validity of the Revised Fear Survey Schedule for Children (FSSC—R). *Behaviour Research and Therapy, 21,* 685–692.

Ollendick, T. H., & Cerny, J. A. (1981). *Clinical behavior therapy with children.* New York: Plenum.

Ollendick, T. H., & Francis, G. (1988). Behavioral assessment and treatment of childhood phobias. *Behavior Modification, 12,* 165–204.

Ollendick, T. H., & Greene, R. (1990). Behavioral assessment of children. In G. Goldstein & M. Hersen (Eds.), *Handbook of psychological assessment* (2d ed., pp. 403–422). Elmsford, NY: Pergamon Press.

Ollendick, T. H., Hagopian, L. P., & Huntzinger, R. M. (1991). Cognitive-behavior therapy with nighttime fearful children. *Journal of Behavior Therapy and Experimental Psychiatry, 22,* 113–121.

Ollendick, T. H., & Hersen, M. (1983). An historical introduction to child psychopathology. In T. H. Ollendick & M. Hersen (Eds.), *Handbook of child psychopathology* (pp. 3–12). New York: Plenum.

Ollendick, T. H., & Hersen, M. (Eds.) (1984). *Child behavioral assessment: Principles and procedures.* Elmsford, NY: Pergamon Press.

Ollendick, T. H., & Hersen, M. (1993). *Handbook of child and adolescent assessment.* Elmsford, NY: Pergamon Press.

Ollendick, T. H., & King, N. J. (1990). School phobia and separation anxiety. In H. Leitenberg (Ed.), *Handbook of social and evaluation anxiety* (pp. 179–214). New York: Plenum.

Ollendick, T. H., & King, N. J. (1991). Origins of childhood fears: An evaluation of Rachman's theory of fear acquisition. *Behaviour Research and Therapy, 29,* 117–123.

Ollendick, T. H., King, N. J., & Frary, R. B. (1989). Fears in children and adolescents: Reliability, and generalizability across gender, age and nationality. *Behaviour Research and Therapy, 27,* 19–26.

Ollendick, T. H., Matson, J. L., & Helsel, W. J. (1985). Fears in visually impaired and normally-sighted youth. *Behaviour Research and Therapy, 23,* 375–378.

Ollendick, T. H., & Mayer, J. A. (1984). School phobia. In S. M. Turner (Ed.), *Behavioral theories and treatment of anxiety* (pp. 367–411). New York: Plenum.

Ollendick, T. H., & Yule, W. (1990). Depression in British and American children and its relation to anxiety and fear. *Journal of Consulting and Clinical Psychology, 58,* 126–129.

Ollendick, T. H., Yule, W., & Ollier, K. (1990). Fears in British children and their relationshp to manifest anxiety and depression. *Journal of Child Psychology and Psychiatry, 32,* 321–331.

O'Reilly, P. P. (1971). Desensitization of a fire bell phobia. *Journal of School Psychology, 9,* 55–57.

Partridge, J. M. (1939). *Truancy. Journal of Mental Science, 85,* 45–81.

Patterson, G. R. (1976). The aggressive child: Victim and architect of a coercive system. In E. J. Mash, L. A. Hammerlynck, & L. C. Hardy (Eds.), *Behavior modification and families* (pp. 267–316). New York: Brunner/Mazel.

Patterson, G. R. (1982). *Coercive family process.* Eugene, OR: Castalia.

Paul, G. L. (1969). Outcome of systematic desensitization: I. Background and procedures, and uncontrolled reports of individual treatments. In C. M. Franks (Ed.), *Behavior therapy: Appraisal and status.* New York: McGraw-Hill.

Perkins, G. J., Rowe, G. P., & Farmer, R. G. (1973). Operant conditioning of emotional responsiveness as a prerequisite for behavioural analysis: A case study of an adolescent school phobic. *Australian and New Zealand Journal of Psychiatry, 7,* 180–184.

Perry, M. A., & Furukawa, M. J. (1980). Modeling methods. In F. H. Kanfer & A. P. Goldstein (Eds.), *Helping people change* (2d ed., pp. 131–171). Elmsford, NY: Pergamon Press.

Phillips, D., & Wolpe, S. (1981). Multiple behavioral techniques in severe separation anxiety of a twelve-year-old. *Journal of Behavior Therapy and Experimental Psychiatry, 12,* 329–332.

Poznanski, E. O. (1973). Children with excessive fears. *American Journal of Orthopsychiatry, 43,* 428–438.

Prins, P. J. M. (1985). Self-speech and self-regulation of high- and low-anxious children in the dental situation: An interview study. *Behaviour Research and Therapy, 23,* 641–650.

Prins, P. J. M. (1986). Children's self-speech and self-regulation during a fear-provoking behavioral test. *Behaviour Research and Therapy, 24,* 181–191.

Puig-Antich, J., Perch, J. M., Lupatkin, W., Chambers, W. J., Tabrizi, M. A., King, J., Goetz, R., Davies, M., & Stiles, R. L. (1987). Imipramine in pre-pubertal major depressive disorders. *Archives of General Psychiatry, 44,* 81–89.

Quay, H. C., & Peterson, D. R. (1983). *Manual for the Revised Behavioral Problem Checklist.* Unpublished manuscript.

Quay, H. C., & Werry, J. S. (Eds.) (1979), *Psychopathological disorders of childhood* (2d ed.). New York: Wiley.

Quinn, D. M. P. (1986). Prevalence of psychoactive medication in childhood. *Canadian Journal of Psychiatry, 31,* 575–580.

Rachman, S. (1977). The conditioning theory of fear acquisition: A critical examination. *Behaviour Research and Therapy, 15,* 375–387.

Reynolds, C. R., & Paget, K. D. (1983). National normative and reliability data for the Revised Children's Manifest Anxiety Scale. *School Psychology Review, 12,* 324–336.

Reynolds, C. R., & Richmond, B. O. (1978). "What I think and feel": A revised measure of children's manifest anxiety. *Journal of Abnormal Child Psychology, 6,* 271–280.

Reznick, J. S. (Ed.) (1989). *Perspectives on behavioral inhibition.* Chicago: University of Chicago Press.

Reznick, J. S., Kagan, J., Snidman, N., Gersten, M., Baak, K., & Rosenberg, A. (1986). Inhibited and uninhibited children: A follow-up study. *Child Development, 57,* 660–680.

Richmond, B. O., & Millar, G. W. (1984). What I think and feel: A cross-cultural study of anxiety in children. *Psychology in the Schools, 21,* 255–257.

Richmond, B. O., Sekume, S., Ohmoto, M., Kawamoto, H., & Hamazaki, T. (1984). Anxiety among Canadian, Japanese, and American children. *Journal of Psychology, 116,* 3–6.

Richter, N. C. (1984). The efficacy of relaxation training with children. *Journal of Abnormal Child Psychology, 12,* 319–344.

Riddle, M. A., Nelson, J. C., Kleinman, C. S., Rasmusson, A., Leckman, J. F., King, R. A., & Cohen, D. J. (1991). Sudden death in children receiving Norpramin®: A review of three reported cases and commentary. *Journal of the American Academy of Child and Adolescent Psychiatry, 30,* 104–108.

Rimm, D. C., & Masters, J. C. (1974). *Behavior therapy: Techniques and empirical findings.* New York: Academic Press.

Rodriguez, A., Rodriguez, M., & Eisenberg, L. (1959). The outcome of school phobia: A follow-up study based on 41 cases. *American Journal of Psychiatry, 116,* 540–544.

Roehling, P. V., & Robin, A. L. (1986). Development and validation of the Family Beliefs Inventory: A measure of unrealistic beliefs among parents and adolescents. *Journal of Consulting and Clinical Psychology, 54,* 693–697.

Rosenstiel, A. K., & Scott, D. S. (1977). Four considerations in using imagery techniques with children. *Journal of Behavior Therapy and Experimental Psychiatry, 8,* 287–290.

Rutter, M., Tizard, J., & Whitemore, K. (Eds.) (1970). *Education, health, and behaviour.* London: Longman.

Ryall, M. R., & Dietiker, K. E. (1979). Reliability and clinical validity of the CFFS. *Journal of Behavior Therapy and Experimental Psychology, 10,* 303–309.

Sarason, S. B., Davidson, K. S., Lighthall, F. F., Waite, R. R., & Ruebush, B. K. (1960). *Anxiety in elementary school children.* New York: Wiley.

Scherer, M. W., & Nakamura, C. Y. (1968). A Fear Survey Schedule for Children (FSSC): A factor-analytic comparison with manifest anxiety (CMAS). *Behaviour Research and Therapy, 6,* 173–182.

Seligman, M. E. P., Peterson, C., Kaslow, N. J., Tanenbaum, R. L., Alloy, L. B., & Abramson, L. Y. (1984). Attributional style and depressive symptoms among children. *Journal of Abnormal Psychology, 93,* 235–238.

Shaffer, D. (1974). Suicide in children and early adolescence. *Journal of Child Psychology and Psychiatry, 15,* 275–291.

Shapiro, E. S. (1984). Self-monitoring. In T. H. Ollendick & M. Hersen (Eds.), *Child behavioral assessment: Principles and procedures* (pp. 106–123). Elmsford, NY: Pergamon Press.

Sheehan, D. V., Coleman, J. H., Greenblatt, D. J., Jones, K. J., Levine, P. H., Orsulak, P. J., Paterson, M., Schildkraut, J. J., Uzogara, E., & Watkins, D. (1984). Some biochemical correlates of panic attacks with agoraphobia and their response to a new treatment. *Journal of Clinical Psychopharmacology, 4,* 66–75.

Silverman, W. K. (1991a). *Anxiety Disorders Interview Schedule for Children (Child Version).* Albany, New York: Graywind Publications.

Silverman, W. K. (1991b). *Anxiety Disorders Interview Schedule for Children (Parent Version).* Albany, New York: Graywind Publications.

Silverman, W. K. (1991c). Diagnostic reliability of anxiety disorders in children using structured interviews. *Journal of Anxiety Disorders, 5,* 105–124.

Silverman, W. K., & Eisen, A. R. (1992). Age differences in the reliability of parent and child reports of child-anxious symptomatology using a structured interview. *Journal of the American Academy of Child and Adolescent Psychiatry, 31,* 117–124.

Silverman, W. K., & Nelles, W. B. (1988). The Anxiety Disorders Interview Schedule for Children. *Journal of the American Academy of Child and Adolescent Psychiatry, 27,* 772–778.

Simeon, J. G., & Ferguson, H. B. (1985). Recent developments in the use of antidepressant and anxiolytic medications. *Psychiatric Clinics of North America, 8,* 893–907.

Simeon, J. G., Ferguson, H. B., Knott, V., Roberts, N., Gauthier, B., Dubois, B. A., & Wiggins, D. (1992). Clinical, cognitive, and neurophysiological effects of alprazolam in children and adolescents with overanxious and avoidant disorders. *Journal of the American Academy of Child and Adolescent Psychiatry, 31,* 29–33.

Skinner, H. A., Steinhauer, P. D., & Santa-Barbara, J. (1983). The family assessment measure. *Canadian Journal of Mental Health, 2,* 91–105.

Sleator, E. K. (1985). Measurement of compliance. *Psychopharmacology Bulletin, 21,* 1089–1093.

Smith, S. D., Rosen, D., Trueworthy, R. C., & Louman, T. (1979). A reliable method for evaluating drug compliance in children with cancer. *Cancer, 43,* 169–173.

Smith, S. L. (1970). School refusal with anxiety: A review of sixty-three cases. *Canadian Psychiatry Association Journal, 15,* 257–264.

Smucker, M. R., Craighead, W. E., Craighead, L. W., & Green, B. J. (1986). Normative and reliability data for the Children's Depression Inventory. *Journal of Abnormal Child Psychology, 14,* 25–39.

Spivack, G., & Shure, M. B. (1974). *Social adjustment of young children: A cognitive approach to solving real-life problems.* San Francisco: Jossey-Bass.

Spivack, G., & Shure, M. B. (1982). The cognition of social adjustment: Interpersonal cognitive problem-solving thinking. In B. B. Lahey & A. E. Kazdin (Eds.), *Advances in clinical child psychology* (vol.5, pp. 323–372). Elmsford, NY: Pergamon Press.

Staley, A. A., & O'Donnell, J. P. (1984). A developmental analysis of mothers' reports of normal children's fears. *Journal of Genetic Psychology, 144,* 165–178.

Strauss, C. C. (1988). Social deficits of children with internalizing disorders. In B. B. Lahey & A. E. Kazdin (Eds.), *Advances in clinical child psychology* (vol.11, pp. 159–191). New York: Plenum.

Strauss, C. C., Forehand, R., Frame, C., & Smith, K. (1984). Characteristics of children with extreme scores on the Children's Depression Inventory. *Journal of Clinical Child Psychology, 13,* 227–231.

Swann, G. E., & MacDonald, M. L. (1978). Behavior therapy in practice: A rational survey of behavior therapists. *Behavior Therapy, 9,* 799–807.

Tahmisian, J. A., & McReynolds, W. T. (1971). Use of parents as behavioural engineers in the treatment of a school phobic girl. *Journal of Counseling Psychology, 18,* 225–228.

Taylor, J. A. (1951). The relationship of anxiety to the conditioned eyelid response. *Journal of Experimental Psychology, 42,* 183–188.

Thomas, A., & Chess, S. (1977). *Temperament and development.* New York: Brunner/Mazel.

Tiller, J., Maguire, K., & Davies, B. (1990). A sequential double-blind controlled study of moclobemide and mianserin in elderly depressed patients. *International Journal of Geriatric Psychiatry, 5,* 199–204.

Trueman, D. (1984). What are the characteristics of school phobic children? *Psychological Reports, 54,* 191–202.

Tyrer, P., & Tyrer, S. (1974). School refusal, truancy, and adult neurotic illness. *Psychological Medicine, 4,* 416–421.

Vaal, J. J. (1973). Applying contingency contracting to a school phobic: A case study. *Journal of Behavior Therapy and Experimental Psychiatry, 4,* 371–373.

Versiani, M., Oggero, U., Alterwain, P., Capponi, R., Dajas, F., Heinze-Martin, C. A., Marque, M. A., Poleo, M. A., Rivero-Almanzor, L. E., Rossel, L., Schmid-Burgk, W., & Ucha-Udabe, R. (1989). A double-blind comparative trial of moclobemide v. imipramine and placebo in major depressive episodes. *British Journal of Psychiatry, 155* (suppl. 6), 72–77.

Walk, R. D. (1956). Self-ratings of fear in a fear involving situation. *Journal of Abnormal and Social Psychology, 52,* 171–178.

Warnecke, R. (1964). School phobia and its treatment. *British Journal of Medical Psychology, 37,* 71–79.

Warren, W. (1965). A study of adolescent psychiatric inpatients and the outcome six or more years later. 1. Clinical histories and hospital findings. *Journal of Child Psychology and Psychiatry, 6,* 1–17.

Waters, B. (1990). Pharmacological and other treatments. In B. J. Tonge, G. D. Burrows, & J. S. Werry (Eds.), *Handbook of studies on child psychiatry* (pp. 387–402). Amsterdam: Elsevier.

Watson, D., & Clark, L. A. (1984). Negative affectivity: The disposition to experience aversive emotional states. *Psychological Bulletin, 96,* 465–490.

Watson, J. B., & Rayner, R. (1920). Conditioned emotional reactions. *Journal of Experimental Psychology, 3,* 1–14.

Weist, M. D., Ollendick, T. H., & Finney, J. W. (1991). Toward the empirical validation of treatment targets in children. *Clinical Psychology Review, 11,* 515–538.

White, J. H. (1980). Psychopharmacology in childhood: Current status and future perspective. *Psychiatric Clinics of North America, 3,* 443–453.

Wolf, M. M. (1978). Social validity: the case for subjective measurement or how applied behavior analysis is finding its heart. *Journal of Applied Behavior Analysis, 11,* 203–214.

Wolfe, V. V., Finch, A. J. Jr., Saylor, C. F., Blount, R. L., Pallmeyer, T. P., & Carek, D. J. (1987). Negative affectivity in children: A multitrait-multimethod investigation. *Journal of Consulting and Clinical Psychology, 55,* 245–250.

Wolpe, J. (1958). *Psychotherapy by reciprocal inhibition.* Stanford, CA: Stanford University Press.

Wolpe, J. (1969). *The practice of behavior therapy.* Elmsford, NY: Pergamon Press.

Wolpe, J., & Lang, P. J. (1964). A fear survey schedule for use in behavior therapy. *Behaviour Research and Therapy, 2,* 27–30.

Woolfolk, A. E., Woolfolk, R. C., & Wilson, G. T. (1977). A rose by any other name . . . Labeling bias and attitudes toward behavior modification. *Journal of Consulting and Clinical Psychology, 45,* 184–191.

Yates, A. J. (1970). *Behavior therapy.* New York: Wiley.

Zatz, S., & Chassin, L. (1983). Cognitions in test-anxious children. *Journal of Consulting & Clinical Psychology, 51,* 526–534.

Zatz, S., & Chassin, L. (1985). Cognitions of text-anxious children under naturalistic test-taking conditions. *Journal of Consulting and Clinical Psychology, 53,* 393–401.

Author Index

Abramovitz, A., 82, 83
Achenbach, T. M., 28, 55, 56, 102, 129, 148
Adams, P. L., 21
Agras, S., 9
Aman, M. G., 128
American Psychiatric Association, 10
Anders, T. F., 32
Angelino, H., 4, 6
Atkinson, L., 2, 21, 22
Ayllon, T., 58, 65, 84, 85, 87

Baker, H., 19, 21, 22
Ballenger, J. C., 120
Bandura, A., 88
Barnett, D., 120
Barrett, C. L., 17, 56, 107
Bartels, M. G., 125, 132
Bauer, D., 4
Beck, A., 45
Beck, A. T., 45
Beidel, D., 39
Beidel, D. C., 52, 53
Berg, I., 2, 3, 9, 18, 19, 21, 22, 23, 60, 61,
    66, 95, 109, 140, 141
Berganza, C. E., 32
Bernard, M. E., 92
Berney, T., 122, 123
Bernstein, D. A., 68
Bernstein, G., 14, 120
Bernstein, G. A., 9, 13, 14, 18, 61, 123,
    124, 126, 129, 140, 141
Bigger, J. T., 125, 132
Birleson, P., 45
Blackman, M., 15
Blagg, N., 1, 16, 33, 81, 109, 145, 146
Blagg, N. R., 84, 108, 109
Bolstad, O. D., 60
Borchardt, C. M., 123, 124, 126, 129

Borkovec, T. D., 68
Bornstein, P. H., 79
Braswell, L., 150
Briant, R., 113
Broadwin, I. T., 1, 46, 47
Burke, A. E., 2, 46
Burr, C., 1
Butler, A., 18, 22, 66

Campbell, M., 117, 118
Campbell, S., 32
Cantwell, D. P., 45
Carlson, C. I., 60
Carlson, G. A., 45
Carr, R., 114, 121
Casleneda, A., 43
Cautela, J. R., 68, 69
Cerny, J. A., 28, 29, 31, 73, 75, 76, 150
Chassin, L., 18
Chazan, M., 8, 9
Chess, S., 15
Chiles, J. A., 45
Clark, L. A., 46
Cone, J. D., 30, 51, 57
Coolidge, J. C., 8
Costello, A. J., 34
Cox, G. B., 45
Cutherbert, B. N., 54
Cutter, H. S. G., 68
Cyr, J. J., 2, 22

D'Amato, G., 126
Davies, B., 121
Davison, G. C., 16, 79, 81
De Giovanni, I. S., 7, 91
Desai, N., 120
Deutsch, S. I., 117, 118
Dietiker, K. E., 40

173

DiNardo, P. A., 34
Doerfler, L. A., 45
Dollins, J., 4, 6

Edelbrock, C., 34
Edelbrock, C. S., 55, 102
Edwards, G. L., 45
Eisen, A. R., 39
Eisenberg, I., 65
Eisenberg, L., 21, 108
Elizur, J., 7, 63
Elliott, G. R., 124, 132
Elliot, S. N., 147
Estes, H. R., 2
Esveldt-Dawson, K., 9, 89, 90
Evans, I. M., 31
Eysenck, H. J., 17, 18

Farmer, R. G., 138
Feldman, L., 5
Ferguson, H. B., 115
Fielding, D., 21
Finch, A. J. Jr., 45, 46
Finney, J. W., 29
Flakierska, N., 23
Flament, M. F., 122
Forehand, R. L., 58
Francis, G., 21, 22, 39, 43, 88
Frary, R. B., 6, 40, 43, 44
Frommer, E. A., 121, 126
Furukawa, M. J., 88, 91

Garcia, K. A., 7, 91
Garfield, S. L., 128
Garfinkel, B. D., 9, 13, 14, 18, 61, 123,
    124, 126, 129, 140, 141
Gelfand, D. M., 5
Gillberg, C., 23
Gilman, A. G., 115
Gittleman, R., 115, 116
Gittleman-Klein, R., 4, 18, 121, 122, 123,
    124, 140
Glaser, K., 108
Glassman, A. H., 125, 132
Glennon, B., 59
Goeke, K. E., 57
Goldfried, M. R., 57, 79
Goldman, B., 4
Granell de Aldaz, E., 4, 5, 6, 7, 8, 18,
    19, 21

Graziano, A. M., 7, 91
Green, W. H., 117, 118
Greene, R., 34
Groden, J., 68, 69
Gross, A. M., 31
Grolevant, H. D., 60
Gullone, E., 4, 8, 46, 110, 111, 147

Hagopian, L. P., 39
Hahn, P. B., 8
Hall, G., 22
Hamilton, D. I., 7, 30, 68, 76, 81, 88
Hampe, E., 17, 22, 56, 107
Hayes, S. C., 50
Haylett, C. H., 2
Healy, W., 1
Hedlund, M. A., 68
Helsel, W. J., 40, 43
Herjanic, B., 34
Hersen, M., 21, 27, 28, 30
Hersov, L., 146
Hersov, L. A., 2, 8, 16, 22, 121
Hirshfeld, D. R., 16
Hodges, K., 34
Hollingshead, A. B., 21
Holmes, F. B., 27
Howell, C. T., 28
Huey, W. P., 21
Huntzinger, R. M., 39

Ingram, R. E., 46

Jackson, A., 22, 23
Jacob, T., 60, 61
Jacobsen, V., 22
Jarrett, R. B., 50
Jersild, A. T., 4
Johnson, A. M., 2
Johnson, S. M., 60
Jones, M. C., 27, 76
Joyce, M. R., 92

Kagan, J., 16
Kanner, A., 115, 116, 123, 124, 128, 129
Katkin, E. S., 57
Kazdin, A. E., 45, 60, 90
Kearney, C. A., 8, 46, 47, 50, 54, 67, 68,
    81, 98, 102, 106
Kendall, P. C., 60, 89, 92, 138, 150
Kennedy, W. A., 8, 19, 21, 108, 109

Kent, R. N., 57
King, N. J., 2, 4, 6, 7, 8, 17, 30, 40, 43, 44, 46, 68, 76, 81, 88, 110, 111, 145, 147
Klein, D., 4
Klein, D. F., 121, 122, 123, 124
Klein, R. G., 24, 123, 124, 128, 129
Knapp, M., 79
Koeppen, A. S., 69, 73
Koplewicz, H. S., 123, 124, 128, 129
Kovacs, M., 34, 45, 98, 101
Kraft, I. A., 126
Kratochwill, T. R., 6, 68, 76, 77, 81, 87
Kunzelman, H. D., 51, 54

Lang, M., 7, 18, 19, 21, 45, 66, 140
Lang, P. J., 40, 54
Lapouse, R., 7
Last, C. G., 8, 12, 13, 14, 18, 21, 22, 24, 43, 61, 66
Lazarus, A. A., 16, 79, 81, 82, 83
Lazovik, A. D., 54
Lederer, A. S., 52, 53
Ledwidge, B., 91
Leton, D. A., 21
Leventhal, T., 10
Lick, J. R., 57
Linehan, M., 31
Linström, M., 23
Loftus, J. J., 4
Lucas, A. R., 128
Luiselli, J. K., 76
Lukens, E., 18, 94, 95

MacDonald, M. L., 31
Madle, R. A., 57
Maguire, K., 121
Malcarne, V. L., 46
Mansdorf, I. J., 18, 94, 95
Marks, I. M., 68
Martin, G., 87
Mash, E. J., 27, 30
Masters, J. C., 68, 76, 87, 92
Matson, J. L., 40, 43, 90, 151
Mayer, J. A., 1, 4, 7, 11, 12, 13, 14, 19, 40, 56, 84
Maziade, M., 15
Mech, E. V., 4, 6
Millar, G. W., 44
Miller, L., 22

Miller, L. C., 17, 22, 56, 106, 107, 117
Miller, M. L., 45
Mitchell, S., 7, 19
Monk, N., 7
Moore, T., 7
Morris, R. J., 6, 68, 76, 77, 81, 87
McCandless, B. R., 43
McConaughy, S. H., 28
McDonald, N. F., 21
McGuire, R., 9, 141
McMahon, R. J., 56, 58
McNamara, E., 54, 79

Nakamura, C. U., 40
Neal, A. M., 52, 53
Neisworth, J. T., 57
Nelles, W. B., 34, 39, 98, 101
Nelson, R. O., 31, 50
Nichols, K., 2, 3, 9, 19, 21, 22, 95, 109
Nichols, K. A., 9, 22

O'Donnell, J. P., 7
O'Farrell, T. J., 68
Ollendick, T. H., 1, 2, 3, 4, 6, 7, 8, 11, 12, 13, 14, 17, 19, 21, 27, 28, 29, 30, 31, 34, 39, 40, 42, 43, 44, 46, 56, 68, 73, 75, 76, 81, 84, 88, 91, 98, 101, 117, 145, 150, 151
Ollier, K., 6, 40, 43, 44
O'Reilly, P. P., 79

Paget, K. D., 44
Palmero, D. S., 43
Partridge, J. M., 1
Pasley, F. C., 128
Patterson, G. R., 32
Paul, G. L., 77
Pear, J., 87
Peck, A. L., 8
Perkins, G. J., 138
Perry, M. A., 88, 91
Peterson, D. R., 56, 98
Petti, T. A., 45
Polefka, D. A., 16, 79, 81
Popper, C. W., 124, 132
Poznanski, E. O., 16
Prins, P. J. M., 18
Pritchard, C., 2, 3, 9, 19, 21, 22, 95, 109
Pritchard, J., 18, 66
Puig-Antich, J., 121

Quarrington, B., 2, 22
Quay, H. C., 21, 56, 98
Quinn, D. M. P., 128

Rachman, S., 17
Rayner, R., 27
Redlich, F., 21
Reich, W., 34
Reynolds, C. R., 43, 44, 98, 101, 123
Reznick, J. S., 16, 100
Richmond, B. O., 43, 44, 98, 101, 123
Richter, N. C., 76
Riddle, M. A., 125
Rimm, D. C., 68
Robin, A. L., 62
Rodriguez, A., 21, 108
Rodriguez, M., 21, 108
Roehling, P. V., 62
Rogers, M., 58, 65, 84, 85, 87
Rogers, T. R., 46
Rosenstiel, A. K., 84
Rowe, G. P., 138
Rutter, M., 19
Ryall, M. R., 40

Santa-Barbara, J., 60
Sarason, S. B., 6
Saylor, C. F., 45
Scherer, M. W., 40
Scott, D. S., 84
Seligman, M. E. P., 46
Shaffer, D., 9
Shapiro, E. S., 51
Sheehan, D. V., 127
Shepherd, M., 7, 19
Sills, M., 10
Silverman, W., 2, 46
Silverman, W. K., 8, 34, 36, 38, 39, 46,
        47, 50, 54, 67, 68, 81, 98, 101,
        102, 106
Simeon, J. G., 115, 127
Skinner, H. A., 60
Sleator, E. K., 119, 129
Smith, D., 58, 65, 84, 85, 87
Smith, S. D., 119
Smith, S. L., 8, 19, 20, 21, 22
Smucker, M. R., 45
Snidman, N., 16
Staley, A. A., 7

Steinhauer, P. D., 60
Strauss, C. C., 9, 13, 14, 21, 43, 46, 61
Svingen, P., 13, 18, 61, 141
Swann, G. E., 31

Taylor, J. A., 43
Taylor-Davies, A., 120
Tennenbaum, D. L., 60, 61
Terdal, L. G., 27, 30
Thomas, A., 15
Tiller, J., 121
Tisher, M., 45
Tizard, J., 19
Trueman, D., 21
Tyrer, P., 23, 24
Tyrer, S., 23, 24

Unis, A. S., 90

Vaal, J. J., 84
Versiani, M., 121
Vivas, E., 5

Walk, R. D., 54
Warnecke, R., 21, 22
Warren, W., 22
Waters, B., 115, 116, 119, 120, 121, 124,
        126, 128
Watson, D., 46
Watson, J. B., 27
Weist, M. D., 29
Weisz, J. R., 59
Werry, J. S., 21, 128
Wheler, G. H. T., 15
White, J. H., 113
Whitemore, K., 19
Wills, V., 19, 21, 22
Wilson, G. T., 147
Wisner, K. L., 90
Wolf, M. M., 110
Wolfe, V. V., 46
Wolpe, J., 40, 54, 76
Woolfolk, A. E., 147
Woolfolk, R. C., 147

Yates, A. J., 17
Yule, W., 6, 40, 43, 44, 46, 84, 108, 109

Zatz, S., 18

Subject Index

Agoraphobia, 10
Antidepressants, 120–126
Anxiety Disorders Interview Schedule for
    Children, 34–39, 50, 95–101,
    102–105
Anxiolytics, 126–128
Avoidant disorder, 10, 95–101

Behavioral assessment, 27–63
    behavioral interviews, 31–34
    behavioral observations, 57–60
    behavioral ratings, 54–57
    definition, 27–29
    diagnostic interviews, 34–39
    family assessment, 60–63
    self-monitoring, 51–54
    self-report instruments, 39–51
Behavioral ratings, 54–57
    Child Behavior Checklist, 55–56,
        102–105
    Louisville Fear Survey Schedule for
        Children, 56
    Revised Behavior Problem Checklist,
        56, 95–101
Behavioral treatments, 65–112
    case illustrations, 94–105
    cognitive restructuring, 91–94, 95–101
    contingency management, 84–87,
        95–101
    emotive imagery, 81–84
    families, 140–144
    functional analysis, 67–68, 95–101,
        102–105
    issues in treatment, 135–153
    maintaining treatment gains, 149–152
    modeling, 88–91, 102–105
    relaxation training, 68–76, 95–101,
        102–105

research support for, 105–112
school consultancy, 144–148
shaping, 84–87, 95–101, 102–105
systematic desensitization, 76–81,
    102–105

Child Behavior Checklist, 55–56
Children's Assessment Schedule, 34
Children's Depression Inventory, 44–46,
    95–101, 102–105
Children's Manifest Anxiety Scale, 43–44,
    95–101, 102–105
Cognitive restructuring, 91–94, 95–105,
    106–112
Contingency management, 84–87, 95–105,
    106–112

Diagnostic and Statistical Manual, 10–11,
    24, 34
Diagnostic Interview for Children and
    Adolescents, 34

Emotive imagery, 81–84, 105–112

Family assessment measures, 60–63
    Family Assessment Measure, 60–62
    Self-Administered Dependency
        Questionnaire, 60–62
Fear Survey Schedule for Children, 4–6,
    40–43, 50, 95–101, 102–105, 117
Functional analysis, 67–68, 95–98,
    102–103

Generalized anxiety disorder, 10

International Classification of
    Diseases, 10
Interview Schedule for Children, 34

Issues in treatment, 135–153
  family context, 140–144
  future directions, 152–153
  maintaining treatment gains, 149–152
  problems encountered, 136–140
  school consultancy, 144–149

Louisville Fear Survey Schedule for
    Children, 56, 117

Major depressive disorder, 10–13
Modeling, 88–91, 105–112

Neuroleptics, 128

Obsessive-compulsive disorder, 10
Overanxious disorder, 10, 95–101

Pharmacotherapy, 114–133
  action of drugs, 115–116
  administration issues, 117–120
  antidepressants, 120–126
  anxiolytics, 126–128
  case illustration, 130–132
  cautions for use, 129–130
  drug safety, 116–117
  neuroleptics, 128
  side effects, 116–117
  stimulants, 128–129
Post-Traumatic Stress Disorder, 10
Preschool Observation Scale of
    Anxiety, 59

Relaxation training, 68–76
  cognitive procedure, 69–73
  muscle procedure, 73–76
  research support for, 105–112
Revised Behavior Problem Checklist, 56,
    95–101

School refusal
  age of onset, 20

age trends, 3–7
behavioral assessment, 27–63
behavioral treatment strategies, 65–112
clinical presentation, 7–10
definition, 1–3
developmental issues, 3–7
diagnostic considerations, 10–15, 35–39
epidemiology, 19–22
etiology, 15–19
gender issues, 3–7
issues in, 135–153
overview, 1–25
pharmacotherapy of, 114–133
relationship to adult psychopathology,
    22–24
socioeconomic factors, 3–7
School Refusal Assessment Scale, 47–51,
    95–101, 103
Self-Administered Dependency Question-
    naire, 60–61
Self-monitoring, 51–54
Self-report instruments, 39–51
  Children's Depression Inventory, 44–46,
    95–101, 102–105
  Children's Manifest Anxiety Scale,
    43–44, 50, 95–101, 102–105
  Fear Survey Schedule for Children,
    40–43, 50, 95–101, 102–105
  School Refusal Assessment Scale,
    47–51, 95–101, 102–105
Separation anxiety disorder, 10, 102–105
Shaping, 84–87, 95–101, 102–105,
    106–112
Simple phobia, 10
Social phobia, 10, 95–101
Stimulants, 128
Systematic desensitization, 76–81
  anxiety hierarchy, 76–78
  case study, 105–112
  relaxation, 76
  research support for, 105–112

DATE DUE